FOOLISH
FIGLEAVES?

FOOLISH FIGLEAVES?

Pornography in –and out of–Court

Richard H. Kuh

THE MACMILLAN COMPANY, NEW YORK

COLLIER - MACMILLAN LTD., LONDON

Library of Congress Catalog Card Number: 67-24286

FIRST PRINTING

The Macmillan Company, New York
Collier-Macmillan Canada Ltd., Toronto, Ontario

Printed in the United States of America

TO

Joyce and The Folks

CONTENTS

PART IV. PROPOSED ACTION—WHY AND HOW

PART V. THE FUTURE

Foreword

A FEW YEARS ago, in New York City's criminal courts, an aging defendant who had been convicted of a minor crime came on for sentencing. The presiding judge read his "yellow sheet" aloud— the record of his prior brushes with the law. A lifetime of transgressions, serious as well as petty, with repeated terms in jail, was revealed. In all, the defendant had spent far more time inside prison walls than on the outside. When all had been orally catalogued, the judge looked up wearily, asking the routine question of what, if anything, the defendant wished to say for himself. The sunlight through the courtroom blinds momentarily flashed from the prisoner's gold front teeth as his face broke quickly into a broad smile. "Well, Judge, Your Honor," he said, "ain't none of us is perfect."

So it is with the criminal law as it is with the people who provide its provender: little if any of it is perfect. And in its attempts at dealing with the obscene, the imperfections are not to be readily ignored.

In this book I have chronicled the law's all too imperfect efforts to express—and to repress—that which it deems pornographic. I have ventured, however, more than a book about obscenity and censorship. In anti-obscenity enforcement are many of the dilemmas that besiege the administration of criminal justice today. Freedom of personal action is juxtaposed against community protections—whether necessary or fancied. The law and its execution places in question whether the state has any business penalizing conduct that does no direct harm to bystanders, and possibly none even to participants. Should the law try to enforce *morality*, always an amorphous concept, and one now leading all America a merry chase through change? Has the judge a proper role as a law-*maker?* Is ours truly a system of laws, and not of men, when what the law *is* depends upon what the swing judge (in a five to four split) *says* it is? To what extent may a prosecutor, sworn to uphold the law, ignore those statutes with which he has little sympathy? How, when years are spent nursemaiding cases through trial and appellate delays, and the ultimate outcome is anybody's guess, can the penal law deter? Do pressure groups, by underscoring extreme positions, better serve our democracy than they might through conciliatory efforts? The passions of the Bill of Rights and of the United States Constitution seethe through the pornography-free speech brouhaha.

And so this book, written about enforcement of the laws against the obscene, is painted on a broader canvas. It is, however, formed from brushstrokes and pigments that have had eternal interest for man and woman. Sex, after all, is fundamental to pornography. Moreover, crammed as is the criminal law with unresolved problems (narcotics enforcement, the interrogation of suspects, wiretapping, the bail system, the "insanity" defense, the free press-fair trial dilemma, to mention a few), in none are the public emotions on each side so strong, so widely shared, and so persistent as they are concerning obscenity and censorship; in none have the words of the statutes proven so inadequate; in none has the impact of the United States Constitution remained so uncertain despite so many rulings from our nation's highest Court; and in none do the decisions of the judges throughout America so unrelentingly defy consistency.

This book is not proferred as an exhaustive scholarly compilation, accumulating all that judges from Maine to California have said about the obscene. Nor is it one of these verbal collages constructed from banned excerpts, handpicked and looped together with threads of anti-censorship text. Rather, in weighing the law and pornography, not only have I considered some of the broader questions, the dilemmas that far transcend obscenity enforcement, but I have told something of the persons whose actions and interests have helped to shape today's obscenity picture. Some of the courtroom and out-of-court incidents are viewed—some of the humor and some of the frustrations—that add warmth to the law's processes. "The life of the law," Holmes had noted, "has not been logic: it has been experience." To those wise words, the whole spectrum of obscenity confusion replies with a trumpet-tongued, "Amen."

The law's *proper* role in the control of pornography remains a mystery—still officially unsolved. As with any mystery, the writer's solution, my own viewpoint and mode of reconciling all the meaningful "clues" or values, is not fully disclosed until the book's latter portions. By that point, all the necessary elements have been presented, and the paradoxes and the near futilities of present efforts have been laid bare. For those who like problems, intellectual as well as practical, both emotional and reasoned, obscenity poses a world-beater. It is, to use the phrase Li'l Abner made famous, indubitably "amoozin' but confoozin'."

RICHARD H. KUH

New York City
1967

PART I

The Problem

1. The Antagonists in the Obscenity-Censorship Battle

I am persuaded that divers of you, who lead the people, have laboured to build yourselves in these things wherein you have censured others, and established yourselves upon the Word of God. Is it therefore infallibly agreeable to the Word of God, all that you say? I beseech you, in the bowels of Christ, think it possible you may be mistaken.

> —Oliver Cromwell, *Letter to the General Assembly of the Church of Scotland*, August 3, 1650

SEX—filmed or still-photographed, its joys savored both autobiographically and fictionally, its sounds and breaths captured on phonograph records, its tensions monologued—is one of the law's greatest frustrations. Hardly anyone involved in either what the law does about it or leaves undone is satisfied.

Anti-censors find most police and prosecutors, and many trial judges, irritatingly meddlesome and needlessly repressive. They magnify official blue-pencilings into dangers to those essential freedoms that contrast our way of life with that in thought-controlled dictatorships. In the opposite camp, the pornographic and the obscene[1] are deemed the breeding grounds of crime, and any degree of official permissiveness is castigated as the sheerest folly, if not such moral weakness as to jeopardize the very fabric of our society.

United States Supreme Court Justices Hugo L. Black and William O. Douglas have long urged that free speech, guaranteed by the United States Constitution's First Amendment, is meant to be absolutely free, and that any censorship is inconsistent with our American democracy.[2] Pushing this view to the very outskirts of reason, there are those absolutists who have urged that society should go along "if people would want to publicly perform intercourse on a nightclub stage, or to defecate or anything like that,"[3] and "Who cares if people want to copulate in public on TV? Why not? The Controllers can always turn off the screen if it doesn't please them. . . ."[4]

Eberhard and Phyllis Kronhausen, high priest and priestess in the laissez-faire war on censorship (a husband and wife team of popular psychologists), have ferreted out historical data supporting this extreme, showing that "exhibitions of human intercourse for the entertainment of special guests were not at all rare occurrences . . . through part of the 18th century in France, and it is well to remember that these exhibitions took place before mixed audiences of men and women."[5] And, not to neglect the teenagers, the Kronhausens have urged that books such as Frank Harris's *My Life and Loves,* which narrates with as much relish as physical and sensuous detail the author's remembrances of philanderous sexual encounters, would be "the ideal supplement to what the average enlightened home or school offers in the form of sex education" for boys and girls.[6]

The Kronhausens are not lone enthusiasts of full permissiveness for the young. Their grounds are psychiatric. Emanuel Redfield, counsel to the New York Civil Liberties Union, has urged a constitutional basis in support of the same conclusions. Redfield is the able and dedicated attorney who succeeded, in 1964, in temporarily making the long-banned erotic novel *Fanny Hill,* with its page after page of detailed descriptive data concerning lesbianism, masturbation, attempted rape, and intercourse, lawful literature for New York State's teen-agers. In his brief, which brought victory over the state statute barring the sale to youngsters of matters describing "illicit sex or sexual morality," Redfield urged:

Classification means censorship. Censorship, no matter how small or desirable, is still censorship; and once the barriers are breached, an insidious entering wedge is provided for more censorship. . . . Since the Constitution, born out of a history that knew censorship, rejects censorship, it follows that the classification for under 18 year olds must fail.[7]

(Although the court knocked out the statute, it did so on grounds narrower than those Redfield had urged.)[8]

The American Civil Liberties Union seemingly concurred in this all-embracing anti-censorship position when, in 1962, it declared: "Any governmental restriction or punishment of any form of expression on the ground of obscenity must require proof beyond a reasonable doubt that such an expression would directly cause, in a normal adult, behavior which has validly been made criminal by statute."[9] The impact—and sophistry—of this statement is clear. Normal American males, even when roused by the most bizarre and erotic that any bacchanalian bachelor party may offer, are unlikely to run amuck, ravishing such females as may cross their paths. Certainly, to "prove beyond a reasonable doubt" that even such carnal revels "would directly cause" criminal violence would far transcend the powers of law—or of psychiatry. And so the usually direct and outspoken American Civil Liberties Union, in the course of its battle for untrammeled freedom of expression for others, has shied from clear expression for itself, elliptically phrasing what is obviously its own position: to the Union, under no circumstances should any obscenity *ever* be criminally punishable.

But all the extremists in the battle raging over obscenity are not to be found among the anti-censors. The absurd lengths to which pornography's dedicated enemies have gone have been often rehearsed. Dr. Thomas Bowdler's nineteenth century expurgations both of Shakespeare's plays and of Gibbon's *Decline and Fall of the Roman Empire* have preserved his name in the word "bowdlerizing," the process of eviscerating for delicacy's sake. And more than thirty years ago, an assistant collector of customs for the United States began a letter by stating, "Sirs: There is being detained . . . 2 packages addressed to you, containing obscene photobooks, 'Ceiling Sistine Chapel,' Filles-Michael Angelo, the importation of which is held to be prohibited under the provisions of the Tariff Act."[10] Similarly, proper persons in British customs read a book title, *Rape Round Our Coasts,* and seized the book—a volume dealing with soil erosion.[11] Understandably, Aldous Huxley quipped, "To the Puritan, all things are impure."

In 1956, a United States Senate subcommittee investigating juvenile delinquency, indulging in that mathematical fantasy so dear to those who love to startle with statistics, estimated pornography to be a half-billion dollar annual racket in this country.[12] This figure, of at least questionable validity, has been commonly quoted by many who are alarmed at pornography's seeming omnipresence, suggesting a cost in the neighborhood of ten dollars a year for every American family's pornography diet—considering pornography, momentarily, as a family staple. J. Edgar Hoover, in his 1960 New Year's greetings to all America's law enforcement officials, embraced it:

> In 1957 there were nearly eight forcible rapes per 100,000 inhabitants in the United States. In 1958 this figure increased ten and one-half percent, a forcible rape occurring every 36 minutes! This truly shocking and shameful state of affairs is made even more deplorable by the knowledge that sex crimes and obscene and vulgar literature often go hand in hand.
> The time for half-hearted, oblique actions against dealers in depravity is past. Although their despicable trade reaps $500 million a year, this diabolical business is costing the Nation much more than money. It is robbing our country and particularly our younger generation of decency—it is a seedbed for delinquency among juveniles and depravity among all ages.[13]

In May 1964, the *Reader's Digest,* apparently dissatisfied with the earlier Senate committee estimate, quadrupled it, noting that "the smut industry is approaching an estimated two-billion-dollar-a-year volume" (this time figuring more than ten dollars annually for each *man, woman, adolescent,* and *newborn child* in the

United States!). It went on to quote a Senate committee report that "the moral fiber of the country is being undermined by a deluge of vile and filthy books, pictures and other pornographic material. Worst of all, up to 75 percent of it falls into the hands of minors."[14] This despair has been shared by members of the judiciary. Judge John F. Scileppi of New York State's highest appellate court, in July of the same year in dissenting from a decision that approved the sale of *Fanny Hill*, stated:

> The majority opinion here, in my view, sounds the death knell of the long-honored standards of American decency which have remained an integral part of our national heritage . . . .
>
> In balance, public decency and morality are more important than the deprivation resulting from the banning of noxious publications which seem to appeal to the small segment of our people whose baser instincts make reading of obscenity and pornography their favorite pastime.[15]

Inevitably, with this strength of feeling running on both sides, both those who have restrained censorship and the censors have come under strong personal attacks. In 1959, United States Senator Herman E. Talmadge of Georgia complained of what he termed a "shocking and unconscionable decision of the Supreme Court of the United States" that year.[16] The opinions that drew the Georgian's sparks had vitiated censorship of the motion picture of *Lady Chatterley's Lover*. The film, like the book, portrayed adultery favorably. "By that edict," Senator Talmadge's attack continued, "that Court, which already has set itself above the laws of man, undertook also to set itself above the laws of God."[17]

And one more professionally accredited in the laws of God than is the Senator, Francis Cardinal Spellman of the New York diocese, criticizing the high Court's majority in several 1964 obscenity rulings,[18] ventured, "The regrettable but obvious conclusion is that the community standards prevailing among the Supreme Court judges who voted in such a way are substantially below the standards of the communities over which they sit in judgment."[19]

This sort of personal malediction is a two-way street. Anti-censors have similarly zeroed in on the censors' personalities. Obscenity arrests (as Part III of this book describes) are often accompanied by a staccato of the most vitriolic anti-police, anti-prosecution denunciations. And America's two most diligent researchers and leading academic writers in the area of pornography, Dean William B. Lockhart and Professor Robert C. McClure, both of the University of Minnesota, have described the typical censor as "seldom a person who appreciates esthetic values or understands the nature and function of imaginative literature. His interests lie elsewhere. Often an emotionally disturbed person, he sets out to look for smut and consequently finds it almost everywhere." "He is rarely an educated person. . . . He is often an . . . intemperate person with a paranoid personality."[20] Across the ocean, a British barrister, H. Montgomery Hyde, one who also has written well (although with no claim of objectivity) on obscenity, has noted that "those who are most prominent in condemning pornography are usually the most eager to read a 'banned' book."[21]

These attacks pose a dilemma for public officials charged with anti-pornography chores. Should they, as censors, fail to show full familiarity with an appreciable portion of the flood of marginal items that now appear, they invite the sophisticate's contempt: they are know-nothings, wielding the censor's shears, possibly for political reasons, in abject ignorance of our contemporary milieu. If, on the other hand, they suggest that they have read deeply on the subject they will undoubtedly lay themselves open to Montgomery Hyde's accusation.

"A fanatic," Finley Peter Dunne reported his Mr. Dooley as philosophizing, "is a man that does what he thinks th' Lord wud do if He knew th' facts iv th' case."[22] Both censorship and anti-censorship fanatics, boiling at their opposition's inability to see things their way, have, in their resort to personal abuse, taken paradoxically untenable positions. Anti-censors have sought to embarrass their opponents, to silence them by crude reflections on their intelligence, their emotional balance, and their integrity. Free speech champions, they have ignored the wise words attributed to Voltaire, "I disapprove of what you say, but I will defend to the death your right to say it." And those who see pornography threatening to engulf America in lawlessness have acted to diminish respect for law and order in attributing judicial decisions to chinks in the personal morality of our highest judges. The decisions have soft spots enough; it is bad advocacy —as well as cowardice—to attack them by focusing on their authors' imagined personal frailties.

In this war waged by extremists, each side is well dug in. The anti-censors, taking their lead from Supreme Court Justices Black and Douglas (rather than from the high Court's majority) deify freedom of speech and freedom of the press. Their new religion demands that these freedoms exist in pristine, uncompromised condition. A public forum for this viewpoint is easy to come by; generally, the media of communications, press, radio, and television, tend to be friendly: for the most part they fear the foot in the door of any censorship. And articulate sympathizers are many; the doctrinaire liberal is as quick to make himself part of a chorus of resentment against interference with absolute freedom as he is to accept such other dogma as his particular liberal gods have predigested for him. (The militant liberal today, aiding all the right causes, mouthing all the right thoughts, idolizing all the right heroes, and all the while bursting with pride at his own independence of mind, is kin to George Bernard Shaw's proud Briton—"Englishmen never will be slaves: they are free to do whatever the Government and public opinion allow them to to."[23])

Keeping pornography on the books as a penal violation, enforced by police, prosecutors, and the courts, conjures to the anti-censor spectral reminders of fascism—of the police state, with its controlled press and its stifling of free thought. These

images are haunting, so much so that the anti-censor distrusts
efforts at line drawing between the obscene and the non-obscene;
he is terrified lest once delineation starts it may get out of hand.
Moreover, he is conscious that future history may well mirror
the past, and may reflect the folly, when weighed against the
standards of another age, of not having drawn the lines a good
deal more permissively.

Those on the other side, the hordes of people urging jail for
pornographers, bombard police and prosecutors on a year-in,
year-out basis, with a flood of wires, letters, phone calls, and
visits that, regularly, is greater than that which accompanies any
other single area of law enforcement. Some of the communications are spontaneous—from parents shocked to discover what
the "plain wrappers" received through the mails by their children, ofttimes unsolicited, contain. But a large part of the volume
is stimulated by the host of local committees that have germi-
nated to combat "filth for money's sake." The main theme is that
struck by J. Edgar Hoover: that "sex crimes and obscene and
vulgar literature often go hand in hand," that pornography "is a
seedbed for delinquency among juveniles and depravity among
all ages." Often psychiatric testimony, such as that of Dr. Nicholas G. Frignito, chief neuropsychiatrist and medical director of
the Philadelphia municipal court, is relied upon to support this
conclusion—although psychiatrists are also available to testify on
the other side of the question.[24] Testifying before a House committee in Washington, Dr. Frignito noted that his court "has case
histories in which sexual arousal from smutty books led to criminal behavior from vicious assault to homicide. Some of these
children did not transgress sexually until they read suggestive
stories and viewed lewd pictures in licentious magazines."[25]

Those pressing for brisk crackdowns against the pornographic
are troubled by its impact on the emotions of the young. Before
a United States Senate subcommittee in 1955, Norman Thomas,
clearly no book-burner, testified:

I am not at all impressed by the degree to which defenders of certain kinds of comic books, and even of pornography, pure and simple, want to press the first amendment. I do not think the first amendment gives any guaranty to men to seduce the innocent and to exploit the kind of unformed mind and unformed emotions of children and adolescents.

I think there is a great deal of dangerous nonsense in this appeal to the first amendment and to freedom of the press when one is dealing with [this] kind of thing . . . .

I do not believe that in order to protect the fundamental liberties of the press we have to turn our children, who are, in a sense, the ward of all our society, over to the kind of visual exploitation of base emotion, and the arousal of base emotion to which, of course, this literature, this pornographic literature, these films and cards, and all the rest are directed.

• • •

I think in these times, with this terrible increase of juvenile delinquency, with this immensely profitable flood of pornography, using techniques never before available to the seducers of the innocent, I think it is nonsense to say that we are so bound by a very extreme interpretation of the freedom of the press that we cannot act.[26]

Thus, the two sides: The anti-censor, seeing no clear proof that any censorship is needed, fears that the slightest invasion of press and speech freedom may accelerate to the point of constituting thought control. The pro-censor, desperately fearful that our heritage of decency is receding, is convinced that this disintegration can be stopped or at least slowed by some governmental rein.

With these the fears and the emotions, neither side has been prone to seek compromise. Those for controls, self-righteously certain that sex was never meant to be either dinner-table conversation nor after-dinner reading, talk of present-day growing permissiveness as only a temporary "swing of the pendulum." Charles S. Desmond, then chief judge of New York State's highest court, dissenting when New York found *Fanny Hill* not to be obscene, said, "I refuse to believe that all this can continue to be the law. I predict that the wheel will turn and the pendulum swing back."[27] Those opposing any controls are equally certain that these are no pendulum swings but massive shifts, glacial in character, far too slow possibly, but moving inexorably in a single direction, never to be reversed. These conflicting certainties (the wish is father to the thought) discourage compromise. Each side believes that with time working for its viewpoint, nothing need be surrendered.

This conflict is taking place in a setting that, if not hospitable to clear obscenity, is certainly extremely tolerant of closely related items. Walter Allen, a British editor and critic, was to write:

After half a million years of man on earth, during which time every single human being has been produced by sexual intercourse, one might have expected that by now sex would present no difficulty; but, as we all know, outside dirty jokes sex is no laughing matter, and in public discussion of the subject a tone of the most righteous high-mindedness is obligatory to all taking part, whatever their point of view, repressive or permissive. Repressives and permissives alike unite in condemning the constant and all-pervading exploitation of sex that is one of the most striking aspects of the public face of Western society. Indeed, there are times when one feels that our old friend, the Man from Mars, dropped down in London or New York to visit the theaters and cinemas, travel the escalators in the Underground, inspect the bookstalls, read the newspapers and magazines and listen to the pop songs, could hardly not conclude that he had been projected into a society whose members were permanently on heat and in which the condition of being on heat, was regarded as the highest felicity.[28]

Items not pornographic in themselves, although deemed in poor taste by substantial portions of the population, seem to pursue the citizenry. Living, palpitating decolletage enters the most staid parlors, through the medium of television. Nudity—be it of Australian bushmen (and women) or Hollywood sex symbols—lands on the coffee table, on or between the covers of large-circulation magazines. Massive billboards adorning movie marquees or high above the city's streets spill over with fleshy charms. (One gigantic display, a completely undraped head-to-toe replica of actress Jane Fonda, appeared above New York City's theater district until the real-life actress, well-covered by public relations personnel, sued to have it removed.) Well-stocked book and magazine racks in corner stationery and drugstores, featuring cover pictures of well-stacked and uncovered ladies, attract the youngsters as did the glass candy cases of an age gone by. Nude photographs of men and boys can be found in other magazines by those with less conventional leanings. Foreign films, formerly the province of espresso-serving art theaters in a few major metropolises but now shown throughout the land (sometimes matched by those from Hollywood) display nudity and depict—occasionally with sensitivity—the most intimate and erotic of themes.

John Crosby, free-thinking and -speaking columnist, has complained:

I habitually take my thirteen-year-old daughter, Maggie, to the movies on Friday night; yet, in the enormous city of New York, with scores of movies to choose from, there is often hardly a single one fit to show a girl of that age. In fact, I'm afraid Maggie has seen a lot of movies that I don't approve her seeing because—well how do you know in advance?

• • •

I think that we who defend freedom of speech, freedom of expression, and all that, have been booby-trapped in the case of movies by labelling almost everything that deals with sexual freedom "adult," when most of the American movies which are lascivious are the exact opposite of adult. They are childishly prurient, adolescent quiverings —peeping-Tom-type movies, if I make myself clear, and it's not going to be easy. This is why a censor's work is difficult—in fact, impossible —to do intelligently. Because in one picture seduction is high art, great theater, great literature. In another, it's just dirty. The difference lies in intent, in honesty, in craftsmanship, in art.[29]

The uncertainty of any pornography-crime causal connection, supplemented by this increased public exposure to the "childishly prurient," does not alleviate the law's obscenity dilemma. Rather, these factors intensify it. Were it possible to establish that pornography inevitably or even regularly led to crime, little disagreement would exist as to its criminality. Freedom of speech has not, for example, immunized inciting to riot or conspiracy to commit crime, instances in which the nexus between some utterance and violence is clear. And the vast numbers of provocative items that today exist safely outside the penumbra of illegality heat those persons urging governmental controls to fever pitch. To them, these items serve as daily reminders of a spreading satyriasis, ready to loose all bonds if limits are not established and enforced.

Obviously, much that today's candor licenses is art or literature. Equally clearly, much is not. Much is seriously offensive to only the most straight-laced, and is tolerated, ignored or enjoyed by the balance of our populace. Considering the entire potpourri, from the most erotic or scatological trash to the most artful in realism or eroticism (and viewing everything including Sunday *Times* magazine section bra ads and *Ladies Home Journal* advice for females with frigid husbands), is intelligent sorting feasible? Is censorship, as John Crosby has said, "impossible"? Now, in the 1960s, has the law, evolved by man to draw so many lines in so many areas between permissible and impermissible conduct, a valid function to perform? If it has, can it do so with such clarity that the governed will be able to anticipate what it is they can do, and what they are barred from doing?

PART II

The Law's Confusion

2. Underpinnings of the Obscenity Law—Rulings Before *Roth*

Every freeman has an undoubted right to lay what sentiments he pleases before the public: to forbid this, is to destroy the freedom of the press: but if he publishes what is improper, mischievous, or illegal, he must take the consequence of his own temerity. To subject the press to the restrictive power of a licenser . . . is to subject all freedom of sentiment to the prejudices of one man, and make him the arbitrary and infallible judge of all controverted points in learning, religion, and government. But to punish (as the law does at present) any dangerous or offensive writings . . . is necessary for the preservation of peace and good order, of government and religion, the only solid foundations of civil liberty.
—Sir William Blackstone, *Commentaries on the Laws of England*, vol. iv, p. 152 (1765–69)

THE JUSTICES OF THE United States Supreme Court have, during the past decade, been devoting far more of their time to pornography than formerly. The cases that led to this intensified concern by the nation's highest tribunal were argued in Washington in April of 1957, and decided by the Justices two months later. In one, the defendant was Samuel Roth, a New York mail order dealer in obscene and near obscene books; the other involved David S. Alberts, engaged in a similar business three thousand miles away in California.

Although today's understanding of the law of obscenity in America dates largely from the opinions in those two cases, its seeds are found in earlier litigation. Claims of criminal obscenity had, of course, been carried through the lower federal and state courts, and fought to the Supreme Court, long prior to the *Roth* and *Alberts* decisions. The earlier cases, although indicating that some statutory restraints upon the pornographic were in order, had failed to venture any definition of the word "obscene."

For example, in February of 1957, just two months before *Roth* and *Alberts* were argued in Washington, the Justices had unequivocally rejected one definition of "obscene." All nine—reflecting a unanimity that was later to become a rarity in obscenity cases—joined together in reversing the Michigan conviction of a bookseller named Alfred E. Butler.[1] Butler had been found guilty of selling a novel, John Griffin's *The Devil Rides Outside*. This well-written book told the moral story of a young man's struggle against lust while staying in a French monastery. A Detroit trial judge had held the book's sale to be in violation of a statute that had barred sales to the general public of books "containing obscene, immoral, lewd or lascivious language, or . . . descriptions, tending to incite minors to violent or depraved or immoral acts, manifestly tending to the corruption of the morals of youth. . . ." In a short opinion, the late Justice Felix Frankfurter wrote:

The State insists that, by thus quarantining the general reading public against books not too rugged for grown men and women in order to shield juvenile innocence, it is exercising its power to promote the general welfare. Surely, this is to burn the house to roast the pig . . . . We have before us legislation not reasonably restricted to the evil with which it is said to deal. The incidence of this enactment is to reduce the adult population of Michigan to reading only what is fit for children.

"Obscene," when intended to restrict adult reading, could not be defined in terms of an item's fitness for those of tender age.

The Supreme Court, more than a third of a century earlier, had articulated another limitation on measures designed to restrict freedom of publication. Such measures, the high Court had held, could not predict, sight unseen, that something was going to be scurrilous or obscene, and in anticipation ban its publication.[2] In Minneapolis, one J. M. Near had been turning out a weekly hate sheet that regularly excoriated the Jews. ("I simply state a fact when I say that ninety per cent of the crimes committed against society in this city are committed by Jew gangsters . . . . It is Jew, Jew, Jew, as long as one cares to comb over the records . . . . I have withdrawn all allegiance to anything with a hook nose that eats herring.") Municipal officials sued to have the paper, including future issues, suppressed. Successful in Minnesota, they were reversed in Washington. The high Court's Justices split, five to four, but the majority ruled against all *prior restraints,* saying:

The fact that the liberty of the press may be abused by miscreant purveyors of scandal does not make any the less necessary the immunity of the press from previous restraint in dealing with official misconduct. Subsequent punishment for such abuses as may exist is the appropriate remedy, consistent with constitutional privilege.

Seventeen years later, but still almost a decade before the *Roth-Alberts* decisions, finding a criminal statute too vague, the Supreme Court had knocked out a New York law directed against sadistic literature.[3] (When the statute thus doomed fell, nineteen similar laws that had existed in other states fell along with it.) New York had, by statute, declared it to be a misdemeanor to sell any publication "principally made up of criminal news, police reports, or accounts of criminal deeds, or pictures, or stories of deeds of bloodshed, lust or crime . . . ." In 1941, Murray Winters, operator of a bookshop, was convicted under that statute. He had been found in possession of more than two thousand copies of *Headquarters Detective,* a magazine hardly designed as a law enforcement aid. "The stories are embellished with pictures of fiendish and gruesome crimes," New York's intermediate appellate judges had observed, "and are besprinkled with lurid photographs of victims and perpetrators. Featured articles bear such titles as 'Bargains in Bodies,' 'Girl Slave to a Love Cult,' and 'Girls' Reformatory.'" The New York courts sustained Winters' conviction, only one of the state's seven highest judges deeming the statute too vague to be enforceable. At first the United States Supreme Court itself seemed somewhat uncertain of the statute's adequacy. After hearing this case argued for the first time in March 1946, it called for further argument and heard it in November of the following year. Then in March 1948, split six to three, it ordered Winters' conviction reversed. In so doing, the majority noted:

. . . we find the specification of publications, prohibited from distribution, too uncertain and indefinite to justify the conviction of this petitioner. . . . [W]e think fair use of collections of pictures and stories would be interdicted because of the utter impossibility of the actor or the trier to know where this new standard of guilt would draw the line between the allowable and the forbidden publications . . . . When stories of deeds of bloodshed, such as many in the accused magazines, are massed so as to incite to violent crimes, the statute is violated. It does not seem to us that an honest distributor of publications could know when he might be held to have ignored such a prohibition. Collections of tales of war horrors, otherwise unexceptionable, might well be found to be "massed" so as to become "vehicles for inciting violent and depraved crimes." Where a statute is so vague as to make criminal an innocent act, a conviction under it cannot be sustained.

One further important Supreme Court decision to come twenty-one years prior to the *Roth-Alberts* cases, and involving another and different limitation on censorship, must be considered. In *Hannegan* v. *Esquire, Inc.*[4] the impact of the high Court's holding was to declare that an item was not censorable solely because it failed to "contribute to the public good and the public welfare." The *Esquire* magazine of the early '40s was that generation's progenitor of today's *Playboy*, although, as is so often true of the older generation, it was not quite as "far out." Sex tended to dominate a fair number of its stories and articles; its cartoons and photographs featured nudes—firm-breasted, long-legged, winsome, desirable. Its layout was attractive, its advertisements utterly respectable, and its authors foreshadowed the magazine's present literary standing. Spicy or lusty—yes; obscene—emphatically, no. Yet the postal authorities were irked at its free-swinging sexuality and resented subsidizing it continually by granting it second-class mailing privileges, at a saving to *Esquire* of about a half million dollars annually. So the Postmaster General nixed these privileges. His theory in doing so was that

Congress had provided them for magazines "published for the dissemination of information of a public character, or devoted to literature, the sciences, arts or some special industry," and that *Esquire* made no contribution "to the public good and the public welfare." The Supreme Court rejected this contention. Deprivation of the lower postal rate constituted an economic embargo, it held; the effect of the postal ruling was censorship. And it was unsound to permit such censorship based on the Postmaster General's judgment as to what contributed—and what didn't—to the public good and the public welfare.

In brief, prior to deciding the *Roth* and *Alberts* cases in June of 1957, the Supreme Court had held that adult reading could not be restricted to a level fit for children (*Butler*), that unpublished items could not be prevented from ever seeing the light of day (*Near*), that restrictions imposed on freedom of expression were void if vague and uncertain (*Winters*), and that a publication could not have its circulation impeded merely because of a public official's opinion that it lacked affirmative public value (*Esquire*). But the highest Court had given no definitive meaning to the word "obscene," a word that, in the lower federal courts and in some of the state courts, was in the process of taking on a narrowed meaning.

For generations the American courts had accepted the meaning of "obscenity" promulgated by the English almost a century ago. In 1867, in Wolverhampton, England, 252 copies of a pamphlet entitled *The Confessional Unmasked; shewing the depravity of the Romish priesthood, the iniquity of the Confessional, and the questions put to females in confession* had been seized and ordered destroyed by a local magistrate, Justice Benjamin Hicklin. Although about half of the pamphlet was argumentative and not obscene, in magistrate Hicklin's view, the remainder of it, discussing intercourse and fellatio—among other topics—was such as to render the entire work taboo. Although Hicklin's action was reversed by an intermediate reviewing court, the case was appealed, and in 1868 the Chief Justice, Sir Alexan-

der James Edmund Cockburn, reinstated Hicklin's orders of seizure and destruction.) In so doing, Cockburn framed a test that
was to endure in England until 1959 and did not breathe its last
in America until the 1957 *Butler* and *Roth-Alberts* opinions
served to inter it. "I think the test of obscenity is this," the Lord
Chief Justice said, "whether the tendency of the matter charged
as obscenity is to deprave and corrupt those whose minds are
open to such immoral influences, and into whose hands a publication of this sort may fall." That standard well serves those who
see a threat to youth in any mention of sex, and who would steep
adults solely in the pristine literature of childhood in order to
protect the young. But its defects, today, are obvious. Not only
would it reduce adults to the reading level of their children, but
it would completely ignore artistic, literary, scientific, or other
values. As long as something would tend to "corrupt" a child, it
would be regarded as obscene; other benefits that it might
bestow would be irrelevant. Anthony Comstock's crusading,
book-burning slogan, "Morals, not Art or Literature,"[6] is but a
simplification of the *Hicklin* rule.

Although by the start of the twentieth century, some American
courts had disowned *Hicklin*, Judge Learned Hand, in 1913, held
it to be still binding.[7] At that time, Hand, who in a judicial
career spanning a half-century was to become one of America's
most venerated appellate jurists, was sitting as a federal trial
judge. Before him was an indictment for mailing an allegedly obscene book. Defense counsel's attack conceded that the defendant had mailed the book in question, but urged that as it was not
obscene, the mailing was not criminal. In rejecting this defense,
Hand acted in obedience to the *Hicklin* rule, although in an
opinion he effectively formulated his own strong misgivings:

> . . . I hope it is not improper for me to say that the rule as laid down,
> however consonant it may be with mid-Victorian morals, does not
> seem to me to answer to the understanding and morality of the pres-
> ent time, as conveyed by the words, "obscene, lewd, or lascivious." I
> question whether in the end men will regard that as obscene which is

honestly relevant to the adequate expression of innocent ideas, and whether they will not believe that truth and beauty are too precious to society at large to be mutilated in the interests of those most likely to pervert them to base uses. Indeed, it seems hardly likely that we are even to-day so lukewarm in our interest in letters or serious discussion as to be content to reduce our treatment of sex to the standard of a child's library in the supposed interest of a salacious few, or that shame will for long prevent us from adequate portrayal of some of the most serious and beautiful sides of human nature. That such latitude gives opportunity for its abuse is true enough; there will be, as there are, plenty who will misuse the privilege as a cover for lewdness and a stalking horse from which to strike at purity, but that is true today and only involves us in the same question of fact which we hope that we have the power to answer.

Yet, if the time is not yet when men think innocent all that which is honestly germane to a pure subject, however little it may mince its words, still I scarcely think that they would forbid all which might corrupt the most corruptible, or that society is prepared to accept for its own limitations those which may perhaps be necessary for the weakest of its members . . . . [S]hould not the word "obscene" be allowed to indicate the present critical point in the compromise between candor and shame at which the community may have arrived here and now? . . . To put thought in leash to the average conscience of the time is perhaps tolerable, but to fetter it by the necessities of the lowest and least capable seems a fatal policy.

(Long years after this decision, in an off-the-bench comment, a much older Learned Hand, whose lusty humor provided relief from the majesty commanded by his appearance, his manner, and his incisive mind, was to suggest that the appropriate judicial test for obscenity was to see whether the disputed matter physically aroused the judge, not any judge, but an exceedingly old, old—old—one!)

(In 1933 when the United States customs authorities sought to exclude James Joyce's *Ulysses* from these shores as an obscene book, both the federal trial judge and the United States appellate court (of which Hand was then a member) rejected the *Hicklin* rule.[8] Trial Judge John M. Woolsey delivered an opinion that ranged tastefully, and with simple clarity, over the problems raised when an obscenity charge was pressed against a highly literate work. In describing a day in June 1904, in the lives of a handful of Dubliners, Judge Woolsey observed that Joyce had used, "with astonishing success," a stream of consciousness technique, revealing "not only what is in the focus of each man's observation of the actual things about him, but also in a penumbral zone residue of past impressions, some recent and some drawn up by association from the domain of the subconscious." Joyce's technique, the judge noted, "has required him incidentally to use certain words which are generally considered dirty words and has led at times to what many think is a too poignant preoccupation with sex in the thoughts of his characters. . . . Joyce has been loyal to his technique, and has not funked its necessary implications." Rejecting the claims of obscenity, Judge Woolsey said:

. . . in "Ulysses," in spite of its unusual frankness, I do not detect anywhere the leer of the sensualist. I hold, therefore, that it is not pornographic.

• • •

The words which are criticized as dirty are old Saxon words known to almost all men and, I venture, to many women, and are such words as would be naturally and habitually used, I believe, by the types of folk whose life, physical and mental, Joyce is seeking to describe. In respect of the recurrent emergence of the theme of sex in the minds of his characters, it must always be remembered that his locale was Celtic and his season Spring.

• • •

. . . I have not found anything that I consider to be dirt for dirt's sake. Each word of the book contributes like a bit of mosaic to the detail of the picture which Joyce is seeking to construct for his readers.

Up to this point, the opinion had dealt largely with Joyce's artistry. Woolsey then analyzed the claims of obscenity. In doing this the judge did not use the *Hicklin* test of the impact of passages upon "those whose minds are open to such immoral influences," but viewed the work as a whole, and weighed its sexual impact as upon the average person:

Whether a particular book would tend to excite such impulses and thoughts must be tested by the court's opinion as to its effect on a person with average sex instincts—what the French would call *l'homme moyen sensuel*—who plays, in this branch of legal inquiry, the same role of hypothetical reagent as does the "reasonable man" in the law of torts and "the man learned in the art" on questions of invention in patent law.

• • •

. . . reading "Ulysses" in its entirety, as a book must be read on such a test as this, did not tend to excite sexual impulses or lustful thoughts, but . . . its net effect . . . was only that of a somewhat tragic and very powerful commentary on the inner lives of men and women.

It is only with the normal person that the law is concerned. Such a test . . . therefore, is the only proper test of obscenity in the case of a book like "Ulysses" which is a sincere and serious attempt to devise a new literary method for the observation and description of mankind.

I am quite aware that owing to some of its scenes "Ulysses" is a rather strong draught to ask some sensitive, though normal, persons to take. But my considered opinion, after long reflection, is that whilst in many places the effect of "Ulysses" on the reader undoubtedly is somewhat emetic, nowhere does it tend to be an aphrodisiac.

The government appealed. The higher federal court judges to hear the appeal were Learned Hand, his cousin, Augustus N. Hand (who, although not generally accredited with Learned's primacy in the rolls of America's most celebrated judges, was throughout long years on the appellate bench a highly astute, urbane, and distinguished jurist), and Martin T. Manton. (Some years later Manton's career was to explode in disgrace; his own moral lapses led to his conviction, for conspiring to obstruct justice, and his federal imprisonment.)

The two Hands joined in sustaining Judge Woolsey; Manton,

dissenting, urged reversal. Although the Augustus Hand opinion reflected less certainty than had Woolsey's that *Ulysses* was a latter day classic ("It may be that Ulysses will not last as a substantial contribution to literature, and it is certainly easy to believe that, in spite of the opinion of Joyce's laudators, the immortals will still reign . . . ."), the court below was sustained in all legal points:

That numerous long passages in Ulysses contain matter that is obscene under any fair definition of the word cannot be gainsaid; yet they are relevant to the purpose of depicting the thoughts of the characters and are introduced to give meaning to the whole, rather than to promote lust or portray filth for its own sake. The net effect even of portions most open to attack . . . is pitiful and tragic, rather than lustful . . . . The book as a whole is not pornographic, and, while in not a few spots it is coarse, blasphemous, and obscene, it does not, in our opinion, tend to promote lust. The erotic passages are submerged in the book as a whole and have little resultant effect . . . .

• • •

. . . We think that Ulysses is a book of originality and sincerity of treatment and that it has not the effect of promoting lust. Accordingly it does not fall within the statute, even though it justly may offend many.

Apparently, the government had learned from this appeal. It did not risk the further lambasting that might have come had *Ulysses*' odyssey been prolonged by efforts to bring the book before the United States Supreme Court.

3. The *Roth* and *Alberts* Cases—Obscenity is Not Constitutionally Protected Free Speech, But What is It?

Polonius. What do you read, my lord?
Hamlet. Words, words, words.
        —Shakespeare, *Hamlet,* Act 2, sc. ii.

MORE THAN A SCORE OF YEARS was to pass after the *Ulysses* litigation, until, in 1957, the Supreme Court formulated a test for the obscene. The cases in which the high Court acted did not involve the imaginative genius of James Joyce. They were those of Sam Roth, publisher of erotica whose wares had included sensual excerpts torn from Joyce's *Ulysses,* and David Alberts, co-proprietor with his wife of an unadorned, non-literate West Coast mail-order business in filth.[1]

In 1956, Roth had been convicted for sending pornography through the mails, and had been sentenced by the federal court in New York City to serve five years in prison and to pay a five thousand dollar fine. His conviction and sentence had been affirmed by the intermediate appellate court. During his considerably more than a quarter of a century of writing, pirating, editing, publishing, advertising, and selling borderline items by mail order, Roth had had several bouts with the law on obscenity and fraud charges (the latter for promising more in his advertising throwaways than his merchandising in fact delivered), and had previously served time in prison. Wispily moustached, a thin, emotional, cerebral-looking man, proud of his frequent martyrdom in the financially prosperous cause of free speech, Roth had tendered his mail-order customers everything erotic—with pretensions of literary merit, antiquity's approval, artistry, or scientific value—from aphrodisiac cookbooks to sexual scenes or imaginings wrenched from classics, ancient and modern.

Roth's appeal from his conviction for misusing the mails was argued before the United States Supreme Court in Washington on a day in spring, 1957. On that same vernal day, the Court heard the case of David Alberts, convicted for violating the obscenity statutes of the State of California. Alberts and his wife, like Roth in the East, had been engaged—courtesy of the United States post office's resolute couriers—in a similarly extensive mail-order pornography trade. Alberts was not prosecuted under postal statutes, however; a large quantity of his wares had been seized by Los Angeles deputy sheriffs, armed with search warrants. The books and pictures that led to Alberts's conviction had no possible literary or artistic pretensions. They consisted of bondage and torture pictures (showing young women, partially clad, sometimes in leather garments and with uncomfortably high spike heels, sometimes chained or bound, whipping and otherwise maltreating each other), books of sadistic and masochistic tales (containing descriptions of similar activity), and pictures of nude and partially nude girls, some of unusually gifted development. (One such picture, simply and directly described by the trial judge, was of "a nude girl facing the camera, and there is a table or a counter before her on which there are two champagne glasses, and she had one breast in each of the two glasses—large breasts."[2] Alberts's conviction, and his sentence to sixty days' imprisonment, a five hundred dollar fine, and two years on probation, had been affirmed by the California courts.

From the appeals of these two tawdry defendants the Supreme Court fashioned principles that—despite their vagueness—have to this day been proclaimed as dominant in determining what can, and what cannot, be done in the theater, the cinema, literature, and the graphic arts, without running afoul of the anti-pornography laws of the United States or of any of the fifty states.

In neither Roth's nor Alberts's cases were the materials the most shocking available in the pornography market. Yet neither defendant placed significant reliance on arguments that the particular items that led to his conviction were not obscene. Rather, both trained their guns upon the constitutionality of *any* anti-pornography legislation. If, unimpressed by the exhibits that had led to these two convictions, the Justices had accepted the defense contentions and had invalidated the particular federal and state obscenity statutes, all similar laws throughout America would have similarly been vitiated. As both statutes before the Court were typical American anti-pornography laws, the floodgates would have been burst wide. (There would, for example, have then remained no ban on the showing of "stag" movies. Such films might—with the obscenity laws scuttled—have been shown to the public commercially, to adults, and possibly even to children, drawn to movie theaters by ads and billboards featuring the choicest film moments.)

The United States' assistant solicitor general, Roger D. Fisher, in opposing Roth's appeal, foresaw the repercussions of an adverse decision and displayed the imaginative tactics of the true advocate. Fisher, now professor of law at the Harvard Law School, took an unusual step. His brief ranged far beyond the materials before the Court. He noted that items proscribed by the federal mail statute included not only borderline photographs but literary works focusing on "sex conduct in a vocabulary based on four-letter words," and "hard-core" pornography; motion and still pictures of sex acts, erotic objects, and books and pamphlets of singular detail and offensiveness.[3] To demonstrate vividly this last and largest category, Fisher sent the high Court's Justices something that had not appeared in the trial record in either case—a carton brimful of the most obnoxious, disgustingly pornographic items the postal authorities had collected.[4] The Court was on notice of the impact its decision might have!

The Justices consolidated the *Roth* and *Alberts* cases for argument and for decision and wrote a single set of opinions to govern both (spoken of, generally, as those in the *Roth* case). No portion of the decisions was unanimous: four opinions, occupying (with notes) thirty-eight printed pages in the official Supreme Court reports, were filed. Associate Justice William J. Brennan, Jr., wrote for the majority of five of the nine Judges (himself, and Felix Frankfurter, Harold Burton, Tom C. Clark and Charles E. Whittaker). Chief Justice Earl Warren concurred in the result, but wrote separately, suggesting narrower grounds. Associate Justice John M. Harlan, in another opinion, concurred in affirming Alberts's conviction, but dissented in Roth's case. And Associate Justice William O. Douglas, writing for himself and Hugo L. Black, dissented emphatically from the views of all of his colleagues.

CONSTITUTIONALITY OF ANTI-OBSCENITY LAWS

Roth's lawyers had urged that federal penal laws, with obscenity as their target, contravened the First Amendment to the United States Constitution, that "Congress shall make no law . . . abridging the freedom of speech, or of the press." Similarly, counsel for Alberts had argued that state laws with the same aim conflicted with the Fourteenth Amendment's inhibition, "nor shall any State deprive any person of life, liberty, or property without due process of law." Had the Supreme Court Justices bought these arguments, and declared that any restraints on expression directed against pornography were unconstitutional, they would have instantaneously voided all American strictures on the obscene, *with no possibility of restoring any of them* through the passage of new and more imaginative legislation.

After noting that the high Court had not previously squarely ruled on this question of constitutionality, Justice Brennan's ma-

jority opinion briefly surveyed the early history of free speech in
America, pointing out that by 1792 when fourteen of the states
had ratified the Constitution, most of them prosecuted for libel,
and made blasphemy criminal:

> In light of this history, it is apparent that the unconditional phras-
> ing of the First Amendment was *not* intended to protect every utter-
> ance.
>
> • • •
>
> All ideas having even the slightest redeeming social importance—
> unorthodox ideas, controversial ideas, even ideas hateful to the pre-
> vailing climate of opinion—have the full protection of the guaranties,
> unless excludable because they encroach upon the limited area of
> more important interests. But implicit in the history of the First
> Amendment is the rejection of obscenity as utterly without redeeming
> social importance . . . . *We hold that obscenity is not within the area
> of constitutionally protected speech or press.*

The majority unequivocally rejected the contention that as anti-
obscenity laws punished "incitation to impure sexual *thoughts*,"
constitutional guarantees were violated unless there was "proof
either that obscene material will perceptibly create a clear and
present danger of anti-social *conduct* or will probably induce its
recipients to such conduct" (a contention that, today, as has been
noted, is still pressed by the American Civil Liberties Union).
The "clear and present danger" test, the majority said, did not
apply to *unprotected* speech (and obscenity was unprotected)
but only to constitutionally *protected* speech.

All but Justices Black and Douglas concurred in the opinion
that obscenity was *not* constitutionally protected free speech. The
Chief Justice stated that "the State and Federal Governments *can*
constitutionally punish such conduct." And Justice Harlan wrote
that "nothing in the broad and flexible command of the Due
Process Clause [of the Fourteenth Amendment] forbids California to prosecute one who sells books whose dominant tendency might be to 'deprave or corrupt' a reader." Federal power to
curb obscenity existed but in Harlan's view was extremely lim-

ited: "I do not think that the federal statute can be constitutionally construed to reach other than what the Government has
termed 'hard-core' pornography."

Passionately rejecting the conclusions of their colleagues, Justices Douglas and Black proclaimed:

. . . Government should be concerned with anti-social conduct, not
with utterances. Thus, if the First Amendment guarantee of freedom
of speech and press is to mean anything in this field, it must allow
protests even against the moral code that the standard of the day
sets for the community. In other words, literature should not be
suppressed merely because it offends the moral code of the censor.

• • •

. . . The First Amendment, its prohibition in terms absolute, was designed to preclude courts as well as legislatures from weighing the
values of speech against silence. The First Amendment puts free
speech in the preferred position.

• • •

I would give the broad sweep of the First Amendment full support.
I have the same confidence in the ability of our people to reject
noxious literature as I have in their capacity to sort out the true from
the false in theology, economics, politics, or any other field.

But Justices Douglas and Black were only two of nine. And the
degree of passion with which a belief is embraced does not out-
weigh the impact of a judicial nose count.

Counsel for both Roth and Alberts had also urged that the
statutes under which each had been convicted were unconstitutional because of vagueness. This was the argument that Murray
Winters, distributor of the lurid magazine *Headquarters Detective*, had successfully used before the same Court nine years earlier. If a penal statute is so uncertain in its scope that it gives no
warning telling persons what it is that they can, and what they
cannot, do, it is void. Its very vagueness threatens to deprive
persons of liberty without "due process of law": a defendant has
no way of knowing his act is unlawful until long after he has
done it, when a court declares it to have been violative of the

laws. Two separate statutes were before the high Court, one federal and one state, both in language typical of America's obscenity laws: the federal statute barred from mails "Every *obscene, lewd, lascivious,* or *filthy* book, pamphlet, picture, paper, letter, writing, print or other publication of an *indecent* character"[5]; the California provision declared it criminal for anyone to write, publish, sell, or otherwise distribute or issue "any *obscene* or *indecent* writing, paper, or book."[6]

Profuse use of adjectives had been adequate for obscenity enforcement at a time when post-Victorian thinking still assured all but universal agreement that most representations or descriptions of sex or nudity (other than in classical painting or sculpture) were *per se* obscene, indecent, and so forth—and so taboo. But by the 1950s those sweet and simple conditions had passed. That which one man might find obscene would be deemed mere realism by a second, and by a third would be praised as an artistic triumph.

However, having in sight that carton of smut sent to them by the assistant solicitor general, and possibly mindful of the pornographer's field day that a finding of vagueness would have assured, the Court's majority searched beyond the wording of the statutes and established its own definition for determining when actionable obscenity existed. Then having, judicially, imparted meaning to the word "obscene," the Justices proceeded to reject the contention that the statutory language, *language that had necessitated their own formulation,* was too vague to be legislatively sound. Speaking for the majority, and examining the statutes, Justice Brennan said:

These words, applied according to the proper standard for judging obscenity . . . give adequate warning of the conduct proscribed and mark ". . . boundaries sufficiently distinct for judges and juries fairly to administer the law . . . . That there may be marginal cases in which it is difficult to determine the side of the line on which a particular fact situation falls is no sufficient reason to hold the language too ambiguous to define a criminal offense . . . ."

Whether the Justices were whistling up their own convictions; whether, in fact, the "boundaries [are] sufficiently distinct for judges and juries fairly to administer the law" is, as both later cases and police and prosecution experience were to prove, subject to extremely substantial doubts.

Nine years before the *Roth* decision, during the course of another Supreme Court obscenity argument, the late Associate Justice Robert H. Jackson, questioning counsel for a book that had been banned, asked: "Does your argument mean that we have to take every obscenity case and decide the constitutional issues on the merits of the literary work? It seems to me," the Justice continued, "that would mean that we would become the High Court of Obscenity."[7] Examination of the standards fixed by the *Roth* case as giving meaning to "obscene" (and to its synonyms, "lewd," "lascivious," "indecent," and all those other dirt-describing words), reveals that the *Roth* decision created problems at least as rapidly as it solved them. And as the ultimate solution to each of those problems rests with the Supreme Court, such examination also presages the extent to which the solemn, black-robed, near-omnipotent Justices, sitting in the law's holy-of-holies in the nation's capital, were to become judges of America's "High Court of Obscenity."

THE Roth TEST FOR OBSCENITY

The *Roth* formulation, at first glance, may not seem difficult. Legally actionable obscenity exists, the five Justices declared, if *"to the average person, applying contemporary community standards, the dominant theme of the material taken as a whole appeals to prurient interest"* and is *"utterly without redeeming social importance."*

The words are simple—but their sense is not.

Who is "the average person"? Are pictures of male nudes, designed for sale to deviates, to be tested by questioning their impact on the man-in-the-street, or on an effete interior decorator?

Are lurid stories of flagellation and of singed flesh to be examined by gauging their effect on the normally sexed male, or on
hip-booted cultists of the scourge and the bullwhip? To the
typical adult, such items are likely to arouse naught but curiosity; in quantity, they will be found boring; at worst, revolting.
They are unlikely to goad him into acts condemned by society.
But the steady market for sadistic and homosexual pictures,
books, and magazines testifies that their prurient appeal to the
aberrant is great and, probably, is getting greater. Should there
be any danger to our social fabric from these items, it lies in the
stimulation to offbeat actions that they may provide for the immature and for the deviate; it is not from the boredom they
produce in the typical adult.

The same words, "the average person," create a second difficulty at the other end of the spectrum. Where in the "average
person" test is there leeway for the sale of concededly obscene
material to that professionally asexual scholar—the sociologist,
the librarian, or (sometimes) the lawyer—who has a serious,
legitimate, and impersonal interest in studying or collecting the
obscene? It is all the same, taking the *Roth* wording literally,
whether the material is offered for sale to the village sex maniac
or to the psychiatrist who is trying to comprehend his conduct.
Rome's Vatican Library and Indiana's Kinsey Institute each has
extensive and growing pornography collections. The "average
person" standard does not, however, in its phrasing distinguish
such connoisseurs from quite different collectors who may use
pornography to stimulate themselves and those whom they may
be entertaining. How, as long as the standard fails to spell out
exceptions based on the identity of the particular customer, can
sales to the Vatican Library or to the Kinsey Institute be legiti-
matized without simultaneously warping the high Court's formulation?[8]

The "average person" portion of the *Roth* standard has a third
defect. The same person, known in the law of torts as the "reasonable man," is expected to live up to certain minimal standards

of behavior when behind the wheel of his car, regardless of the mood he may be in. These are the standards that the law imposes on all drivers. (If he does not, and someone is injured, he will be held liable.) When we talk of the "reasonable man" driving a car, we are thinking of the "reasonable driver." But when we speak of the impact of alleged pornography on the "average person," we ignore the fact that the average person does not himself regularly buy, or read, or see, such items. Margaret Mead has commented that pornography appeals to "the dreaming adolescent, the frightened, the impotent, the bored and sated, the senile . . . not yet old enough to seek sexual partners, or [who] has lost the precious power of spontaneous sexual feeling."[9] Testing pornography's impact on "the average man" becomes a wholly artificial exercise. Focusing on a completely unreal situation, we cannot make any *real* finding of fact. We can only hypothesize, only theorize. Indeed, even our theorizing is thrown askew by another factor: can we predict how the "average person," with deviant strains neither greater nor less than those Dr. Kinsey has found typical, is expected to act while reading pornography? Wise Judge Curtis Bok of Pennsylvania noted the vast variability of any single person's reactions:

If he reads an obscene book when his sensuality is low, he will yawn over it or find that its suggestibility leads him off on quite different paths. If he reads the Mechanics' Lien Act while his sensuality is high, things will stand between him and the page that have no business there. How can anyone say that he will infallibly be affected one way or another by one book or another?[10]

If we are to search for, and to make, a meaningful finding of fact, we should have to focus on the alleged pornography's impact on those persons for whom the questioned material was designed. Shifting our focus in this way from the "average person" to the actual purchaser, or to the person at whom the advertising was directed, would remove us from an unreal area of speculation, and put us in an area in which some realistic fact-finding was possible.

But the "average person" portion is only one of the defects of the *Roth* formulation. That standard goes on to talk of this "average person *applying contemporary community standards*." What is the "community" of which this speaks? If we are talking of a book or of a picture, is our concern with the literary or artistic community? A community so delineated is certain to be more tolerant than is a community defined geographically, consisting of everyone in the neighborhood—art-lovers, literati, occasional readers, newspaper scanners, *Look*-and-*Life*-lookers, comic book devotees, and plain non-readers—all fused in cross-sectional proportions. If it is a geographically defined community, is it the community of Mauch Chunk, Pennsylvania, that of Keokuk, Iowa, or that of Jackson, Mississippi; or is the New York City community, or that of Westport, Connecticut? When a publication has nationwide circulation, impact may vary as widely as the geography over which it ranges. Or are all of these suggested "communities" too narrow? Does the *Roth* case refer us to the standards of a national community: blending rural, suburban, urban, and megalopolitan, and further blending everyone in all of these places from the most sensitive of art-lovers to the most earthbound of non-readers? Clearly there could rarely be a conglomerate consensus *as to obscenity* from such an admixture of unmixables. How, then, can evidence establish *beyond a reasonable doubt* (the measure of proof required in any criminal case), just how such a "community" would react to any particular questioned material?

Assuming however that a community, of whatever dimensions, can be described, how are its standards to be made known? Are juries, or are judges sitting without juries, sufficiently attuned to the necessary pulses to perceive unaided what such a community's standards are? If not, who are the experts to whom the standards are most likely to be revealed? Are they the community's clergymen (in well-balanced and politically aware fashion, one of each faith), or its sociologists or psychologists? Or are they its standard-makers: its magazine, newspaper, and television columnists and critics?

The questions multiply if the *Roth* standard—this formula *designed to clarify* the meaning of the word "obscene'"—is examined further. *Roth* requires a determination of "the dominant theme of the material taken as a whole." How is such dominance discovered? When is one theme merely a vehicle for another? Sampling best-selling novels of recent years, solely with reference to this portion of the standard, illustrates the problem. Was, for example, sexual dalliance the dominant theme of *Forever Amber,* or was it life at the royal court of England several centuries ago? Was illicit sex the dominant theme of *Peyton Place,* or was it life in a small New England community? Were sexual tournaments the dominant theme of *The Carpetbaggers,* or was it the career of an eccentric and daring Hollywood tycoon? Turning to more hotly litigated novels, was sexual fulfillment the theme of *Lady Chatterley's Lover,* or was it the lot of the English gamekeeper or the impact of the industrial revolution on England? Was commercially variegated sex the dominant theme of *Memoirs of a Woman of Pleasure (Fanny Hill),* or—if there is a difference—was it a view of eighteenth century middle class English indoor life?

What is "the dominant theme . . . taken as a whole" of materials that have a multitude of themes, none apparently dominant, such as anthologies, far ranging and disjointed monologues, magazines in which conscious efforts have been made to achieve some balance in their contents?

Two key phrases of the *Roth* standard have not yet been discussed. When does allegedly obscene material "appeal to the prurient interest?" And when is it "utterly without redeeming social importance?"

"Prurient" is still another synonym, of sorts, for the statutory terms "obscene," "indecent," "lewd," "lascivious," and all of the others. Webster's, for instance, defines "prurient" as "Itching; longing; uneasy with desire or longing; of persons, having itching, morbid or *lascivious* longings; of desire; curiosity, or propensity, *lewd.*" This dictionary definition not only defines "prurient" in terms of the statutory words "lascivious" and "lewd" that "prurient" was supplied to clarify (thus coming full circle), but it fails to specify whether only lust-inciting is intended, or whether "prurient" also includes items that are disgusting or vile. It is clear, for example, that titillatingly sensual descriptions are likely to be deemed of prurient appeal; but what of overly graphic word-pictures of either excretory functions or of sadistic conduct, and what of the interminable use of those four-letter words that we know as "obscenities"? Are they equally banned pornography? A footnote to the *Roth* majority opinion does not quite answer this question, although it strongly points to the conclusion that these areas too would be deemed to possess "prurient appeal."[11]

Clearly, the most difficult portion of the *Roth* standard is its statement that nothing is actionable obscenity unless it is "utterly without redeeming social importance." The difficulties are two-fold: first, the language itself is unclear—the phrase's few words are internally inconsistent; second, the question of "social importance" in the area of obscenity is one on which no unanimity of thought can ever be anticipated.

As to the incongruity in wording: "utterly" is an absolute concept; it recognizes no middle ground, no compromise; "redeeming," on the other hand, is the essence of compromise; it intimates a variable amount (if one price, for example, will not redeem, doubling it, or tripling it, may); "importance" too (defined, in part, in Webster's as "consequence; weight; moment; significance") is a word of degree. The phrase "utterly without redeeming social importance" thus juxtaposes an absolute concept against two variables. What, then, is its meaning? Further analysis is bound to come out as gobbledygook because of this inconsistency, but we can try: if something is not "utterly without" *any* social value, but has so little as to fail to constitute "importance," it would then be "utterly without redeeming social importance"; but how does one decide, when an item has *some* social value, that it has so little as not to be enough to give it the necessary "redeeming social importance"? (Had the Court meant that anything having *any* "social value" could not be deemed actionably obscene, it could have readily so said, omitting the words "redeeming" and "importance" and using the simpler phrase, "utterly without social value."[12]

If all this is not as sparkling clear as springwater, the use of the testimony of experts on "social importance" is unlikely to filter out any of its murkiness. With all art forms today—the novel, music, dance, theater, painting, sculpture, photography, movies— in the throes of continuing experimentation, accredited prophets of the avant-garde will, *testifying in complete good faith,* find literary or artistic importance in almost anything that serves to shatter convention. Overtly dealing in the sensual or in those bodily organs or functions that custom dictates be kept private, is now—and may remain for a few years to come—one certain way of garnering acclaim. One instance will suffice. Consider a tiny-budgeted far-out movie, *Flaming Creatures* (a movie so offbeat that it hadn't played in any of the expresso theaters), a movie that periodically throughout its near random sequences repeatedly flashed close-ups of male penises and female breasts. Courageously non-conforming critic and sensitive novelist Susan Sontag had this to say:

The only thing to be regretted about the close-ups of limp penises and bouncing breasts, the shots of masturbation and oral sexuality, in Jack Smith's *Flaming Creatures* is that it makes it hard simply to talk about this remarkable and beautiful film; one has to *defend* it. But in defending as well as talking about the film, I don't want to make it seem less outrageous, less shocking than it is. . . . But even if *Flaming Creatures* were pornographic, that is if it did . . . have the power to excite sexually, I would argue that this is a power of art for which it is shameful to apologize. Art is, always, the sphere of freedom. In those difficult works of art, works which we now call avant-garde, the artist consciously exercises his freedom. And as the price the avant-garde artist pays for the freedom to be outrageous is the small number of his audience, the least of his rewards should be freedom from meddling censorship by the philistine, the prudish and the blind.[13]

Although critics, like Susan Sontag, express their bona fide critical convictions, surely their strong empathies for the censored and antipathies toward censorship are likely to goad them into desperately imaginative hunts for "social importance" in anything touched by the censor's hand.

Obviously, if any censorship is to remain, literary, artistic, or other social significance should not be ignored in determining what items must remain beyond its reach. Cavalierly dismissing such values, as did the English *Hicklin* test, or seeking deliberately to override them as in the Comstock slogan of "Morals, not Art or Literature," are follies of an age irretrievably gone. But using the measuring stick of whether the material is "utterly without redeeming social importance" may not be the wisest way of handling claims of merit made on behalf of items otherwise possibly deemed pornographic.

The *Roth* formula, and all of the uncertainties it entails, provided by the Justices to salvage America's obscenity laws, illustrates the vice of trying to use judicial curettes to scrape clean legislative abortions. Everyone would be happier had either the need for the surgery been avoided, or had it been properly done in the first place. When legislators, year after year, in almost all of the states, leave our statute books glutted with laws directed against the "obscene," "lewd," and "lascivious," without specifying just what they have in mind, they force the courts into attempting to do their work for them: either the judges must provide definitions, or must declare the statutes void. And the Supreme Court has done the former. Unhappily, however, the uncertainties that remained once the *Roth* standard had been formulated were as great as those that had led to its formulation.

The very existence of the *Roth* test for obscenity reveals the error of those who wail that the high Tribunal's Justices are cynical men, reshaping America into a latter-day Sodom and Gomorrah. What the majority did proves quite the contrary. Had the Justices failed to provide a formula defining obscenity, the attacks on both the federal and California statutes for vagueness, logically, should have been sustained. The majority's formulation, illusory as it may have been, seemed to shape flesh around the bare bones of inadequate although typical statutes. In so doing, it appeared to give obscenity some ascertainable meaning, and afforded the Court some basis for rejecting the claim that the statutes were void for vagueness.

4. The *Nights of Horror* Case—Prohibiting, Not Prosecuting, Prurience

There are a thousand hacking at the branches of evil to one who is striking at the root. . . .
   —Henry David Thoreau, *Walden (Economy)* (1854)

ALTHOUGH ITS DECISION in the *Roth* and *Alberts* cases has been, despite its vagueness, the Supreme Court's most important single pronouncement in the pornography field, certain others of the high Tribunal's recent rulings require attention. One such was in a case argued the very day on which the *Roth* and *Alberts* cases were heard, and decided the same date, June 24, 1957, when the high Court handed down its decision in those obscenity landmarks. On that day, which saw a divided Court produce four separate *Roth-Alberts* opinions, the Justices split five to four, and producing four more (somewhat shorter) opinions, affirmed New York's action in enjoining the distribution of a series of paperback books that had been marketed under the title, *Nights of Horror*.[1]

The title was apt. When the City of New York had sought to ban the sale of those booklets, the injunctive action was taken before state trial court justice Matthew M. Levy. In his 1955 opinion, ordering the injunction, Judge Levy had described the content of these booklets, in part, in these words:

"Nights of Horror" is no haphazard title. Perverted sexual acts and macabre tortures of the human body are repeatedly depicted. The books contain numbers of acts of male torturing female and some vice versa—by most ingenious means. These gruesome acts included such horrors as cauterizing a woman's breast with a hot iron, placing hot coals against a woman's breasts, tearing breasts off, placing hot irons against a woman's armpits, pulling off a girl's fingernails with white-hot pincers, completely singeing away the body hairs, working a female's skin away from her flesh with a knife, gouging and burning eyes out of their sockets, ringing the nipples of the breast with needles . . . . Sucking a victim's blood was pictured; and so was pouring molten lead into a girl's mouth and ears; and putting honey on a girl's breasts, vagina and buttocks—and then putting hundreds of great red ants on the honey. Sodomy, rape, lesbianism, seduction prevail. Youngsters disrobing in the presence of and to the detailed recorded delight of elderly males was described. Incidental training of the teen-ager to narcotic addiction and sexual perversion was part of the activities engaged in.[2]

(In August 1954, New Yorkers were stunned to learn of the wanton savagery of four Brooklyn teen-agers who horsewhipped, beat, kicked, and burned their several victims, ultimately drowning one of them—all for amusement. The eighteen-year-old leader of the group, Jack Koslow, who described the killing by drowning as "the supreme adventure," boasted of having read every volume in the *Nights of Horror* series. A psychiatrist who examined him found "the parallelism is complete" between *Nights of Horror* texts and pictures and the methods used by the youthful killers.[3] Koslow's January 1955 life imprisonment sentence, on his first degree murder conviction, was ultimately reduced to ten to twenty years.)

The New York statute that was under attack in the case—section 22-a of the state's penal law—set up a procedure for *preventing the distribution* of existent obscene materials, rather than simply arresting each dealer for each sale of an allegedly obscene item. It authorized the confiscation and destruction of the seized contraband. The United States Supreme Court majority's opin-

ion, written by the late Justice Felix Frankfurter, rejected the
contention that such injunctive processes involved "prior restraints" like those the Court had declared void in its opinion
in the case against anti-Semitic publisher J. M. Near, a quarter
of a century earlier. Sustaining New York's right to move to
prevent alleged pornography from being distributed (here the
injunction was against Kingsley Books, Inc., purveyors of the
Nights of Horror pamphlets), the Frankfurter opinion said:

> . . . Instead of requiring the bookseller to dread that the offer for
> sale of a book may, without prior warning, subject him to a criminal
> prosecution with the hazard of imprisonment, the civil procedure as-
> sures him that such consequences cannot follow unless he ignores a
> court order specifically directed to him for a prompt and carefully
> circumscribed determination of the issue of obscenity . . . .
>
> Criminal enforcement and the proceeding under §22-a interfere
> with a book's solicitation of the public precisely at the same stage.
> In each situation the law moves after publication; the book need not
> in either case have yet passed into the hands of the public . . . .

Two contributions to the law—or, rather, to the potential for
change and development in the law—were found in the *Kingsley
Books* opinions. One was in the majority opinion, the other was
a suggestion made in two of the three dissents.

In sustaining New York's then novel injunctive procedures,
the Supreme Court majority demonstrated that the Constitution
had not fossilized anti-pornography enforcement methods in the
form they customarily took in dealing with the obscene. Procedures were shown to be viable: new ones, adaptable to fit newly
realized needs, were not to be held defective merely because,
in the area of sacredly protected free speech, they were departures from tradition.

Two of the dissenting opinions touched on an important point
that had been ignored in the same day's formulation by the *Roth*
majority. Speaking only for himself, Chief Justice Earl Warren,
who in his *Roth* concurrence had made the same point, noted:

> . . . the same object [an allegedly obscene item] may have wholly

different impact depending upon the setting in which it is placed. Under this statute, the setting is irrelevant.

It is the manner of use that should determine obscenity. It is the conduct of the individual that should be judged, not the quality of art or literature . . . .

And in the dissent delivered by Justice William O. Douglas (joined by Justices Black and Brennan), the same point was somewhat differently made:

In New York City the publisher may have been selling his tracts to juveniles, while in Rochester he may have sold to professional people. The nature of the group among whom the tracts are distributed may have an important bearing on the issue of guilt in any obscenity prosecution . . . .

Hence four of the high Court's nine Justices, on the very day that *Roth* was handed down, suggested that any particular item was not, necessarily, to be deemed obscene under *all* circumstances simply because it was obscene under *some*. This approach was to be further developed nine years later, in March 1966, by a majority of the Justices (the Chief Justice, and Justices Brennan, Clark, White, and Fortas), with Justices Douglas and Black among those taking sharp issue with it.

Judicial tolerance for experimentation with hitherto untested approaches that are aimed at removing the virus from the pornography traffic, and judicial appreciation of the wisdom of a variable obscenity standard (one that will inspect the advertising, the customer, the media, and the viewing circumstances, as well as the purported contraband), both lend encouragement to those statutory proposals that Part IV of this volume suggests and discusses. The Justices, in their several *Kingsley Books* opinions, strongly intimated that in dealing with alleged pornography, legislative imaginations may be liberated from old molds and new means ventured when the old answers prove to be no answers at all.

5. *Smith* v. *California* — the Case of the Unknowing Pornographer

Where ignorance is bliss,
'Tis folly to be wise.
—Thomas Gray,
On a Distant Prospect of Eton College (1742)

IN DECEMBER 1959, two and a half years after the decisions in the *Roth, Alberts,* and *Kingsley Books* cases, in reviewing the conviction of a Los Angeles bookseller named Eleazer Smith, the Supreme Court imposed a new restraint on obscenity enforcement.[1] Although all nine Justices agreed that the bookseller's conviction could not stand, their reasoning so varied that five separate opinions were filed. A bare majority, five, of the Judges (Earl Warren, William J. Brennan, Jr., Tom C. Clark, Potter Stewart, and Charles E. Whittaker) concurred in the law as reported in an opinion written by Justice Brennan.

Eleazer Smith, who ran a retail store selling new and used books and magazines, had been convicted for violating a municipal ordinance. The Los Angeles statute had required no proof of an actual sale, but had made criminal the mere possession, in certain carefully listed places, of any "obscene" or indecent" writing. The places specified included all areas within three hundred yards of schools, parks, and playgrounds, and the interiors of candy stores, movie theaters, and record shops (all frequented by youngsters)—as well as of billiard halls, liquor stores, bars, etc. Obviously ignorant of the true identity of his customer, Smith had sold a policeman a book, *Sweeter Than Life* (its publisher used the name "Vixen Press"), that dealt with lesbianism. Not so obviously, but according to Smith's sworn trial testimony, his customer's identity was not the full extent of his ignorance: Smith disowned any knowledge of the character of the content of this pulp novel—although he had instructed his clerk to permit no one under twenty-one to handle the books or magazines.

As it had done in the *Roth-Alberts* and *Kingsley Books* cases, the high Court majority once again avoided ruling on the obscenity of the material, accepting the findings of the California courts that the book was obscene.

Moving to an area not foreshadowed in *Roth*, Justice Brennan wrote:

. . . our holding in *Roth* does not recognize any State power to restrict the dissemination of books which are not obscene; and we think this ordinance's strict liability feature would tend seriously to have that effect, by penalizing booksellers, even though they had not the slightest notice of the character of the books they sold . . . . For if the bookseller is criminally liable without knowledge of the contents, and the ordinance fulfills its purpose, he will tend to restrict the books he sells to those he has inspected; and thus the State will have imposed a restriction upon the distribution of constitutionally protected as well as obscene literature. . . . If the contents of bookshops and periodical stands were restricted to material of which their proprietors had made an inspection, they might be depleted indeed. The bookseller's limitation in the amount of reading material with which he could familiarize himself, and his timidity in the face of his absolute criminal liability, thus would tend to restrict the public's access to forms of the printed word which the State could not supress directly. The bookseller's self-censorship, compelled by the State, would be a censorship affecting the whole public, hardly less virulent for being privately administered. Through it, the distribution of all books, both obscene and not obscene, would be impeded.

And so, the *Smith* majority held, a defendant could not be convicted of an obscenity violation without proof that he knew the "character" of the material on which the charge was bottomed; legally phrased, "scienter" (knowledge of the item's contents) was necessary to establish guilt under the obscenity laws. The Los Angeles ordinance had not required scienter, purporting to make *all* possession criminal without regard for the defendant's knowledge, or lack of it. Therefore, the Court declared, that ordinance was invalid.

Once again, the high Court's ruling, although giving some guidance (obscenity statutes, henceforth, either expressly or by implication, would have to require proof of scienter), suggested a number of questions. Must firsthand knowledge of the particular item's content be proven? No, said the majority:

> Eyewitness testimony of a bookseller's perusal of a book hardly need be a necessary element in proving his awareness of its contents. The circumstances may warrant the inference that he was aware of what a book contained, despite his denial.

Just what "circumstances," of course, was the jugular question. As the high Court was to require something not specified in the statutes, just what was it that they were requiring? Unfortunately, for those in law enforcement who must know what is expected of them, the Court was silent as to the answer.

Justice Frankfurter, concurring in the reversal of Smith's conviction, took the majority to task for this evasion:

> Obviously the Court is not holding that a bookseller must familiarize himself with the contents of every book in his shop. No less obviously, the Court does not hold that a bookseller who insulates himself against knowledge about an offending book is thereby free to maintain an emporium for smut. How much or how little awareness that a book may be found to be obscene suffices to establish scienter, or what kind of evidence may satisfy the how much or the how little, the Court leaves for another day.
>
> . . . I submit invalidating an obscenity statute because a State dis-

penses altogether with the requirement of scienter does require some indication of the scope and quality of scienter that is required. It ought at least to be made clear, and not left for future litigation, that the Court's decision in its practical effect is not intended to nullify the conceded power of the State to prohibit booksellers from trafficking in obscene literature.

Obscenity having become as uncomfortable a problem as it had, the Brennan opinion in the *Eleazer Smith* case was understandable. It would keep most of our nation's anti-obscenity statutes on the books, necessitating at most their amendment to include the requirement of scienter. Yet it would serve to narrow the area in which *Roth's* standards, with all of their uncertainties, would have to be invoked: if knowledge was not demonstrable, that would end it—the difficult question of whether or not an item was legally "obscene" would never have to be reached.

The trouble was, as Justice Frankfurter foresaw, guides were lacking to indicate just what scienter meant. When could knowledge be soundly inferred, and just how much knowledge would be necessary?

The celebrated obscenity cases, those the public reads about in the news reports and in columnists' diatribes against the censor, rarely embrace any scienter difficulties. In such cases, generally involving claims of literary or artistic merit, full knowledge of the contents of the disputed items is almost certain to be conceded, both prosecution and defense seeking a court ruling on whether or not actionable obscenity exists. But even lacking this voluntary cooperation on the part of the defense, the knowledge requirement poses no real problem if the alleged obscenity is in a popularly shown movie or in a significantly advertised book. When the obscenity dispute centers on an item that has been greeted by pre-release fanfare—as were the reissues of *Tropic of Cancer* and *Fanny Hill*—proof of the necessary knowledge is unlikely to be troublesome.

When, however, the alleged pornography is covertly published trash, marketed by those bookshops that major in merchandising muck, proving scienter can pose a number of difficulties. Is the "general character" of a store legitimately the subject of proof, and if so, can scienter be inferred from the fact that the store specializes in retailing books, pictures, and magazines dealing with sex and nudity? Although the bookseller's string of prior arrests—or convictions—for other obscenity sales may demonstrate convincingly that he knows exactly what he is doing, ordinarily these cannot be proven without running afoul of rules of evidence that bar proof of other crimes.

The Supreme Court has not yet said what its Justices meant by scienter. And trial judges and justices of intermediate appellate courts who do not like being reversed on appeal by the higher courts, are in practice likely to play it safe by requiring a goodly amount of proof of knowledge, enough to satisfy *any* appellate judge who may give scienter its broadest construction. If such proof is lacking, they will find that the state has failed to prove knowledge adequately, and out goes the case.

A word of clarification, concerning criminal appeals, is in order. If, after a criminal trial has been started, a judge dismisses the case, finding that the state's proof is legally insufficient to sustain the charges, the constitutional right against being placed twice in jeopardy on the same charge protects the defendant against any further prosecution. Having been once tried, his freedom is secure. It is of no consequence that the trial judge's ruling was shockingly erroneous; the error cannot be appealed, the defendant cannot be retried. On the other hand, if the judge fails to dismiss the charge, and there is a conviction, the defendant can *always* appeal, getting the trial judge's action reviewed, and possibly reversed. This difference affords trial judges, not all of whom are noted for either their courage or their legal acumen, the simplest of means for shielding their possible errors from the gaze of the appellate courts. "When in doubt, throw it out," is the trial judge's safety slogan. Applying this to the scienter problem, if the trial judge throws out an obscenity charge, stating that the proof was not legally adequate to constitute scienter, he *cannot* be reviewed or reversed. If he tries the case, however, and there is a conviction, he risks reversal—and embarrassment—at the hands of appellate judges who may read Justice Brennan's opinion as requiring more proof than was thought necessary at the trial.

Thus scienter, with its still protean shape, causes difficulties in the trial courts. Yet these are minor compared to the scienter problem on the streets, the true locus of law enforcement. What sort of evidence can a diligent policeman collect to prove—to an uncertain, unspecified degree—what has been going on in the mind of an accused smut merchant? Police attempts to deal with this practical difficulty themselves create new problems.

In early fall, 1966, the high Court heard argument in two cases—one from New York and one from Kentucky—dealing with the scienter question. Seven months later, on May 8, 1967, its decision was handed down. Ducking scienter completely, and thus arousing the dander of two dissenting Judges (Justices Harlan and Clark) who urged that "the issues for which the cases were taken should be decided," the Supreme Court ruled that the items—particular girlie magazines and pulp novels—were not in fact obscene.[2] The riddle of scienter remained.

6. Pictured Male Nudes—Their Lack of "Patent Offensiveness"

> All the world is queer save me and thee; and sometimes I think thee
> is a little queer.
> —Anonymous

In June 1962, two and a half years having gone by since it promulgated the *Smith* scienter rule, the high Tribunal in Washington ventured its first major post-*Smith* obscenity decision. (In the interim there had been one case in 1961 significant for its impact on search warrants as commonly used in pornography investigations.[1])

The 1962 decision, in the case of *Manual Enterprises* v. *Day,* had its wellsprings in Post Office Department action barring from the mails three magazines for homosexuals, *MANual, Trim,* and *Grecian Guild Pictorial,* both because of their alleged obscenity and because they advertised where allegedly pornographic pictures might be purchased.[2] The Justices, although voiding action that had been taken by both the federal courts and the postal authorities, were unable to muster majority support for any single reason for so doing. Seven members of the Court, split four ways, participated in the decision: Justice John M. Harlan wrote for reversal for himself and Justice Stewart; Justice William J. Brennan, Jr., concurred in the Harlan-Stewart action, but for quite different reasons, writing for himself, the Chief Justice, and Justice Douglas; Justice Hugo L. Black also concurred, but this time without stating his grounds. Justice Tom C. Clark dissented. Although in writings about the law the adjective "vigorous" is so commonly wedded to the noun "dissent" that the latter seems uncomfortably puny unless so beefed up, Justice Clark wrote what must, truly, be termed a "vigorous dissent." It lead off with the pungent comment:

> While those in the majority like ancient Gaul are split into three parts, the ultimate holding of the Court today, despite the clear congressional mandate . . . requires the United States Post Office to be the world's largest disseminator of smut and Grand Informer of the names and places where obscene material may be obtained.

How egregious were the materials that provoked Justice Clark to be so uncharitable to his colleagues? Justice Harlan, whose opinion was one of the two that reversed the mail ban, had noted:

> . . . the following administrative findings . . . are supported by substantial evidence . . . which we, and indeed the parties, for the most part, themselves, accept: (1) the magazines are not, as asserted by petitioners, physical culture or "body-building" publications, but are composed primarily, if not exclusively, for homosexuals, and have no literary, scientific or other merit; (2) they would appeal to the "prurient interest" of such sexual deviates, but would not have any interest for sexually normal individuals; and (3) the magazines are read almost entirely by homosexuals, *and possibly a few adolescent males;* the ordinary male adult would not normally buy them.
>
> • • •
>
> . . . Our own independent examination of the magazines leads us to conclude that the most that can be said of them is that they are dismally unpleasant, uncouth, and tawdry.

Describing the photographs in the magazines, the Harlan opinion, in a footnote, quoted these graphic words from the United States' brief:

Many of the photographs were of nude male models, usually posed
with some object in front of their genitals . . . a number were of nude
or partially nude males with emphasis on their bare buttocks . . . .
Although none of the pictures directly exposed the model's genitals,
some showed his pubic hair and others suggested what appeared to
be a semi-erect penis . . . . Two of the magazines had pictures of
pairs of models posed together suggestively . . . . The magazines also
contained photographs of virtually nude models wearing only shoes,
boots, helmets or leather jackets . . . . There were also pictures of
models posed with chains or of one model beating another while a
third held his face in his hands as if weeping . . . .

And Justice Clark, in his dissent, found these facts in the trial
record:

Turning to Womack, the president and directing force of all three
corporate publishers . . . Mr. Womack admitted that the magazines
were planned· for homosexuals, designed to appeal to and stimulate
their erotic interests. To improve on this effort, he made suggestions
to photographers as to the type of pictures he wanted. For example,
he informed one of the studios listed in his publications that "phy-
sique fans want their 'truck driver types' already cleaned up, show-
ered, and ready for bed . . . [and] it is absolutely essential that the
models have pretty faces and a personality not totally unrelated to
sex appeal." Womack had also suggested to the photographers that
they exchange customer names with the hopes of compiling a master
list of homosexuals. He himself had been convicted of selling obscene
photographs via the mails . . . . More recently he had pleaded not
guilty by reason of insanity to like charges . . . . Furthermore, he
was warned in March, April, and July of 1959 that a number of his
photographer advertisers were being prosecuted for mailing obscene
matter and that he might be violating the law in transmitting through
the mails their advertisements.

Six of the Justices voted to overturn the Post Office's bans.
The Brennan opinion closely traced the relevant mail statutes'
histories, and concluded that Congress, having created penal
sanctions, had given no administrative authority to the postal
authorities to ban seeming obscenity from the mails. Limited to

consideration of postal legislation, the restrained Brennan opinion threw no general light on the problem of pornography. In contrast, Justice Harlan's opinion dealt squarely with the obscenity question; whether light was shed or shadow intensified, however, may be the subject of legitimate dispute.

As officially chronicled in the printed bound opinions of the United States Supreme Court, the Harlan views appear first, the position traditionally reserved for the views of the Court majority. This placement priority seems to make his the "prevailing" opinion, although it speaks for but two of the Justices. His opinion has commonly—although incorrectly—been deemed the holding of the high Court.

The intermediate appellate court had held that, in dealing with items designed to appeal to deviates, the "average person" in the community whose prurient interests were relevant was the "average homosexual." This made sense; both experience and common sense showed that items appealing to the pruriency of deviates sell to deviates. The "average person," even in sophisticated metropolitan New York City, will rarely be exposed to more than the cover, with its body-building façade, of the homosexual magazines. Insofar as such magazines may stimulate any conduct or heighten any emotions or attitudes, they do so through their real audience of homosexuals, not through any theoretical *Roth* standard audience of "average persons." But Justice Harlan expressly passed up the opportunity of deciding the case on this ground; had he done so his opinion might have helped to resolve one of *Roth's* riddles. Harlan virtually ignored the action of the court below; his opinion rested on another basis. Another four years were to slide by before, in the *Mishkin* case dealing with sado-masochistic pulp literature, a majority of the Justices was finally to rule that "the appeal of this type of material [is] to be assessed in terms of the sexual interests of its intended and probable recipient group."[3]

As had been done by the Supreme Court's majority in the *Smith* case, Justice Harlan (and, with him, Justice Stewart) once again sought and found a means of avoiding entanglement with the vague and multi-problem *Roth* standard. The means were quite similar to those invoked in *Smith*. Another hitherto unarticulated obscenity requirement, to be satisfied in addition to satisfying the *Roth* standards, was shaped. Finding this new prerequisite not met, the Justices were able to state, without seriously fretting over *Roth*, that the magazines and the male nudes they pictured were not unlawfully obscene:

. . . For we find lacking in these magazines an element which, no less than "prurient interest," is essential to a valid determination of obscenity . . . . These magazines cannot be deemed so offensive on their face as to affront current community standards of decency— a quality that we shall hereafter refer to as "patent offensiveness" or "indecency." Lacking that quality, the magazines cannot be deemed legally "obscene." . . .

• • •

Obscenity under the federal statute thus requires proof of two distinct elements: (1) patent offensiveness; and (2) "prurient interest" appeal. Both must conjoin before challenged material can be found "obscene." . . . In most obscenity cases, to be sure, the two elements tend to coalesce, for that which is patently offensive will also usually carry the requisite "prurient interest" appeal. It is only in the unusual instance where, as here, the "prurient interest" appeal of the material is found limited to a particular class of persons that occasion arises for a truly independent inquiry into the question whether or not the material is patently offensive.

This finding of a new requirement, "patent offensiveness" or "indecency," as an additional one to those of the *Roth* case, has set the law of obscenity running round in circles. *Roth* had been evolved both to give meaning to the federal statute's language that was directed against "every obscene . . . book . . . or other publication of an *indecent* character," and to give meaning to the similar language of a state statute dealing with "any obscene or *indecent* writing." Yet in *Manual Enterprises* the two Justices suggested that "indecency," or "patent offensiveness" (the synonym they expressly created for it), *was something more than the language the Court had itself evoked earlier to define indecency.* In other words "indecency" became, in some fashion, greater than itself! The tail was truly chasing the dog chasing the tail.

Consider Justice Harlan's observation that when dealing with "most obscenity" the prurient interest test and the patent offensiveness test "tend to coalesce," but that when the claimed dirty books are of deviate appeal then "patent offensiveness," as something going beyond prurience, will be required. This poses a paradox: magazines that stimulate deviate activity, activity that is itself *un*lawful in most of the states, are more readily found to be *lawful* than are items that stimulate heterosexual activity, although such activity itself is, universally, legal.

Were this incongurity the law, it would bear unwelcome fruit: homosexual magazines masquerading as body-building journals seen (as Justice Harlan noted) by "possibly a few adolescent males," are particularly pernicious for the young whose sexual proclivities are just taking shape. Yet such magazines would be given greater license than their less damaging heterosexual counterparts.

In its *Roth* case brief, the United States government had noted that the federal mail pornography statute had condemned a variety of obscene materials, including those of the crassest kind, termed by the brief "hard-core" pornography. In his own *Roth* opinion, Justice Harlan (then writing alone) had taken up that new term: "I do not think that the *federal* statute can be constitutionally construed to reach other than what the Government has termed as 'hard-core' pornography." Since that case, and before *Manual Enterprises* had reached the Supreme Court in Washington, New York State's highest tribunal was to enshrine the phrase "hard-core" in its own case law. In *People* v. *Richmond County News, Inc.,*[4] decided in 1961, New York's top court, split four to three (its majority, further splintered, producing two opinions each speaking for two judges only), had affirmed the reversal of a girlie magazine distributor's conviction that had followed the sale of the April 1957 issue of *Gent* magazine. The first of the three New York opinions (one of those for reversing the conviction), had described the magazine:

> The photocover of "Gent" is similar to that of numerous other magazines which loudly proclaim their dedication to coarse sensuality. The contents, like the cover, exhibit the same attempt to pander to and commercialize upon man's taste for the bawdy and the ribald behind a bare disguise of aesthetic respectability.[5]

(This sort of opening gambit, describing the materials in strong or even repellent terms, is one often employed in obscenity cases. It serves as a prelude to the casting of a judicial ballot for a conviction's reversal, demonstrating that the allegiance of the judges to constitutionally protected free expression forces them to overcome personally harbored disgust.) Both opinions constituting the majority used the term "hard-core" (each giving it different meaning) in describing the only obscenity New York could bar.

With this precedent for language stronger than "prurient appeal," Justice Harlan let precise limits remain undefined:

> Whether "hard-core" pornography, or something less, be the proper test, we need go no further in the present case than to hold that the magazines in question, taken as a whole, cannot, under any permissible constitutional standard, be deemed to be beyond the pale of contemporary notions of rudimentary decency.

And so, to lend clarity to such legislatively supplied, uncertain, but commonly used adjectives as "obscene," "lewd," "lascivious," "indecent," and all the others, we have been supplied judicially with similarly imprecise, but *less common phrases,* such as "prurient appeal," "hard-core," "patently offensive," and "beyond the pale of contemporary notions of rudimentary decency." Is every evolution an improvement? How much more guidance is provided by the phrases than by the words they interpret? If one species of repetition, the stringing out of adjectival analogues for "obscenity," does not make everything clear, will garlands of phrases do much better?

7. The *Jacobellis* and *Tropic of Cancer*
Decisions — Chaos Triumphant

It behooves any critic of the Court's performance to close on a note
reminiscent of the wall plaque of frontier times: 'Don't shoot the
piano player. He's doing his best.' It is still possible, however, to
wish that he would stick to the piano and not try to be a one-man
band. It is too much to ask that he take piano lessons.
  —Philip B. Kurland, *The Supreme Court, 1963 Term, Harvard
          Law Review*, vol. 78, p. 176 (1964)

THE CASE OF *Jacobellis* v. *Ohio*,[1] decided in June 1964, reversed,
six to three, the conviction of a Cleveland moving picture
theater manager, one Nino Jacobellis, who had had the temerity
—and the business sense—to show and to advertise a French
film, *Les Amants (The Lovers)*, that told the tale of a married
woman, her regular paramour, and her most recent lover. The
picture contained, as two of the Supreme Court Justices under-
standingly noted, "*an explicit* love scene in the last reel." (More
colorfully, a pair of their dissenting colleagues had quoted from
the films ballyhoo, heralding " 'When all conventions explode . . .
in the most daring love story ever filmed!' 'As close to authentic
amour as is possible on the screen.' 'The frankest love scenes
yet seen on film.' 'Contains one of the longest and most sensuous
love scenes to be seen in this country.' ") There were multiple
and sharply clashing opinions; an even half dozen of them this
time, from eight of the Justices. (Justice Byron R. White, having
so many assorted viewpoints to pick among, chose simply to be
noted as "concurs in the judgment.") However, this potpourri

of views afforded little light by which a local policeman, or prosecutor, or trial judge might learn what was expected of him, on the next occasion that vaguely similar circumstances might arise.

Since the Court (lumping the various opinions) reversed a movie exhibitor's obscenity conviction, the case apparently does hold that movies, along with books and other writings, are within the constitutional mantle of protected free speech (if not removed from it by pornographic content). But that the Court had earlier indicated.[2] Beyond that, the Justices disagreed on just about everything; they were unable to marshal majorities for any of their reasoning. Tempers, apparently, were provoked, and concomitant umbrage taken.

For example, on the over-all role of the Court in obscenity matters, Justice Hugo Black (and with him, Justice Douglas), wishing that all echelons of government would get out and stay out of the obscenity field, and quoting the favorite authority of most legal writers, one's own earlier writings, declared:

. . . My belief, as stated in *Kingsley International Pictures Corp.* v. *Regents* . . . is that "If despite the Constitution . . . this Nation is to embark on the dangerous road of censorship . . . *this Court is about the most inappropriate Supreme Board of Censors that could be found.*"

The Chief Justice, Earl Warren, joined by Justice Clark (both dissenting) also urged the high Tribunal's inappropriateness as a censor:

. . . protection of society's right to maintain its moral fiber and the effective administration of justice require that this Court not establish itself as an ultimate censor . . . .

But their reasons for so contending were quite different from Justice Black's; Supreme Court reversal of lower court action was only appropriate, they suggested, when the results reached by the courts below lacked evidence to support them. Justices Brennan and Goldberg, however, urging that the high Court's role was to be more active, expressed personal pique at their four colleagues' attacks on what they were doing:

Nor can we understand why the Court's performance of its constitutional and judicial function in this sort of case should be denigrated by such epithets as. "censor" or "super-censor." . . . Use of an opprobrious label can neither obscure nor impugn the Court's performance of its obligations to test challenged judgments against the guarantees of the First and Fourteenth Amendments . . . . [T]his Court cannot avoid making an independent constitutional judgment on the facts of the case as to whether the material involved is constitutionally protected.

A question unanswered by *Roth*, whether obscenity was to be judged by local or national "community standards," no longer went unnoticed. Because of the continued impasse, however, it remained unresolved. "We do not see how any 'local' definition of the 'community' could properly be employed in delineating the area of expression that is protected by the Federal Constitution," said Justices Brennan and Goldberg, in urging that the standard must be a national one. "It is my belief," countered the Chief Justice (and Justice Clark), "that when the Court said in *Roth* that obscenity is to be defined by reference to 'community standards,' it meant community standards—not a national standard, as is sometimes argued. I believe that there is no provable 'national standard,' and perhaps there should be none." With this latter position Justice Harlan seemed to nod agreement, noting that he had "heretofore expressed the view that the States are constitutionally permitted greater latitude in determining what is bannable on the score of obscenity than is so with the Federal Government."

Had the hard-core test become the legal litmus by which both federal and state enforcement was to be tested? Here, too, the opinions covered a spectrum. *Yes,* said Justice Stewart, "I have reached the conclusion, which I think is confirmed at least by negative implication in the Court's decisions since *Roth* and *Alberts* . . . that under the First and Fourteenth Amendments

criminal laws in this area are constitutionally limited to hard-
core pornography." (He supported his opinion by citing the
Harlan opinion in *Manual Enterprises,* along with three other
cases in which the high Court had reversed obscenity convictions *without* writing opinions!) *No,* said his Chief, Earl Warren,
along with Justice Clark, "We are told that only 'hard core
pornography' should be denied the protection of the First
Amendment. But who can define 'hard core pornography' with
any greater clarity than 'obscenity'?" *Maybe,* suggested Justices
Brennan and Goldberg, noting that at least *something* more than
"prurience" was required: ". . . the *Roth* standard requires in
the first instance a finding that the material 'goes substantially
beyond customary limits of candor in description or representation of such matters.'" And Justice Harlan stuck to the guns he
had earlier trained on pornography—the "patent offensiveness"
standard: "I would apply to the Federal Government the *Roth*
standards as amplified in my opinion in *Manual Enterprises.*"

Obscenity received unusual treatment in two of the opinions.
The Chief Justice suggested a variable, but unspecified, standard
of obscenity, a standard that considered the item *in its setting:*
". . . the use to which various materials are put—not just the
words and pictures themselves—must be considered in determining whether or not the materials are obscene. A technical
or legal treatise on pornography may well be inoffensive under most circumstances but, at the same time, 'obscene' in the extreme when sold or displayed to children." And an all-time high
in not bothering to try to explain the law to those who must
follow it was reached by Justice Potter Stewart with his casual,
"I shall not today attempt further to define the kinds of material
I understand to be embraced within that shorthand description
[hard-core]; and perhaps I could never succeed in intelligibly
doing so. But *I know it when I see it,* and the motion picture
involved in this case is not that." Policemen who must decide
whether or not to make an obscenity arrest got no help in
knowing that Justice Stewart boasts a personal obscenity divin-

ing rod. Were police officers today to seek in court to justify any of their police work—in the area of obscenity, or arrest, or search and seizure—by expressing such arrant self-confidence, their police careers would not be notable in courtroom successes.

It is well to pause for a moment, before considering several other aspects of the *Jacobellis* case, in order to note the action the Justices took in the most closely watched obscenity case of this decade—a case decided the same day they handed down their *Jacobellis* opinions. In 1961, Grove Press, a publisher with an expanding line of books hovering uncertainly between pornography and artistry, in extensive pre-publication advertisements announced its forthcoming issuance of Henry Miller's *Tropic of Cancer*. The Miller work, first published in Europe in 1934, had been smuggled into America rather consistently ever after by an endless procession of returning college students. There were critics who praised Miller as uniquely blessed with a gift for expressing the ennui, the loneliness, the futility, the shallow pleasure-snatching, and the degradation and squalor of an American's life in France during the early 1930s. There were those who found him a pornographer, impure and far from simple, relishing shock use of four-letter words, and of passages and chapters creeping with verbal vermin. Actions proliferated throughout America once *Tropic of Cancer* went on sale. Ultimately, the book had been declared obscene in at least one federal circuit and five states, Connecticut, Florida, Illinois, Pennsylvania, and New York;[3] and not obscene in at least three others, California, Massachusetts, and Wisconsin.[4] Then, on June 22, 1964, the United States Supreme Court, split five to four, reversed the Florida finding of obscenity in a single paragraph, in which the Justices were cited as having taken substantially the same positions as those expressed in their *Jacobellis* opinions.[5]

To return to *Jacobellis*. Among the six opinions were other formulations that would, were they the law, have impact on obscenity enforcement. But whether they will ever become the law, only as yet undecided cases may show.

THE RIGHT TO A JURY TRIAL

Has an alleged pornographer, for example, an absolute right to a jury trial? The Warren-Clark dissent, speaking for those two Justices, without weighing any pros or cons, quietly assumed that he had. "If the proceeding involved is criminal," remarked the Chief Justice, *"there must be a right to a jury trial,* a right to counsel, and all the other safeguards necessary to assure due process of law." Using the nose-count method of legal analysis, this viewpoint appears to have majority support. In the *Kingsley Books* case, Justice Brennan, attacking New York's injunction law, but standing his ground alone, had stated: "I believe the absence in this New York obscenity statute of a right to jury trial is a fatal defect." And Justices Black and Douglas would, it may be confidently anticipated, vote to void any obscenity "guilty" finding in any case tried without a jury over the defendant's objections. Two, and one, and two make five; and five constitutes a majority of the high Court in Washington. (Of course, were the jury trial question to be *fully briefed and argued,* the Chief Justice and Justice Clark, both of whom generally line up *against* obscenity and *for* giving the states some leeway in this area might well bounce over to the other side, despite the casual assumption in their *Jacobellis* opinion.)

What are the jury trial arguments?

By way of background, under the federal and most state constitutions, defendants charged with serious crimes—felonies (murder, or robbery, or rape, for example)—crimes for which they may be long imprisoned, are entitled to trial by jury. But those accused of minor crimes only—of misdemeanors (small thefts and minor assaults are examples)—are given no such constitutional right. In New York City alone, more than one hundred thousand misdemeanor cases are disposed of in the criminal courts annually, those actually going to trial running well into the many thousands; they are tried by judges without juries. Were jury trials necessary, existing jury panels, court-rooms, court officers, judges, and prosecutors would be woefully inadequate: trying a case before a jury takes far longer than a non-jury trial.

Obscenity violations, misdemeanors for the most part, arise in goodly numbers in busy jurisdictions. To require that they be tried by jurors would, in New York City for example, break the back of an already overburdened criminal jury calendar. And to do so would be to treat obscenity misdemeanants differently from other misdemeanants, including persons charged with more directly offensive sex crimes: indecent exposure, impairing the morals of minors, and certain statutory rapes. Superficially, however, there is some appeal to the notion that jurors are uniquely suited to reflecting "contemporary community stand-ards." But this impression does not survive close inspection. Judges, most of whom have, pre-judicially, been steeped in poli-tics—in part, the art of knowing how communities of people are likely to react—who daily see and hear battalions of wit-nesses, defendants, and attorneys, and who as judges must examine the multitudinous problems in which people get tan-gled, should be at least as adept in judging community standards as would be most randomly selected laymen. Even so, *were jurors' determinations final,* common sense might favor letting the "good men and true," drawn from the vicinage, determine their own "contemporary community standards." The clutter of opinions from reviewing courts bears witness, however, that ap-pellate judges do not deem themselves the least bit restrained by jury determinations on obscenity questions. No jury finding of "obscene" is inviolate to appellate reversal. And so to give a defendant an absolute right to a jury trial would be to give him a heads-I-win-tails-you-lose advantage; the jurors' special expert-ise in "community standards" would *only* be credited when it resulted in his acquittal! And if either national standards are to be applied, or if prurient appeal is to be judged by the prurience of deviants, then local jurors lack even theoretical special competence.

Moreover, to award jury trials in misdemeanor obscenity cases while continuing to find them not constitutionally required when other minor crimes were charged would be to lose sight of what it is that the criminal trial jury best does. Ordinarily, the jury is solely a fact finder. The requirements in criminal cases that, to convict, all jurors must be unanimous and must be convinced of guilt beyond a reasonable doubt, provide defendants with a substantial cushion of protection. These requirements appropriately safeguard the accused, even at the risk of endangering the community by freeing those whose demonstrable guilt may be far more likely than not. The jurors, functioning under these rules, are to ascertain facts—did the defendant stab, rob, or rape—facts that either did or did not take place, acts that the accused either did or did not do. An all-seeing, irrefutable, infallible, and unimpeachable Big Brother, were one available, could determine such facts with absolute accuracy. But rarely is all that well known, and so our law *wisely* declares that if so much credible evidence is lacking that a reasonable doubt lingers in a single juror's mind, no defendant is to bear the brand of "criminal."

But after all of these pages it should be manifest that in pornography prosecutions, whether or not something is obscene is not the jury's kind of *fact* at all. There is no immutable truth —"obscene" or "not obscene"—lurking somewhere, if only it can be found out. Rather "obscenity" reflects a judgment, an opinion, a classification. It changes with the passage of time, and with the personalities judging it. In appellate courts, when this kind of "fact" is debated, neither requirements of unanimity nor proof beyond a reasonable doubt govern. This is because the "fact" of obscenity is really a legal conclusion—*it is not a fact at all.* Legal conclusions can be reached, under the law, by a mere balancing to determine the preponderance of sound reason; no one expects legal principles to be established beyond a reasonable doubt or pursuant to requirements of unanimity. Sentimentality aside, why—when obscenity is determined this way in the appellate courts—should the United States Constitution be deemed to require the use at trial of the criminal jury with its traditional unanimity requirement?

It is understandable that defense lawyers, retained to keep their clients from being convicted, often favor juries in obscenity cases, particularly in America's greater, more impersonal, cities. Equally understandably, persons are of the same mind who believe that the protection of civil liberties requires, not balance, but the seizing of every means that may improve the chances for exculpation. When juries are used, the defendant is likely to get an extra bite at the apple of acquittal. (This is particularly true in our larger cities in which every panel called for jury duty is almost certain to include at least a sprinkling of ardent libertarians who blanch at the thought of any "censorship." Rural jurors, on the other hand, are likely to view almost all published sex or nudity as such a threat to the American home that they may, without regard for those principles of law charged by the judge, vote "guilty" as a conscience-directed blow, struck against the forces of darkness.) Even when a jury is used, defense arguments that the contraband is not pornographic will, in the first instance, be addressed to the trial judge. This serves the defense as a one-way street: if the trial justice holds the material not to be pornographic, out goes the case. But should he see it differently, he *cannot*, with a jury in the picture, rule the material to be unlawful. The defense loses nothing, and may gain everything, in submitting the obscenity question to a trial jury.

OBJECTIONABLE MATERIAL TO CHILDREN

The *Jacobellis* opinion in which Justice Goldberg joined Justice Brennan suggested an area that lawmakers might spotlight:

We recognize the legitimate and indeed exigent interest of states and localities throughout the Nation in preventing the dissemination of material deemed harmful to children . . . . State and local authorities might well consider whether their objectives in this area would be better served by laws aimed specifically at preventing distribution of objectionable material to children, rather than at totally prohibiting its dissemination.

This particular focus on the immature will be further discussed.

ANY VALUE AS "REDEEMING SOCIAL IMPORTANCE"

That aspect for which the *Jacobellis* case seems best known is the Brennan-Goldberg spotlighting of the phrase "utterly without redeeming social importance," a phrase that *Roth* introduced into the pornography-tester's vocabulary—and left utterly undefined. Said the two Justices in the case's lead opinion (the opinion viewed by hasty lawyers and judges as if it were that of the Court's majority):

We would reiterate, however, our recognition in *Roth* that obscenity is excluded from the constitutional protection only because it is "utterly without redeeming social importance." . . . It follows that material dealing with sex in a manner that advocates ideas . . . or that has literary or scientific value or any other form of social importance, may not be branded as obscenity and denied the constitutional protection. Nor may the constitutional status of the material be made to turn on a "weighing" of its social importance against its prurient appeal, for a work cannot be proscribed unless it is "utterly" without social importance.

In stating that an item's "redeeming social importance" was not to "turn on a *'weighing'* of its social importance against its prurient appeal," Justices Brennan and Goldberg enervated the word "redeeming." At least this was the impact their *Jacobellis* opinion was given by Illinois highest court. On Thursday, June 18, 1964, that bench had unanimously affirmed the Chicago obscenity conviction of Lenny Bruce, a nightclub stand-up comedian (one who had modestly entitled his autobiography, *how to talk dirty and influence people*).[6] In its opinion the Illinois court had stated:

The monologue itself consisted of a number of commentaries upon such unrelated topics as the meeting of a psychotic rapist and a nymphomaniac who have both escaped from their respective institutions . . . why Americans are not respected abroad because our soldiers "——— all their mothers for chocolate bars" (using a slang synonym for sexual intercourse, . . . defendant's intimacies with three married women, a satirical and particularly offensive portrayal of a colored person's experience at a white party where he is asked revolting questions regarding his sexual habits and organs . . . a supposed conversation with a gas station attendant in a rest room which concludes with the suggestion that both Bruce and the attendant put on contraceptives and take a picture, comments regarding homosexuals and the sexual prowess of named movie stars, and a discussion of marijuana.

. . . The testimony also established that defendant repeatedly during his performance made motions indicating masturbation and that these were accompanied by vulgar comments . . . .

• • •

We can conclude only that defendant's mode of expressing his ideas in regard to present attitudes on contemporary social problems by orally making repeated reference to sex and sexual organs and actions indicating masturbation presents a dominant theme indicating a morbid interest in sex which so overbalances the commentary presented, that the performance, when viewed as a whole, must be held obscene under the Illinois statute and prevailing Federal definition.[7]

The Illinois justices so said on a Thursday. The weekend intervened, and on Monday, June 22, 1964, the United States Supreme Court distributed its assorted *Jacobellis* opinions. Two weeks later, on July 7, noting that "The views expressed in the opinions in that case are pertinent to the problem in this case," the Illinois high court vacated its own earlier ruling, and in late November it reversed its June conclusion, stating:

It is apparent from the opinions of a majority [sic] of the court in *Jacobellis* that the "balancing test" rule . . . is no longer a constitutionally acceptable method of determining whether material is obscene, and it is there made clear that material having *any* social importance is constitutionally protected.[8]

If the Illinois justices were correct in concluding that the Brennan-Goldberg opinion spoke for a majority of the nation's highest Court, then a fool-proof escape hatch from obscenity prosecutions would exist. Does a pornographer wish to film and exhibit the hardest of hard-core stag movies, showing, in the most intimate detail, either simple sexual intercourse or an entire sexual olympiad? Fine. Let him utilize an interracial couple, and let him use dialogue and sub-titles to preach supreme happiness from the conquest of color barriers in the ultimate of pleasures. Or let him hedge his obscenity by having the action take place in a rat-infested, plaster-cracking, paint-peeling slum, and as the theme let him stress that the best things in life are free! Absurd? It may be so. But if weighing is no longer proper in evaluating "redeeming social importance," then both of these examples *are* innocent, such stag films being no longer *solely* of prurient appeal in view of their incidental comment on "topics . . . of social importance."

Twenty-one months after the *Jacobellis* opinions, in March 1966, Justice Brennan reaffirmed this usage of the phrase "utterly without redeeming social importance." This time he was joined by the Chief Justice and the Court's newest member, Abe Fortas, Arthur Goldberg's replacement. The case involved the novel *Fanny Hill*. In separate dissents, Justices Clark, Harlan, and White were, however, to quarrel with the Brennan usage, while the remaining three Justices sat out this particular dispute.

The Brennan-Goldberg and Brennan-Warren-Fortas elimination of this "balancing test" mirrors the too common American temptation to escalate, and in so doing to distort sound and thoughtful small steps into dogma. It will be recalled that half a century earlier Judge Learned Hand, in urging the rejection of

the *Hicklin* rule that had given no weight whatever to artistic
or literary value, had questioned "whether in the end men will
regard that as obscene which is honestly relevant to the adequate expression of innocent ideas." Noting that there were
"plenty who will misuse the privilege as a cover for lewdness
and a stalking horse from which to strike at purity," Hand had
observed that such conduct would pose a *question of fact* for
judicial resolution. Judge Woolsey, similarly, in his landmark
Ulysses decision weighed the contribution of every word to the
whole ("Each word of the book contributes like a bit of mosaic
to the detail of the picture which Joyce is seeking to construct
for his readers"). But Justices Brennan, Warren, and Fortas, and
former Justice Goldberg, would, it seems, cast aside such fact
questions; they would reject the test of "honest relevance." For
them, if the broad topics the alleged contraband *touched upon*
had "social importance," that was enough. No further study was
necessary—the material was "redeemed."

8. 1966: *Fanny Hill,* Edward Mishkin, and Ralph Ginzburg—Pandering to Prurience

What is obscenity, anyway? It's not definable, not measurable, a bag of smoke. It's like witchery. There's no such thing, but people got hanged for it. This obscenity issue is so confused that there were fourteen opinions in that ruling today. Fourteen opinions by nine judges. Fourteen.
—Ralph Ginzburg, quoted in the New York *Herald Tribune,*
March 22, 1966, p. 14

WE HAVE SEEN THE SUPREME COURT IN ACTION, steering clear, when it could, of the difficulties posed in applying its own *Roth* standards. (With the late Justice Oliver Wendell Holmes, the high Judges were painfully aware that "General propositions do not decide concrete cases. The decision will depend on a judgment or intuition more subtle than any articulate major premise."[1]) In the nine years from *Roth's* 1957 formulation to 1966, the high Tribunal had promulgated three other tests that, when skillfully invoked, provided a means of ducking a decision on whether or not, under *Roth,* material that came before the Judges was obscene. The first such test had come two and a half years after *Roth.* The case was *Smith* v. *California,* in which five of the high Justices had advanced the scienter test; this was one often available means of never quite reaching the issue of obscenity. Another two and a half years were to pass before two of the Justices in the *Manual Enterprises* case advanced the "patent offensiveness" test. Once again, were this supplemental test not satisfied (and *if* the opinion of the two Judges who announced the Court's action was deemed the law), the materials under scrutiny would be cleared without any determination being made under *Roth* of whether or not they were obscene. And two years after that, in June 1964, a third route away from *Roth* was suggested when, in *Jacobellis*, the *Roth* phrase, "utterly without redeeming social importance" was so refined in meaning (but by only two Justices) that, applying it, *any* colorable claim of value, howsoever slight, would be enough to purge an item of an otherwise obscene characterization.

On the first day of spring, 1966, the Supreme Court continued down this path, articulating another new rule that could be invoked to avoid the need of wrestling *Roth* to the mat. The Justices had before them three major pornography cases, argued the previous December. (The personnel or the subject matter of each had been part of New York County's anti-pornography enforcement experience in the early 1960s; the human, the practical, and the legal problems that each presented will be scrutinized in Part III of this book.) One of the three cases involved a Massachusetts adjudication that the more than two-hundred-year-old pornographic classic *Fanny Hill* was still obscene.[2] The second reviewed New York State's conviction of a busy professional pornographer, Edward Mishkin, America's leading specialist in the manufacture and distribution of the crudest of sadomasochistic booklets.[3] The third brought before the high Court the federal conviction of Ralph Ginzburg, publisher and publicist extraordinary, whose publications included *Eros*, an expensive, artfully "packaged" quarterly on sex, sold to an estimated 150,000 subscribers.[4] Confronted by these three quite different types of adjudicated printed pornography, the high Justices, once again, splintered, writing a total of *fourteen opinions*. *Fanny Hill* was cleared, albeit somewhat conditionally, and the convictions of Mishkin and Ginzburg were affirmed. The Court's new rule, evolved in these three cases, mustered the support of a bare majority of the Justices and authorized the judiciary, both state and federal, to avoid bogging down with *Roth* if there was uncer-

tainty as to whether or not, applying it, something was obscene.
In such cases, the decision as to obscenity was to be reached by
an examination of the purported contraband's advertising and of
the circumstances of its sale. Associate Justice William J. Brennan, Jr., wrote the prevailing opinions in all three of these 1966
decisions. In his *Ginzburg* opinion (in which he was joined by
the Chief Justice and Justices Clark, White, and Fortas), Brennan was to give the fullest exposition of this new obscenity guide:

The deliberate representation [through advertising] of petitioners'
publications as erotically arousing, for example, stimulated the reader
to accept them as prurient; he looks for titillation, not for saving intellectual content . . . . And the circumstances of presentation and
dissemination of material are equally relevant to determining whether
social importance claimed for material in the courtroom was, in the
circumstances, pretense or reality—whether it was the basis upon
which it was traded in the marketplace or a spurious claim for litigation purposes. Where the purveyor's sole emphasis is on the sexually
provocative aspects of his publications, that fact may be decisive in
the determination of obscenity.

• • •

. . . we cannot conclude that the court below erred in taking their
[the defendants'] own evaluation at its face value and declaring the
book as a whole obscene despite the other evidence.

• • •

We perceive no threat to First Amendment guarantees in thus holding that in close cases evidence of pandering may be probative with
respect to the nature of the material in question and thus satisfy the
Roth test . . . . Rather, the fact that each of these publications was
created or exploited entirely on the basis of its appeal to prurient interests strengthens the conclusion that the transactions here were
sales of illicit merchandise, not sales of constitutionally protected
matter.

This "pandering" concept, the examination of purported contraband *in context* to determine whether it was obscene, although new as a high Court rule of law, was no bolt out of the
blue. Concurring in *Roth,* Chief Justice Warren had remarked

that in judging obscenity the materials "draw color and character" from the "context" in which they are seen. The same day, dissenting in the *Nights of Horror* case, he was to make the identical point: "the same object may have wholly different impact depending upon the setting in which it is placed." And, interestingly, Justice Douglas joined by Justice Black, as well as Justice Brennan, had seemed to nod some degree of agreement when, dissenting in the same case, he remarked that "The nature of the group among whom the tracts are distributed may have an important bearing on the issue of guilt." But the three cases decided March 21, 1966, marked the first time that a *majority* of the Justices really developed this *variable obscenity* concept, suggesting, indeed, *holding*, that the advertising, and the prospective customers at whom it was directed, could properly be considered in testing for obscenity.

The anguished cries that met this new rule of law, both from several of the "nine black beetles in the Temple of Karnak" (the late Chief Justice Harlan Fiske Stone's description of the high Judges in their then new Court building[5]), and from outsiders, were predictable.

Although in seeking buyers for his mail-ordered publications, Ginzburg had "unconditionally" guaranteed "full refund . . . if the book fails to reach you because of U.S. Post Office censorship interference" (a guaranty that, the Court noted, was actually a sales message, a promise of prurience), Justice Black was to urge "that Ginzburg . . . is now finally and authoritatively condemned to serve five years in prison for distributing printed matter about sex which neither Ginzburg nor anyone else *could possibly have known* to be criminal." Here at work is seen the penchant for overstatement so common in bitter dissents: quite obviously Ginzburg *did not know* his acts were criminal, he wished to go every inch as far as he could while avoiding jail; but, equally clearly, his "warning" of postal interference proved that he saw the *substantial possibility* that his actions might be found unlawful. In separate dissents, both Justices Harlan and

Stewart were to join the Black condemnation of the decisions as having *ex post facto* impact. Ginzburg, they asserted, was being convicted on a new concept, "pandering," not previously the law. Such answer to this criticism as existed was that the concept of obscenity itself was age-old, and pandering was merely an aid in analyzing it—a judicial exposition of theoretically existent law. Libertarians who had rejoiced at the *narrowing* of the scope given anti-obscenity laws when the other new concepts (scienter, patent offensiveness, and the purgative impact of *any social* value) had come into being, were now to mutter imprecations, and to complain of "vagueness" in the new test. Yet not only were the other once novel concepts similarly vague, but (except for that of scienter) their force was dubious: whether or not they were the law was questionable as they had been voiced by only a minority of the Justices, even though in so-called "prevailing" opinions. One obvious difference existed, however, between the pandering test and these others: the new standard promised some *broadening* in application of state and federal anti-obscenity statutes, while the other Court-made touchstones were *narrowing* ones. Claims of "vagueness," clearly, are influenced by considerations of just whose ox happens to be gored.

This new test of pandering, in the abstract, seems vague, and could—as Justice Harlan suggested—be considerably improved by a legislature's "clear drafting." Yet applied to concrete cases it is far more down to earth than either the *Roth* language or the several post-*Roth* embellishments. It focuses attention *directly* on what a named defendant did at a known place, at a fixed time, with a particular possibly pornographic product. For the first time since *Roth,* we move away from concentration on such theoretical problems as: Can values be found by experts nit-picking their way through a seemingly pornographic book? Would a prurient reaction be evoked in a wholly suppositional "community" (local, statewide, or national; artistic, literary, or cross-sectional)? Can a single *dominant* theme of prurience be isolated in a work with many concurrent themes? For the first time, as to borderline pornography, rather than such fine-spun theorizing, the Court was to focus on *what actually took place*. In deciding upon legality or illegality, a key question would be: In substance, did the publisher (or distributor, or dealer) print an evocative cover, advertise prior banning, display the item massed with other borderline items, and urge in various ways erotic, deviant, or scatological appeal? If so, let him not justify by claiming historical importance, or literary artistry, that, quite obviously, was not even remotely the basis of his sales appeal. "The circumstances of production, sale and publicity are relevant in determining whether or not the publication and distribution of the book is constitutionally protected," Justices Brennan, Warren, and Fortas remarked in the *Fanny Hill* case, adding, "where the purveyor's sole emphasis is on the sexually provocative aspects of his publications, a court could accept his evaluation at its face value."

Justice Potter Stewart was to go far in these three cases toward full comradeship with Justices Black and Douglas in declaring that *all* anti-obscenity legislation was unconstitutional. Hardcore pornography, "and that alone," Stewart urged, was all that "government may constitutionally suppress." Having so said, this Judge, who alluding to pornography in *Jacobellis* had claimed "I know it when I see it," voted to reverse the New York conviction of Edward Mishkin. The sado-masochistic pamphlets there involved, he declared, were *not* hard-core. Yet, in New York, where in 1961 the state's highest tribunal had similarly ruled that pornography was *not* actionable unless it was hard-core,[6] Mishkin's conviction had been *affirmed* in 1964 by that same appellate court *without dissent*.[7] Even hard-core, apparently, was in the eye of the beholder!

Besides firmly introducing the pandering test, the spring, 1966, cases made at least one other contribution to the obscenity law. The *Mishkin* decision finally settled a point left open in *Roth* nine years earlier, one that had been awkwardly ducked by the high Court in its *Manual Enterprises* opinions. Prior to the March

21 rulings, it was still uncertain whether materials intended for deviants were to be judged according to the prurient tastes of average persons or those of average offbeats. In Justice Brennan's opinion, the Court majority (of Brennan, the Chief Justice, and Justices Clark, White, and Fortas, with Justice Harlan separately concurring) unequivocally declared:

> Where the material is designed for and primarily disseminated to a clearly defined deviant sexual group, rather than the public at large, the prurient-appeal requirement of the *Roth* test is satisfied if the dominant theme of the material taken as a whole appeals to the prurient interest in sex of the members of that group . . . . We adjust the prurient-appeal requirement to social realities by permitting the appeal of this type of material to be assessed in terms of the sexual interests of its intended and probable recipient group . . . .

The 1966 decisions embraced a reaffirmation by Justice Brennan, this time joined only by the Chief Justice and the newest of the Justices, Abe Fortas, of his *Jacobellis* idea that *any* social value was adequate to redeem the otherwise pornographic. The Supreme Judicial Court for the Commonwealth of Massachusetts had affirmed a trial court finding that *Fanny Hill* was violative of the Bay State's anti-obscenity laws. The Brennan opinion in the *Fanny Hill* case, in reversing the Massachusetts adjudication (Justices Black, Douglas, and Stewart concurred separately, and on other grounds) commented:

> The Supreme Judicial Court erred in holding that a book need not be "unqualifiedly worthless before it can be deemed obscene." A book can not be proscribed unless it is found to be *utterly* without redeeming social value. This is so even though the book is found to possess the requisite prurient appeal and to be patently offensive. Each of the three federal constitutional criteria is to be applied independently; the social value of the book can neither be weighed against nor canceled by its prurient appeal or patent offensiveness. Hence, even on the view of the court below that *Memoirs* possessed only a modicum of social value, its judgment must be reversed as being founded on an erroneous interpretation of a federal constitutional standard.

But in separate opinions, Justices Harlan, White, and Clark quarreled with this interpetation of the *Roth* phrase, "utterly without redeeming social importance," while the remaining three Justices did not take sides on this point. And so whether or not the phrase is to be given Brennan's twice-urged interpretation has not as yet been decided by a Court majority. Even had it been, however, the Brennan opinion goes on to specify that under the pandering test, if the item is *exploited* for "sexually provocative aspects," for values other than those that allegedly provide its redemption, these claimed positive values will *not* serve to clear it.

Happily, in the *Mishkin* and *Ginzburg* cases the high Court was able to muster bare majorities—five of the Justices—behind the prevailing opinions. It did not do so, however, in the *Fanny Hill* case, nor had it done so two years earlier in the *Jacobellis* and *Tropic of Cancer* cases, nor two years before that in the *Manual Enterprises* decision of 1962. In each of those cases there was a multiplicity of opinions, but none talking for a judicial majority. Judges speaking with so many tongues promulgate little law—beyond the almost purposely narrow holdings that neither the books *Fanny Hill* and *Tropic of Cancer*, nor the picture *Les Amants*, nor the particular issues of the magazines *MANual, Trim,* and *Grecian Guild Pictorial*, were legally actionable. As the Supreme Court of almost two hundred million people is a Court unable to hear more than a handful (far less than two hundred) of the many hundreds of thousands of cases American courts process annually, broad guidance is to be hoped for when it does speak. The Chief Justice, in his *Jacobellis* opinion, had driven this home:

. . . obscenity cases continue to come to this Court, and it becomes increasingly apparent that we must settle as well as we can the question of what constitutes "obscenity" and the questions of what standards are permissible in enforcing proscriptions against obscene matter. *This Court hears such cases as the instant one* not merely to rule upon the alleged obscenity of a specific film or book but *to establish principles for the guidance of lower courts and legislatures.*[8]

But "to establish principles for the guidance of lower courts and legislatures," and for the direction of police, prosecutors, publishers, and booksellers, five Judges must agree. Whether or not one is pleased with the *Mishkin* and the *Ginzburg* results, the fact that the Court action in each was *by a majority*—that *majorities* established the pandering test and ruled that deviant obscenity was to be tested by appeal to deviants—made those cases far more useful, far more realistic, than the *Fanny Hill* case and the obscenity decisions the high Court had handed down in 1962 and 1964. Generally, however, in the obscenity area of recent years Washington has produced an overabundance of judicial talk with a concomitant paucity of clear law, calling into question whether in this field ours is truly a "system of laws and not of men." These doubts are underscored by such items as the Stewart 1964 opinion conceding his probable inability to "intelligibly" provide definitions, but boasting "I know it when I see it." They are further magnified by an examination of the quite consistent pattern of action of Justices Black and Douglas. In their 1957 *Roth* dissent, these two Judges had urged that obsenity was not constitutionally actionable, a view rejected by the Bench's heavy majority. By such rejection, it was declared *not* to be the law of the land. So be it. Nevertheless, no one could fault the two Justices had they, in the privacy of the closed conferences of the Court, clung to their positions, hoping in time to wean a majority over to their thinking, and ultimately getting the Court to reverse itself. But these Justices instead continued to persist publicly, in opinion after opinion, in denying constitutionality to any obscenity legislation or enforcement. More constructively, they might have conceded that anti-obscenity action, under the *present* state of the law, was constitutional, and joined at least one of two of their colleagues in resting their conclusions on other, and more constructive, grounds. Their 1966 opinions matched against their 1957 *Roth* statement, show little growth, no respect for the majorities, and at best slight suggestions of any softening as a result of the nine lean years during which a preponderance of the high

Court's Justices had, year after year, rejected their contentions. (In their 1966 opinions, the two Justices flirted briefly with, but emphatically rejected, *Roth* standards.) Obviously, in the area of pornography, the individual Justices find their private, legally reasoned, convictions far weightier than such law as the Court has articulated. As a result of this primacy of personal viewpoints, anticipating whether or not the high Tribunal will deem untested items obscene tends not to be an exercise in reason or in law, but more than ever, a judicial nose count. Were ours a "system of law, and not of men," in the full flower of the commencement day address sense of that phrase, it would not be ever so.

Five- and six-way splits enervate this noble American oratorical catch-phrase. They also reveal our highest Court as a poor "legislature." If legislation is defined as the making, repealing, or altering of laws, then when the high Justices void statutes, or restrict their applications (more sharply than the state courts have done in interpreting their own states' laws), the Court, after a fashion, legislates. In so doing, it should act with at least a modicum of that precision that is the hallmark of sound legislation, and for the lack of which *the judiciary* regularly strikes down statutes as "vague." There is, alas, no still higher earthly court to call the Justices to account for their frequent failures to get together upon lines of reasoning. But self-restraint, self-imposed discipline, is as appropriate for judges as for policemen. And compromise, so essential in productive legislative bodies, is not enshrined solely as a solon's virtue. Particularly is it called for judicially in areas such as obscenity, in which the courts increasingly second-guess legislative bodies and other courts, both trial and appellate. ("An appeal, Hinnissy," Finley Peter Dunne's Mr. Dooley noted more than a half century ago, "is where ye ask wan coort to show its contempt f'r another coort."[9]) The highest Court's Justices, having been overturning other courts' obscenity judgments with regularity, would (or, at least, *should*) seem to have some obligation either to restrain themselves, or—when overturn they must—to reconcile their differences in order that majorities might be regularly mustered, and *guiding principles spoken with majority concurrences.*

This review of some of the key Supreme Court cases of the past decade witnesses the difficulties in judicially defining obscenity in this vast, diversely peopled nation during an era when the frug and the jerk have given social dancing new movements, when the bikini, the cut-out, and the fish-net (and among the more sophisticated, the topless) have goggled eyes that no longer find the seashore restful, when the busy double bed has become a staple of the motion picture screen, and when high school pregnancies preach that not all hygiene is learned in the classroom. Our legislatures have completely failed to tackle, in modern terms, the definition of obscenity. The problem has been left in courts that are split so profoundly that clear majorities have often been lacking to support any single line of reasoning. Clearly, the simplicity of earlier days has fled. It was *less than two decades ago* when, in an obscenity appeal, an imaginative and plucky youthful appellate prosecutor, Whitman Knapp, dared an oral argument in the United States Supreme Court of unheard-of brevity. He rose and said:

The statute on which the judgment rests is valid. A reading of the book by this Court will demonstrate that the finding of obscenity is reasonable. I therefore submit that the judgment should be affirmed.[10]

And he sat down. That was it. The Court, divided four to four wrote no opinions, and the conviction stood of the publisher of Edmund Wilson's *Memoirs of Hecate County,* which, both qualitatively and quantitatively, were it placed beside *Fanny Hill, Last Exit to Brooklyn,* or the *Story of O,* would seem as if it had flowed from the quill pen of Louisa May Alcott.

PART III

The Censor's Experience

9. An Enforcement Philosophy

All that is necessary for the triumph of evil is that good men do nothing.
—Edmund Burke, *Letter to Thomas Mercer,* between 1790–95

WHAT IS THE POLICEMAN to do (or the prosecutor), having sworn to uphold and enforce the law, but finding it a most elusive changeling?

A case study of sorts, items selected from a metropolitan prosecutor's files involving pornography and seeming pornography, tells the tale. New York County—Manhattan Island—is not only the site of the United Nations headquarters, the world's tallest building, America's leading port of entry, the home of Wall Street, Pell Street, Hester Street, and 42nd Street, but also one of this nation's major entertainment and publishing centers—for the pornographic as well as for the legitimate. For a number of years acting as the prosecutor, the assistant district attorney, charged with handling and supervising the investigation and trial of all New York County misdemeanors, which included obscenity cases, and working closely with New York City's police department, I consumed a substantial fragment of my time and energies and public funds in trying to find my way through this maze.

Before viewing here what we in law enforcement did as "censors" (possibly a dirty word, but a ready label for those—police, prosecutors, or judges—charged with anti-obscenity enforcement) during those years, the philosophy, the approach, that underlay our efforts should be understood.

If a policeman or a prosecutor is not to *be* the law, but is to *serve* it, he must minimize the all-too-human temptations to use his position and authority to reflect his own likes and dislikes, or his own timidities. A law officer abuses his trust when he picks and chooses amongst the criminal statutes, enforcing those he deems wise and ignoring those he deems foolish, contrary to his own sympathies, or inflammatory to known pressure groups. In such hands, ours would take a still further step toward becoming a system of men, and not of laws. Law enforcement's obligation is to enforce *all* the laws. True, there are in the penal laws of most jurisdictions absurdities and anachronisms, such as the criminal penalties for adultery. They, however, are inert; they are unsupported by any clamor for enforcement. Although their passive presence on the statute books may serve to impart some relic of community disapprobation to the practices they condemn, community disinterest has effectively "repealed" them. They are dead letter laws.

But the obscenity laws are clearly not "dead letter." The deluge of mail concerning obscenity, giving voice to community fears and disgusts, has been mentioned; the tremendous judicial activity centering on the pornographic has been described at length. The anti-pornography statutes are among the "live" criminal enactments that police and prosecutors enforce, or should enforce, as diligently as their manpower resources permit. The lawmaking power is that of the legislature; it is not up to a prosecutor to repeal a law by refusing to enforce it. If it is void, that is for the courts to decide. And the courts can make no such decision unless the case is taken to them—by a prosecutor attempting enforcement.

Legal controversies and uncertainties are not settled in America by television panel discussions or by the omniscience of the columnists. They are settled either through new legislation or in the courts through the use of our adversary system. There the law is gradually hammered out before judges who make their rulings after hearing the contending parties. We can rely upon this adversary system because we believe that from the cauldron of debate, sound principles will emerge. Instituting an action in court, then, and later carrying it through the appellate tribunals, is the single way, other than through legislation, of seeking the law's clarification. It is the *sole* mode of securing binding guidance on the impact of the federal and state constitutions. When police turn away rather than make arrests, when prosecutors shun prosecutions rather than pursue them, legal ambiguities are not resolved.

If our system is to work, the role of police and of prosecutors must be to get not only the cut-and-dried issues but the troublesome ones before the courts. A policeman or prosecutor who chooses to ignore a probable violation because he may be pessimistic about its outcome in the courts, may be permitting his own trepidation to void, at least in part, a law that he has sworn to uphold. It is the role of the judge, both trial and appellate, and not that of the prosecutor, to make the decisions whenever *valid* legal issues exist to be decided. That is what the judge is paid (and often well paid) to do. Of course, when no serious argument exists to be made, a policeman or a prosecutor would equally abuse his trust were an arrest to be made and a prosecution initiated solely to harass, or to satisfy vigilante cries for action.

Much of the danger of censorship lies in cloaking personal choices with the force of law. The diligent police or prosecution official does not pick and choose but recognizes that his is the obilgation to enforce all "live" laws. By so doing, he is, in a broad sense, less of a "censor"—*he brings less of his own personal fears and prejudices to his job in law enforcement*—than is his counterpart whose personal inaction, either born of caution or disagreement with the laws, prevents the judiciary from ever determining the proper reach of particular statutes legislatively enacted.

The passive prosecutor, he who chooses not to act, soon finds his *inaction* has had its impact. Forebearance renders our "contemporary community standards" increasingly permissive. Police and prosecutors who fail to take steps against seeming pornography encourage publishers, distributors, and vendors of borderline items. A community, for instance, tolerant of dubious obscenity and as a result saturated with it may find itself hoist by those community standards that these questionable materials *seem* to establish. The courts have recognized this in suggesting, although they have not clearly decided, that in evaluating "contemporary community standards," other works that have been circulating with seeming impunity may be introduced in evidence.[1]

Moreover, and from quite an opposite tack, there is sound law enforcement guidance in the observation of President Ulysses S. Grant, made at the time of his first inaugural in 1869, that "I know of no method to secure the repeal of bad or obnoxious laws so effective as their stringent execution."

10. Sex-in-Action Photographs

. . . anything at all a man and woman wish to do or say in their sexual relations, their love-making, or call it what you please, is exactly their own business and nobody else's. But let them keep it to themselves unless they wish to appear ridiculous at best, at worst debased and even criminal. For sex resembles many other acts which may in themselves be harmless, yet when commited in certain circumstances may be not only a sin, but a crime against human life itself, human feelings, human rights—I do not say against ethics, morality, sense of honour. . . .
                    —Katherine Anne Porter, "A Wreath for the Gamekeeper,"
                                        Feb. 1960 *Encounter* p. 72

IN 1960, WHEN PENGUIN BOOKS announced its intention of openly reissuing D. H. Lawrence's *Lady Chatterley's Lover* in England, the Director of Public Prosecutions brought a criminal action challenging that decision. Penguin's defenders in the Old Bailey did not try a frontal assault on Britain's law against obscenity. Rather, they suggested that although legally, offensive obscenity might exist, *Lady Chatterley* was not obscene. After three days of testimony by defense experts stressing the book's literary value, and three hours of deliberations, the jury acquitted Penguin, and an aging *Lady Chatterley,* whose prior experiences in England had all been under-the-counter, was brought into the sunlight of public sale. For the defense, Mr. Gerald Gardiner, Q.C., in giving his opening statement, told the jurymen:

I do not suppose there is a decent man or woman in this court who does not whole-heartedly believe that pornography, the filthy bawdy muck that is just filth for filth's sake, ought to be stamped out and suppressed. Such books are not literature. They have got no message;

they have got no inspiration; they have got no thought. They have got nothing. They are just filth and ought to be stamped out.[1]

By today's American standards, Gardiner's contention that *Lady Chatterley's Lover* was not among the items that "ought to be stamped out and suppressed"[2] was proper. But what is?

Lawrence himself suggested one answer:

> But even I would censor genuine pornography, rigorously. It would not be very difficult. In the first place, genuine pornography is almost always underworld, it doesn't come into the open. In the second, you can recognize it by the insult it offers, invariably, to sex, and to the human spirit.
>
> Pornography is the attempt to insult sex, to do dirt on it. This is unpardonable. Take the very lowest instance, the picture post-card sold underhand, by the underworld, in most cities. What I have seen of them have been of an ugliness to make you cry. The insult to the human body, the insult to a vital human relationship! Ugly and cheap they make the human nudity, ugly and degraded they make the sexual act, trivial and cheap and nasty.
>
> It is the same with the books they sell in the underworld. They are either so ugly they make you ill, or so fatuous you can't imagine anybody but a cretin or a moron reading them, or writing them.[3]

The most unmistakably "filthy bawdy muck," the clearest "attempt to insult sex, to do dirt on it," that troubles American police and prosecutors has used today's technology to improve on Lawrence's picture postcard. This is the stag film, the most intimate of "home movies," that shows men and women engaging in sexual acts, including (but *only* including) intercourse. Long before the zoom lens was marketed for amateur use, stag moviemakers had brought their cameras breathlessly close, to pick up anatomical detail in action. On occasion, these movies have been done in living color, and even in sound, but more typically they are drab in concept, unlovely in casting, and in black and white. To distinguish one film from another so that purchasers—or party-renters—might know from the title what they have previously seen (the films all, essentially, exhibit only slight variations on the same theme), the sex-in-action that constitutes the bulk of each film is commonly introduced by the most cursory of plots. For example, in the collection the seizure of which is about to be described, one of the films, *Ironing Broad,* opens with a girl ironing; warming, she strips off her blouse and skirt and pursues her chores in the nude until her partner appears; moments later his clothing has apparently been added to the laundry pile and the ironing never gets done. *Strip Poker* similarly proves an apt description for the prologue of a four-handed, four-character movie.

In the winter of 1960-61, the New York County prosecutor's office learned that a sizable manufacturer-distributor of these movies was active in the metropolitan area. Scraps from informants bolstered by long weeks of police surveillance ultimately led to a drifter named George Collins. He was arrested with fifty-nine reels in his possession. Collins not only peddled the finished products, but the previous summer had doubled as "casting director" when eleven new films had been shot in Manhattan. Collins had recruited bar-friends and bed-friends, people who lived (and lived poorly) by their wits and their bodies, to play the male and the female roles. His particular folly in this instance was his having procured the services of a prematurely bedraggled unwed mother, not yet eighteen years of age, to "act" in several of the pictures. This criminally poor casting put Collins, and all concerned with the movies in which she "played" (one of the grand jurors—himself in show business—vigorously protested calling her an "actress"!), in the uncomfortable position of facing not simply the customary misdemeanor charges of producing and selling obscenity, but also as accomplices in the felony charge of statutory rape, with the film itself providing much of the necessary corroborative proof.

Collins's own operations in Lower East Side Manhattan bars led us to the quiet suburban community of Hewlett, Long Island, where a photographer, Fred Barrett, made his home. His garage contained a massive film printer; using the negatives that he had photographed and processed, and other similar films that he had procured, Barrett turned out reels of film to meet the market demand. Although Barrett had had a previous obscenity conviction, his neighbors seemed unaware of it. His business card announced "Photography" as his profession, and legitimate professional activity occupied much of his time; Barrett's specialties, his card proclaimed, were "Weddings and Bar Mitzvahs."

Distribution of the films was handled in Brooklyn. Melvin Dutchkin, the third of these conspirators, ran an unsuccessful television repair business there. On the side, using his store as a supply center, he catered to a handful of uncomfortable little men who made or supplemented their livelihoods by selling hard-core films to local marginal book, photo, and novelty shops, or to anyone who would buy or rent them. Before they were arrested, Barrett, Collins, and Dutchkin had, it was estimated, sold several thousand movie films in and about New York City, reels that rarely brought them more than a few dollars each, although the films would ultimately retail at anything from ten dollars apiece and up, depending upon the customer's hunger and the retailer's greed.

Police, using search warrants simultaneously executed in Hewlett and Brooklyn, seized Barrett and Dutchkin along with more than a hundred film masters, and many hundreds of films made from them, ready for sale and for showing. Interrogated in the prosecutor's office, both were quick to concede their guilt, seeming somewhat relieved that their double lives (not as profitable, they complained, as they had hoped) had been exposed. Shortly thereafter, along with Collins, they eagerly pleaded guilty to multiple misdemeanor charges rather than risking trial on the statutory rape count. All were given indefinite sentences; penitentiary terms with three year maximums.

The Barrett-Collins-Dutchkin case manifests one of the paradoxes of obscenity enforcement. Although, using Lawrence's words, these defendants made human nudity "ugly and cheap . . . ugly and degraded they [made] the sexual act, trivial and cheap and nasty," their pornography had, at most, the *slightest* impact on the metropolitan area in which they operated. And the impact it has was wholly on "volunteers," almost certainly adults, being titillated by it *secretly*. Stag movies are not part of any public display. The actors in them do not become well publicized minor folk-heroes whose employments are likely to serve as trend-setters or exemplars for the immature. The price of the films and their subterranean marketing serve to place them beyond the viewing of most youngsters. Even adult customers require a degree of sophistication (and a contact or two) to learn where to find them. In terms of audience size—circulation figures—compare the stag films with the mass market girlie magazines, available and publicly displayed on many racks and kiosks, and the novels of endless erotic adventure, widely selling for less than a dollar each, in enticingly covered paperbacks. Although the films are clearly "filthy bawdy muck," and the magazines and paperbacks may not be, the movies' limited distribution, and hence impact, is miniscule compared with that of the other merchandise. For this reason, although stag pictures are the farthest-out pornography, they galvanize no extremists into excited action or counter-action. Civic groups do not form to protest them. The *Reader's Digest* runs no articles centering on their perils.

In the opposite corner, the usually eager champions who are strong in their certitude that *any* invasion of freedom of expression endangers the First Amendment, are likely, pitchman-fashion, to mutter "go away boy, you bother me" when confronted with the purposeless filth of these stag films. No committees of libertarians or artists write manifestoes defending the sleezy Barrett-Collins-Dutchkins of this world, although contrasted with many publishers of profitably selling borderline items, these amateurish muck-sellers, functioning in less green financial valleys, and having no palatable defenses if *any* obscenity is constitutionally actionable, need all the outside help they can get.

Lawrence's acknowledgment that he "would censor genuine pornography rigorously," including "the very lowest instance, the picture post-card" because of its "insult to the human body . . . to a vital human relationship," as circumscribed as is the area with which it deals, still leaves its edges undefined. Clearly, single photographs with the same explicit content are in the same league as are the stag motion pictures. But what happens when a veneer of possible artistry is added to this subject matter?

Jonas Mekas, former movie critic for New York City's Greenwich Village weekly, the *Village Voice*, and a leader in the low-low-budget experimental film field, was arrested in the Village in March 1964. His offense was his sponsorship of a public showing of the avant-garde film, *Flaming Creatures*. As has been stated, that film showed matter-of-fact close-ups of male penises being masturbated, and of female breasts being fondled; in one scene an orgy was suggested; another scene showed oral-genital contact. Despite the hosannas of critic Susan Sontag and some others, Mekas—defended by one of New York's ablest and best-known trial lawyers, Emile Zola Berman—was convicted. The three justices of the New York City Criminal Court were unanimous, apparently finding the movie "utterly without redeeming social importance." The guilty verdict was handed down on June 12, 1964, just ten days before that phrase was given added uncertainty by the *Jacobellis* opinions. A year and a half later the conviction was affirmed by the intermediate appellate court.[4] Whether or not the display or sale to the public of *any* photographs of sexual organs actively at play is taboo, or whether *some* artistry or other circumstances may immunize some of them, has not been definitely settled, however, either by our legislatures or in our highest appellate courts.

11. The Offbeat Smut Merchants

> First Murderer: We are men, my liege.
> Macbeth: Ay, in the catalogue ye go for men;
> As hounds and greyhounds, mongrels,
>   spaniels, curs,
> Shoughs, water-rugs and demi-wolves,
>   are clept
> All by the name of dogs.
> —William Shakespeare, *Macbeth*, Act III, sc. i.

IN EACH OF AMERICA's largest cities there are filth merchants who specialize in hawking those books, magazines, and photographs that appeal to offbeat thrill-seekers. In New York City such smut peddlers, styling their establishments "bookstores," cluster about Manhattan's Times Square. The *Nights of Horror* pamphlets that Justice Matthew M. Levy had described in the appropriately grizzly language earlier quoted from his *Kingsley Books* opinion (". . . tearing breasts off . . . completely singeing away the body hairs . . . putting honey on a girl's breasts, vagina and buttocks— and then putting hundreds of great red ants on the honey . . .") were among the items sold in some of the Times Square stores. Kingsley Books itself was a shop located on West 42nd Street, between Broadway and Eighth Avenue. These bookstores, for the most part, are not brightly lit, neatly ordered analogues of Brentano's or Doubleday's with well-arranged display windows decorously showing current best sellers. Traditionally their windows tend to be cluttered with books and magazines, the jackets or covers of which suggest sensual, nudist, deviate, or pseudo-

medical-sexual themes. The window crowding has been deliberate: apart from its display-advertising value, it assists in
obscuring vision into the stores. Sales of special merchandise to
well-known customers, under-the-counter sales of the hardest
hard-core, can proceed with little fear of observation from the
outside. Inside, along with further displays of the window's
wares, are likely to be a number of other crude items for visual
enjoyment: there are the sets of glossy photographs the top pictures of which reveal either nude or underdressed and overdevel-
oped females, and separate sets of photos of male nudes, and
there are the magazines and booklets, dealing with sadism,
masochism, lesbianism, and other perversions. The packaging
both of these books and photographs is significant. Almost always
each item is plastic-wrapped, the combination of transparency
and seal simultaneously stimulating interest and preventing that
too thorough browsing that, undiscouraged, might serve to
quench it. The proprietors and salespeople, all males, are not
remarkable for the courteous or literate impression they convey
in the bookshops—nor is that impression bettered in the courtroom where their arrest and conviction records are likely to
prove considerable, and not solely for pornography.

From April 1963 through August 1964 more than one hundred
and fifty obscenity arrests of salesclerks and proprietors were
made in about two dozen bookstores that clustered about Times
Square. These arrests followed purchases by plainclothes policemen of pictures and booklets that, under the laws, appeared to
be illegal. The contraband items were mostly the cellophane-
packaged sets of photographs, known as "strip-tease nudes," and
the sado-masochistic sex novelettes of a type never reviewed, and
probably never seen, by Sunday book supplement reviewers.

In one of these shops alone, during this period, thirteen arrests
took place, not simultaneously, but on nine separate occasions.
Eight took place in another store. Five or more were made in
each of six others. The cast of characters is interesting. Two of
the individuals were arrested four times each (during this same

period), five three times, and fifteen more twice each. Despite scienter problems, and some search and seizure difficulties, one hundred and twenty of these arrests led to convictions and to sentences, most of which included imprisonment for terms that varied from thirty days to as much as three years.

These sentences would have, had they been served reasonably promptly, removed the offenders from the pornography trade, at least temporarily. By imprisoning *at the same time* a host of convicted store proprietors and managers, along with enough of their help to crimp the recruitment of replacements, a death-knell might have been sounded for the largest portion of this Times Square muck-pushing business. As it was, some of the stores folded. But the activity of others was merely scotched momentarily by their trial convictions. Continuing delays on appeal served to keep most of these defendants at large for months, even years, after they had been found guilty and ordered to jail. During this time they continued to ply their trades to support themselves—and very likely to earn the fees due attorneys and bondsmen for protracted legal services. Defense attorneys, well aware of the merits of the Confucianism, "He who chases justice may catch it," have been true to their tradition of letting appeals lag in cases in which they represent clients *still on the outside.*

MISHKIN, AND THE SADO-MASOCHISTIC LINE OF BOOKS

Edward Mishkin, probably America's leading pornographer of the offbeat, knew the full range of this business long before that 1960 arrest in New York County that, in the winter of 1965-66, was finally to reach the United States Supreme Court. During the decades prior to that arrest, Mishkin had been locked up often, but only once had the pornography charges stuck. That was in 1952. He had not been sent to jail, however, paying instead a $1,600 fine. In 1955, when subpoenaed by the late Senator Estes Kefauver of Tennessee, to testify concerning pornography, Mishkin rested on his Fifth Amendment privilege, refusing even to give customary "pedigree" information, such as his age and marital status.[1] "Mishkin is reputed to gross over $1,500,000 yearly from the pornography traffic," reported the committee; with a partner, the Senators noted, he operated three New York City Times Square bookshops, including Kingsley Books.[2] The *Kingsley Books* case,[3] in the mid '50s, had not involved a criminal proceeding, but had tested out New York's then new injunctive statute. Any warning to Mishkin that might have been implicit in that injunctive action went unheeded. Having learned how profitable the sado-masochistic pornography business could be, and how free of real punishment, Mishkin remained deeply involved.

When arrested in 1960, Mishkin was charged with having published some forty-three different booklets dealing with offbeat sex, and with having sold them, along with items others published, to bookstores, and with having retailed them himself through his own Times Square outlets. (The three stores, incidentally, were at locations at which several years later, during the 1963-64 drive, fresh obscenity arrests and seizures were made. Whether or not during the three year lapse the *real* ownership had changed is unknown; hard-core obscenitors are a hardy breed.) Prior to his 1960 arrest, some seventeen thousand booklets, numerous copies of the forty-three Mishkin titles along with some non-Mishkin books that he distributed, had been seized. The trial testimony proved that this was but a sample of Mishkin's activity. Examined by Assistant District Attorney Melvin Stein, an extremely able, earnest, vigorous prosecutor, who tried the case, Mishkin's printer indicated that print-orders would usually range from one thousand to five thousand copies of each booklet. The printer's charge to Mishkin for the crude black and white offset work would range from fifteen to forty cents a copy; at retail, the booklets would each be marked to bring five, ten, or even fifteen dollars apiece. Writers received no royalties; they were paid one or two hundred dollars (on rare occasions, as much as three hundred), for each book, and the illustrators were paid something less.

Giving evidence in Mishkin's 1960 trial, Hyman Rosen, a writer, told of a conversation with Mishkin:

I came to see Mr. Mishkin and asked him if he wanted a book. He said, "What have you got?" I said, "I have a little novel at home." He said, "Well, spice it up and bring it in." That's exactly what I did.[4]

And a Miss Leotha Hackshaw, a free-lance television writer, testifying to her own conversations with Mishkin, said:

Well, he wanted a book in which there were lesbian scenes, the sex had to be very strong, it had to be rough, it had to be clearly spelled out. In other words, I couldn't be subtle about it; I had to write sex very bluntly, make the sex scenes very strong . . . . He didn't call it lesbian, but he described women making love to women and men were making love to men, and there was spankings and scenes—sex in an abnormal and irregular fashion . . . . In this book he wanted an emphasis on beatings and fetishism and clothing—irregular clothing, and that sort of thing . . . .[5]

Mishkin got what he wanted. Nineteen of the books received in evidence at his trial dealt with women being whipped, beaten, or otherwise tormented. Cover drawings were of females often sufficiently full-bodied to place Jane Russell in shadow, costumed in black corselets and high spiked heels, scourges or other torture equipment at hand. Titles amplified upon the deviate appeal: *Cult of the Spankers, Bound in Leather, Dance with the Dominant Whip* are a few. Sub-titles further teased aberrant curiosity: "The Story of the Creation of a Lesbian," or "The Unusual Story of a Woman Flagellant." Coursing through the Mishkin volumes one finds no imaginable literary merit and little story line. In some there are male-female sexual encounters (conventional, oral-genital, and sado-masochistic) sensually described in abundant detail. In others, there are interminably varied combinations of whipping, paddling, spanking, stretching, gagging, straight-jacketing, manacling, racking, and in other fashions generally abusing the female body, torments inflicted by imperious women upon servile female acolytes. A unanimous three-judge New York City bench, convicting Mishkin in November 1960 on dozens of obscenity counts, wrote:

These books deal with sex in its most corrupt, sadistic, masochistic and dengenerate form. They promote lust and portray filth for its own sake, or as Judge Woolsey called it in the *Ulysses* case . . . "dirt for dirt's sake."[6]

In mid-December 1960, the bench sentenced Mishkin to pay a fine of $12,500 and to serve three consecutive one year prison terms.

By early January, Mishkin's lawyers had secured his release from jail, pending his appeal. That was only the beginning. Recurrent defense postponements stalled the review. When the defense's briefs had finally been filed, the prosecutors handling the appeal, in turn, sought more and more time. Each side was extremely courteous—possibly too courteous—to the other. The extensions were generally agreed to. And, throughout, the appellate courts proved supinely tolerant of this interminable procrastination. "The system of appeals that pervades American jurisprudence," Truman Capote was to observe, "amounts to a legalistic wheel of fortune, a game of chance, somewhat fixed in favor of the criminal, that the participants play interminably. . . ."[7] The *Mishkin* case exemplifies this "wheel of fortune"; rarely in a non-capital case has the art of appellate delay reached such perfection—and produced at least a strong likelihood of dividends generated only by the passage of time. It took almost four years for the case to reach New York State's highest court, where without dissent, the conviction and sentence were affirmed.[8] Mishkin still eluded jail. His counsel secured an order staying his surrender while review was sought in the United States Supreme Court. Argued in the high Court in early December 1965, *five years after Mishkin had been sentenced by the trial judges to imprisonment*, the case was, as has been seen, decided on the first day of spring, 1966. For more than five post-conviction years, Mishkin, sentenced to three years' imprisonment, had remained a free man.

Or, more accurately, had almost remained free. Pornographer that he was, it was the sheerest folly to have expected Mishkin to sit idly by, permitting his own special talents to go to seed, while his case meandered slowly through the appellate courts.

In September of 1962, almost two years after his New York County conviction, Mishkin was arrested again, this time by federal customs officials, charged with conspiring to smuggle English pornography into America. His courier was a seaman on the liner *Queen Mary.* In Southampton the seaman had received a package, along with instructions to deposit it in a New York subway locker, whence he was to proceed to a bookshop at a described location and was there to ask for "Eddie," stating "I have something for you from the boys in England," and was to turn over the locker key. The caper failed, however, when the seaman, his jacket bulging with the poorly concealed package, was spotted by alert customs guards. Arrested, he agreed to carry on with the plan, *in their presence.* As scheduled, he was seen to hand the key to Mishkin, and the following day Mishkin's emissary was observed going to the locker and retrieving the package. In it were a dozen copies of an illustrated book, the title of which reflected both its nature and its British origins: *Thrashed in Many Ways.*

The pace of the federal courts proved quite different from what Mishkin had grown accustomed to. Within a few weeks of the crime, Mishkin's trial was underway. Hoping to keep the book from the jurors' attention, Mishkin's attorney conceded its obscenity. This stratagem failed, however, and Mishkin, convicted of conspiring to import lewd publications, was sentenced to six months' imprisonment to be followed by four and a half years on probation. The federal appeals procedures moved quickly. By October 1963, this conviction and sentence having been affirmed by the federal intermediate appellate court, the

Supreme Court declined review.[9] Remanded to jail, Mishkin served his federal sentence. Imprisonment on the local arrest, an arrest that had preceded by some thirty months the action of the federal customs agents, was still being held at bay by those interminable state-tolerated appellate delays!

Despite his federal difficulties, the slowness of his New York appeal provided Mishkin with obvious new strengths: the community standards with which the *Roth* case had firmly entwined the law were becoming increasingly tolerant. Books like *Fanny Hill* (with its multiple tableaux of male-female, and occasional female-female sex) and *Last Exit to Brooklyn* (explicitly depicting male homosexuality), which could not have been published openly in 1960, were by 1965 being read by a significant portion of America's literate community. Although Mishkin's booklets had no literary merit of any kind, public acceptance of such books as *Fanny Hill* lent some support to the argument that, judged by contemporary community standards, such themes lacked prurience. In the Supreme Court, the Potter Stewart dissent was to remark concerning Mishkin's pamphlets, "However tawdry the books may be, they are not hard-core pornography." The passage of time helped the defendant's chances on review.

Moreover, Mishkin stood to benefit from legal developments that post-dated his conviction. Significantly, three cases decided by the United States Supreme Court *after* Mishkin's New York trial, were to provide his lawyers substantial fuel in argument before the high Court. In one, decided in 1964 and impersonally entitled *A Quantity of Copies of Books* v. *Kansas*,[10] four of the high Court's Justices (with two more, Justices Black and Douglas, concurring on their usual grounds) stated that a seizure of allegedly obscene books was unlawful where the books had been seized *before* their owner had been afforded an opportunity to dispute their obscenity in the courts. Mishkin had had no similar hearing when the more than seventeen thousand paperbacks had been seized from his printer. This 1964 ruling had rested upon a 1961 high Court case, *Marcus* v. *Search Warrants*[11] (decided the year after Mishkin's New York County conviction), in which a majority of the Justices had held that orders for the seizure of obscene books were not to be issued unless the magistrate had actually inspected a copy of *each* of the publications he was ordering seized. In the *Mishkin* case, although search warrants had been used, all forty-three of Mishkin's titles had not been read by the judge before signing the seizure order. Mishkin's very able trial attorney (since elected a New York City judge) had not, on trial, sought to litigate these and other possible technical defects involved in the amassing of evidence against his client. As of 1960, such litigation would have been an utter waste of everyone's time; it was then indisputably clear in New York, and in many other states, that evidence was usable in criminal trials, whether or not it had been lawfully obtained. Then, on the nineteenth of June 1961, seven months after Mishkin's sentencing, in the landmark case of *Mapp* v. *Ohio*[12] the Supreme Court ruled that the state courts could no longer receive in evidence, in criminal trials, anything that had been illegally seized by police. Suddenly, seizure circumstances became important. As to cases pre-dating June 1961 that were still pending on appeal at that time (and Mishkin's was clearly such a case), the Supreme Court later held that illegality of seizure retroactively barred an item's reception in evidence.[13] These cases stood fair to trouble the Supreme Court. But when it had decided to review Mishkin's conviction, the high Bench was interested in pornography, not in procedure. And not compelled to grant review, the Justices neatly sidestepped the seizure questions. "We may, for good reason, even at this stage decline to decide the merits of the issue," the majority opinion stated; and noting that the record before them was almost barren of evidence concerning the seizure, the high Justices concluded, "We think that this is a case for such an exercise of our discretion." This was a close one; although Mishkin's conviction was affirmed by a divided Court, it could well have been reversed *wholly* upon case law developed during the almost interminable—and inexcusable—post-conviction appellate delay.

Thus the five year appellate lag in the *Mishkin* case is seen to illustrate another paradox, one often shared by crimes involving pornography with the entire body of the criminal law. The courts pay lip service to the processing of criminal cases with alacrity. The defendant's Sixth Amendment "right to a speedy . . . trial," and the aphorism, "Justice delayed is justice denied," are regularly mouthed. Yet these are, or should be, two-way streets. That great and sensitive judge, Benjamin N. Cardozo, more than thirty years ago, noted that "justice, though due to the accused, is due to the accuser also."[14] If punishment is to serve some deterrent purpose, reasonable swiftness and certainty of impact are necessary. Yet, today, appellate judges, who are galvanized into acting to remove the motes they spy in the eyes of their lesser judicial colleagues, seem not the least perturbed by the beams that block their own vision. Not only do they fail to compel the processing of appeals with some speed, but their methods, as the *Mishkin* case well shows, tend in practice to *encourage* defendants to move slowly. These methods proclaim that the race today is hardly to the swift; he who hesitates may well thereby be saved.

(As most appeals statutes contemplate getting cases before the appellate tribunals within several months after conviction, attorneys both for the prosecution and for the defense grossly abuse their trusts in permitting them to lag by repeatedly agreeing with each other to adjournments. With simple enabling legislation, were they so inclined, the appellate courts could readily police this by barring extensions of time, regardless of the parties' consent, other than with appeals court approval. And such approval might be parsimoniously parceled out, with appeals being dismissed when defendants were tardy, and convictions being vacated when prosecutors dragged their feet.)

GENOVA AND FRIED AND THE STRIPTEASE NUDE PHOTO SETS

Mishkin's deviantly appealing books are not the only offbeat sex merchandise to have been dragged through the courts. The filth merchants have managed to concoct a near-nude, cursed with their own crudeness, that has similarly moved at snail's pace in the halls of justice. Pictured nudity, certainly when genitals are concealed by prop, costume, or posture, and when sold to adults, is not today deemed obscene. The several decades of Americans who have, in the past, savored *Esquire's* Petty or Vargas girls, the Marilyn Monroe calendar, and *Playboy's* play-mate-of-the month, express male America's enjoyment (and judicial America's ready tolerance) of the provocative, long-legged, full-breasted female nude. But the pornographers have turned this alluring sensual fantasy rancid, substituting for it the murky world of the tawdry hustler.

The transformation is expressed in photographs known in the trade as "striptease nude" sets. As generally sold, they consist of four or six different prints, each showing the same no-longer nubile woman in varying degrees of undress. Although pubic areas are never completely uncovered, breasts or buttocks, commonly somewhat fantastic in size, and rarely noted for firmness, are often exposed. Black panties, bras, and garter belts are shown, not simply serving their customary functions, but frequently—somewhat out of position—utilized to distort, to accentuate, or to focus attention upon the breasts, anal, or genital areas. The poses are often crudely suggestive: the model's hands may be at her nipples, or grasping her crotch. In some, fetishism is involved: high spike heels, or black leather corselets. The pictures are often shot indoors, the subjects crouching, or spread-eagled on worn sofas or unlaundered bed sheets. Lumping the crude poses, the emotionless figures, the tacky interiors, the general crassness, these photographs are barren of any imaginable artistry. They are drab and depressing. In no conceivable way are they things of beauty. They are solely of the flesh, and of the flesh in such crude display as to suggest a tired butcher's concept of the body, not that of the sensualist, the artist, the dreamer, or that of a lusty male. These are the offbeat sex vendor's nudes.

While Mishkin was being tried, in the fall of 1960, another case—that of Robert Genova—was being readied for trial. Genova, much younger, and clearly less the old pro of pornography than Mishkin, had achieved dubious eminence in the area of striptease nudes. Blinds drawn in his studio on the fringes of New York City's garment district, Genova took the pictures that were the first stage of his own vertical operation; he then printed them by the tens of thousands, and ultimately served as his own wholesaler. Whether this industrious pornographer would be convicted, however, was dubious. Criminal trial court judges had had a simple rule of thumb, one for which no appellate authority existed, that they applied when dealing with photographs: no pubic hair—no obscenity. Following this rule, Genova's photos would be innocent. In its mechanical, locational emphasis, this guide ignored the *Roth* principle that obscenity was to be judged by determining whether "the dominant theme of the material taken as a whole appeals to prurient interest." The dominant theme, obviously could be better judged by inspection of an *entire* picture, or set of pictures, than by attempting a somewhat degrading process of visual hair-seeking.

At the end of Genova's trial, the court reserved decision in order to evaluate the legal arguments. Meanwhile, a handful of New York City plainclothes police had been making repeated purchases of books of the Mishkin type, and of pictures of the Genova type, in the Times Square bookstores, stores that had continued to sell them despite the Mishkin conviction and the Genova arrest. On the morning of January 18, 1961 (the date the trial court had set for its *Genova* decision), the police waited near Times Square in order to be able to act promptly. Were the verdict one of "guilty," police would be in a position to move quickly in arresting other wholesalers and retailers before, after learning what had happened in court, they temporarily hid their stocks. As the shops and wholesalers had been profiting from their dealings in borderline merchandise, merchandise tawdry and unnatural in appeal and with no redeeming value whatsoever whether or not legally obscene, it did not seem inappropriate that they bear the hazards of the business in which they had chosen to engage. Obligingly, the headquarters of the Greater New York Council, Boy Scouts of America—just a few blocks from Times Square—was made available to the police for their use as a "staging area." In mid-morning, Genova's conviction reached the police via the Scouts' switchboard. Plainclothesmen promptly fanned into the area, making further purchases of sado-masochistic paperbacks and of photo sets, this time following through immediately with arrests and with seizures of stock. Simultaneously, detectives armed with search warrants appeared at the office-studio-storerooms of Robert Genova, and at those of other major striptease nude wholesalers. In all, twenty-three arrests, four of wholesalers and nineteen of retailers, at thirteen different stores, were made that day. Over two hundred thousand photographs and negatives (well over a hundred packing cartons) were seized. Approximately fifty thousand were taken from Genova alone; in court that morning, once notified of his conviction, he had been released on bail pending sentence, and had returned to his place of employment.

Carefully planned and designed to strangle the continuing nuisance of Times Square, this 1961 effort (anticipating by more than two years the 1963-64 drive already described) fizzled completely. Its failure was the result of a decision made by New York State's highest court some four months later in which the court split three ways, but in the process reversed a key obscenity conviction. Hindsight was later to prove that the reversal, its two-two-three division leaving its meaning obviously clouded, had not even been in point! But by the time that was to become clear, the damage had already been done.

In the case, *People* v. *Richmond County News, Inc.*, New York's highest court majority held for the first time that "hard-core" was the proper obscenity test in New York State, although the meaning of "hard-core" remained the subject of disagreement among the judges.[15] This decision was handed down on May 25, 1961, but the usual delays involved in getting the bailed Times Square defendants to trial had been such that many of those arrests had not yet reached the trial stage. Trial judges, with their customary cautious instinct to play safe and thus avoid reversal, and habituated to characterizing only stag films ("action shots") as "hard-core," reacted instinctively. Acquittals and dismissals followed. Judges who had previously tried and convicted some of the less dilatory of the January defendants recalled and vacated their own prior "guilty" verdicts. Indeed, Genova himself ultimately beat the new charges filed against him. And, paradoxically, his January 18 conviction, the one that had led to the January "raids," was itself reversed when, oddly, the exhibits on which it had been premised could not be located for the appellate courts to review![16]

Striptease nudes, of dubious status in New York before January 18, 1961, but obscene from then until May of that year, seemed in the clear once again. Then, starting in 1962, the law veered once more.

Harry Fried, a midtown bookstore proprietor since 1948, with one prior obscenity conviction and one one hundred dollar fine, was one of those who had been arrested during the "Genova raids" of January 18, 1961. He had that day sold a set of strip-tease nudes to an officer who the previous week had purchased a book from him, *College for Sinners* (described on the back cover as, in part, the story of "an initiation dreamed up by the passion-mad members of The Libertines, a sex club that perverted every concept of decency . . . nights of insane abandon with three of the sex club's beautiful members . . . an orgy of sin shaping their lives with moral decay!"). Fried's lawyer had been successful only to the extent of delaying Fried's trial until more than a post-arrest year had passed. But on March 16, 1962, the attorney found his client in the unhappy position of being on trial, after all of this procrastination, and before the wrong judges. Fried was convicted.

Sentenced a month later to sixty days' imprisonment, and promptly released pending action on his appeal, another year was to slide by before that appeal was perfected and determined. In March 1963 Fried's conviction was affirmed by the intermediate appellate court, both insofar as it rested on his sale of the book, and on that of the striptease pictures.[17] Fried, having been quickly denied permission to appeal further in the state, again had his sentence stayed, this time to permit him to seek review in the United States Supreme Court. In July 1963 Justice Potter Stewart extended the delay of Fried's remand to prison, in order to grant Fried continued freedom while giving the high Court adequate time to decide whether or not it wished to review his conviction. Making that decision took another year. Then, split six to three, the Supreme Court acted on June 22, 1964 (the same date that, badly splintered, it had decided the *Jacobellis* and the *Tropic of Cancer* cases). The Court determined *not* to review the New York conviction.[18] The state decision, that striptease nudes *did* constitute actionable obscenity, remained the law. And finally, three and a half years after his arrest for offering dirty pictures for sale and for selling a dirty book, Fried was committed to serve his sentence—sixty days.

SCIENTER AND THE SMUT MERCHANTS

Before leaving the demi-world of the dealers in offbeat sex, the extremely troublesome requirement of scienter—knowledge —as it relates to them merits comment.

That requirement, at first glance, would seem one unlikely to pose any barriers when dealing with the Times Square's brand of obscenitors. Men employed full time in the dirty-book-and-picture trade, working for or owning stores that have for years been specialists in filth (illegal or borderline), would surely have some idea of what they were about. So common sense would seem to dictate.

But common sense and the law are frequently at odds. For several reasons the scienter requirement is not automatically satisfied by the squalid settings in which so many pornography transactions take place. *First,* prior brushes with the obscenity laws reflected in the fingerprint histories of a number of the dirty-bookstore defendants, although going far to belie an innocent frame of mind, are rarely admissible in evidence.[19] The rule barring their consideration is soundly designed to prevent jurors and judges from stripping away the vital presumption of innocence by reasoning that defendants who have past criminal records are likely to repeat their follies. *Second,* showing that the store in which alleged pornography was sold was otherwise crammed with pictures and titles proclaiming illicit sex, sadism, and semi-nudity, is not generally accepted as proof of scienter. Today's Times Square stores seem "departmentalized." There are racks of glossy photo sets of female nudes, and separate racks for the striptease sets; there are still others exhibiting the male nudes. There are sections for the sado-masochistic books and different areas for books on lesbianism and on homosexuality. Still others display paperback erotica, and there are racks for the marriage manuals and similar tomes. Such evidence would, concededly, bear on the scienter question: salesmen in a store merchandising sex should be on notice as to the likely character of anything they sell. And it is now obviously relevant on the pandering issue. But such proof might multiply side controversies endlessly. Were such items, in fact, being offered for sale? How prominent was their display? Were their apparent themes sexual? Were they in fact pornographic? And so on. Almost eighty years ago, the great Justice Oliver Wendell Holmes, while still a Massachusetts appellate judge, observed that our rules excluding proof at trial of collateral issues were "a concession to the shortness of life."[20] (Holmes retired from the United States

Supreme Court in his ninety-first year!) In the interests of that "concession," trial court judges markedly curtail such proof. *Third,* even were proof of a store's character admitted, it might be legally inadequate to meet the blurry scienter requirement that Justice Brennen suggested, but never got around to defining, in his *Smith* case opinion. In the *Smith* case itself the surroundings were strongly suggestive: the retail store's clerks had been instructed to permit no minors to handle the books or magazines.[21] Proof of scienter may require focusing on the *particular* photograph or volume, and *not solely* on its bookshelf or display counter neighbors. No book or picture is to be deemed known by either the company it keeps or by the company that keeps it.

How, then, are police to show that the defendant knew the character of the particular books, pamphlets, or pictures that led to his arrest? One clear way exists, but it is neither always available nor always adequate. There is also always available another —sometimes questionable—method.

The first way is to prove enough facts (quite apart from any conversations that allegedy took place with the defendant) so that any vendor who was not deliberately shutting his eyes to the nature of the materials he was selling would be alerted. In concurring in the *Smith* case, the late Justice Felix Frankfurter noted, "obviously the Court does not hold that a bookseller who insulates himself against knowledge about an offending book is thereby free to maintain an emporium for smut." Rottenness sufficient to jog the bona fide dealer may be nosed from a number of clues: obvious overpricing, cover illustrations and book titles luridly reflective of sensual promise, unique wrappings (most nonerotic books are not, routinely, sold sealed in plastic), and such prominent display that any defendant salesman would have to be near blind not to have earlier noted the item. New York's key case, in which the state's highest court held the proof of scienter to be adequate, was one against Louis Finkelstein,[22] described by the late Senator Estes Kefauver's juvenile delinquency subcommittee as a former partner of Eddie Mishkin. Involved were two

Mishkin-type books, *Queen Bee* and *Garden of Evil*. Each had carried the printed retail price, "$5.00"; together they were sold for $9.00. Both were paperbacks, each photo-offset on poor stock. Each featured a crude cover drawing of several full- and bare-breasted women, one cover also carrying the legend, "Completely Unexpurgated." (And in the *Fried* case the striptease nudes were plastic-wrapped, the top picture showing; they had been displayed on a counter next to the cash register at which Fried checked out his customers in this self-service bookshop.) Although in the *Finkelstein* and *Fried* cases these facts—*coupled with evidence of some slight conversations*—were found to be sufficient, courts have been known to insist on more. Some trial and appellate judges credulously assume that a book or picture sale may be made *in good faith* by a bookseller who, while somehow spotting the right price, looks past the book's cover illustration and its wrapping, accepting payment—while in all innocence he drops the book into a paper bag.[23]

Scienter may be established, or strengthened, by conversations. Testimony is common that the policeman, on purchasing the book or pictures, asked something such as, "Is this the best you have?" or "Haven't you something hotter?" eliciting the defendant's reply along the lines of "It's great," "It's red hot," or "It's as good as anything we've had." Understandably some judges find this to be normal puffing, common among salesmen of everything from widgets to washing machines, and hence not validly probative of knowledge. Assuming its legal sufficiency, however, along with other factors, to prove knowledge, are such conversations to be believed? Doubts linger that professional pornographers, previously arrested and well aware of the scienter requirements, would be easily drawn into participation in such dialogues. Clearly *sometimes* such things *are* said. Persons (be they book-makers, dope pushers, or pimps) who eke out dishonest livelihoods by the sweat of others' vices are often startlingly stupid. Moreover, the plainclothes policeman's questions are those that might be expected from those deviate patrons, eager to throw their dollars where the prurience is greatest. Yet doubts are intensified when, in the course of hundreds of arrests, vast numbers of conversations are reported, each only slightly varied from the others—all seemingly ad-libbed from the same script.

Once again, obscenity enforcement experience elicits a paradox. To assume that booksellers are ignorant of the general character of items in their stock approaches the absurd; just as Wall-Streeters know the market, and shoemakers know their lasts, booksellers know their inventories. Proving this knowledge *honestly,* however, as to any single book or set of pictures—when familiarity with the law is likely to render even loudmouthed dirty booksellers taciturn—is often impossible. By the scienter requirement the Justices have created an unnatural gap between legal requisites and reality. Inevitably, some of the "conversations" the Court-imposed scienter requirement has produced are wholly the creatures of the imaginations of arresting officers, self-justified by the common sense deduction that the defendant knew precisely what he was doing, whether or not his knowledge was provable. But police perjury, willful lawbreaking in the courtroom by those sworn to uphold the law, is inexcusable. In a system of law, the ends can never justify unconscionable means. Perjury's lack of justification, however, makes it no easier to ferret out: no mysterious alarum sounds for concocted conversations, remaining silent during testimony as to those that actually occurred.

The judicially imposed requirement of scienter can, however, be reconciled *legislatively* to reality, removing temptation from dangerously diligent policemen, and improving the law by conforming it to experience. Along with other legislative suggestions, the mode of accomplishing this will be considered later.

12. Paperback Erotica

THE PAPERBACK REVOLUTION IN PUBLISHING that has brought many great, and a multitude of not-so-great, books at modest prices to drug counters, supermarkets, candy stores, and terminal waiting rooms has also given broad distribution to a particularly vacuous and possibly vicious species of paperback erotica. A number of marginal publishers are engaged in grinding out tons of pulp novels, each of which consists almost wholly of sensuously described and interminably repetitive sexual encounters.

One such publisher was John B. Musacchia, aided and advised by his then attorney-business associate, Irwin Stillman. They adopted the name Kozy Books for their publishing venture. Their motto, "Cozy up with Kozy Books," was imprinted on every one of their paperback covers. Those covers in bright colors almost uniformly showed an alluring girl, partly nude, usually in the act of stripping—(or was it putting her clothes back on?)—while a virile and poised-looking male stood, sat, or sprawled nearby. The titles and blurbs trumpeted their sexual themes; the lure on the back cover of *2-4 Sex*, for example, blared, "It was crazy, it was hopeless. But when he saw her in bed with the bullfighter, he knew he wanted her too . . . if he could only forget her past. That included three husbands and fifteen boyfriends he knew for sure." The front cover of *Rampant Lust*, along with the title and publisher's motto, and a full-color illustration showing a black bra-and-pantied woman watched by an open shirted man, included the come-on "only the most savage and primitive in love-making . . . could succeed in quenching her strange insatiable urges." These paper cornucopias retailed at a mere fifty cents apiece.

Police, executing search warrants, seized a total of 276,178 copies of Kozy Books in mid-January 1961, from several warehouses; the largest haul was made directly across the street from the city's police headquarters, and a second was made just a jump away from New York's criminal courts building. Defense motions to quash the warrants and obtain orders for the return of the books were fruitless. Thirty-nine different expressive titles were among the volumes that were seized: *Desire Under the Palms, Price of a Virgin, The Nude Señorita, and Split-Level Love* were but a few. The books' themes were porridge for the fantasies of the inadequate males who might buy them: repeated encounters between hedonistic, voluptuous, eager girls and their handsome, virile, often shy, lovers. Although no obscene words were to be found, the wildly erotic passages, fulfilling the promise of the jacket blurbs, were abundant. All shared the absence of meaningful plot, of literary artistry, of motivational insight, of any character development. The ending of each episodic novel seemed dictated by the printer's format: including flyleaf (and, in some, a few pages advertising other Kozy titles), every Kozy imprint ran to precisely one hundred and sixty pages. Authors, who received no royalties, were given a few hundred dollars for each manuscript, and used pseudonyms to conceal their identities. In all respects the books were similar to although not as flagrant as *College for Sinners,* the chronicled sex orgies that had, along with the striptease nude sets, been held obscene in the *Fried* case.

Yet, worthless as were these books, were they within the proscriptions of the *Roth* standards? Or were they merely borderline claptrap, harmless entertainment for those chronically adolescent daydreamers who might purchase them, but preferably to be kept away from children? The sex in them was no more explicit than that found in a host of popular contemporary novels, the descriptive details were milder than in many, even though considerably more monotonously sustained and less redeemed.

Several assistant prosecutors, saddled with the tedious task of reading all thirty-nine Kozy titles, agreed that eight appealed solely to prurience, and prurience so unrelieved that, at least arguably, even contemporary community standards were exceeded. The decision on whether to level charges of crime, it was thought, might best be made by the community itself, speaking through a grand jury.

Grand jurors, laymen drawn from the community, do not, as do trial juries, decide guilt or innocence. They belong to an *accusatory* body only, one that levels charges of crime, but does not rule finally on them; the grand jury's ancestry traces back to within a hundred years of the Norman Conquest.[1] Its methods also differ from the criminal trial jury. Unanimity is not required: criminal charges may be returned by a vote of twelve of the grand jury's twenty-three members. Realistically, grand jurors do not act on the trial measure of proof, guilt demonstrated beyond a reasonable doubt; they rarely hear testimony subjected to the truth-testers of cross-examination and opposing witnesses, and usually have only the state's proof before them. All-in-all, as long as our obscenity standards remain as vague as they are, grand juries are well suited to expressing an opinion, *a consensus on behalf of the citizenry,* as to whether alleged obscenity is such that its purveyors *should* be formally charged with violating contemporary community standards.

Although prosecutors can, and often do, sway grand jurors in their decision-making, the purpose of presenting the Kozy investigation to such a jury was to get the reactions of the lay community, largely uninfluenced by any bias that might be entertained by those professionally engaged in law enforcement. The evidence, threfore, in this case, as in those later investigations involving Ralph Ginzburg and Lenny Bruce, was presented to the grand jury "down the middle." Each grand juror was given a set of the eight Kozy books deemed most salacious, along with a copy of the *Roth* opinion; evidence linking Musacchia and Stillman to Kozy was presented.

The decision of the jurors was *against* filing of any obscenity accusation; apparently they found contemporary community life such that these books were not significantly worse than much that was daily stomached. They did, however, charge both defendants with a series of technical misdemeanors: failing to imprint the publisher's or printer's true name and address in each volume, as was required by a separate provision of state law. An almost similar statute, however, had been declared unconstitutional by the United States Supreme Court the previous year,[2] and the probability that the New York statute was similarly void was so overwhelming as virtually to remove this question from the realm of argument. (Our judgment in this regard was later to be redeemed: in 1962, on the *Mishkin* appeal, New York's intermediate appellate court held that the state statute constituted an invalid effort to interfere with constitutionally guaranteed free expression.[3]) Believing that the citizenry would best be served if all copies of these eight novelettes were kept out of circulation, the prosecutor's office stipulated with defense counsel that the technical charges would not be prosecuted in exchange for Kozy's agreement to the destruction of the seventy thousand seized copies of the eight paperbacks. The remaining two hundred thousand books, borderline but more clearly not violative of the obscenity provisions, were returned to the defendants. Although hindsight was to show that this Kozy seizure might better never have taken place, with the consent of Kozy's principals it had succeeded in ridding the community of some thirty-five thousand dollars worth of sleazy and valueless fifty cent books.

But that was not New York City's last enforcement experience with paperback erotica. In September 1963, an extremely able and conscientious, although sometimes "far-out," New York State trial justice, J. Irwin Shapiro, ruling on a much smaller paperback seizure in New York County's neighbor, residential Queens, held similar imprints *not* to be hard-core, and ordered criminal charges dismissed. This time the books were the offspring not of Kozy but of various vague entrepreneurs calling themselves "Nightstand," "Bedside," "Playtime," and "Intimate." Their content surpassed that of the Kozy books in frankness. Along with one-to-one sex (both male-female and lesbianic), these books featured orgies, lineups, and brutality. Literary imagination and skill remained minimal—the constant repetition, in substance, of phrases such as "he could hardly take his eyes off the lavish upsurge of her breasts as they fought against the knit of her sweater," "he kissed her again, feeling her warm body tremble as he held her to him," and "her breasts were brushing his chest, slowly, tauntingly," and that then moved on to both greater specificity and activity. In format, the books resembled the Kozy imprints; the Playtime and Intimate titles ran a fixed one hundred and sixty pages; those of Nightstand and Bedside were thirty-two pages longer. Some retailed at fifty cents, others at sixty and seventy-five. Among the titles involved were *Sex Kitten, Clipjoint Cutie, Passion Pit,* and *Bedroom at the Top.* In the course of a strongly *anti-censorship* opinion, Justice Shapiro commented:

Fully 90% of each book . . . is filled with lurid descriptions of sexual activities, both hetero and homosexual, in sufficient detail to act as an erotic stimulus to those so inclined. However, in all their erotic descriptions they maintain a clever, and apparently deliberate, avoidance of socially unacceptable language, and the descriptions of erotic activity are so similar, in language and action, as to appear to be written by one author using one outline for all the books.
. . . [T]hese books are plain unvarnished trash, but novels and stories of no literary merit have a place in our society. There are those who, because of lack of education, the meanness of their social existence,

or mental insufficiency, cannot cope with anything better. Slick paper confessions, pulp adventure and "comic book" type of magazines provide them with an escape from reality.

. . .

If any of these eight books truthfully picture any considerable segment of our society, we may be doomed to the same destruction which befell the hedonistic voluptarian civilizations of Greece and Rome and Hamlet's disillusionment and disgust with the world as being "no other thing than a foul and pestilent congregation of vapors" could find little dissent.[4]

Clearly, the books lack any redeeming social importance. Clearly, too, their sole appeal is to prurience. Ordinarily, they are not as perverted as are Mishkin's sado-maochistic booklets and not as weirdly voyeuristic as are either the striptease nude sets or the bootlegged sex-in-action films and photos. Possibly, in our increasingly tolerant American community, they are not *too* bad, not hard-core, not patently offensive. Yet their covers, their jacket blurbs, and titles proclaim them as pandering to prurient tastes. About three years after Justice Shapiro had ordered criminal charges dismissed on his theory that even simple folk are entitled to savor the simple tastes of their own particular porridges, that "social importance" lies in the entertainment value to the beholder, a New York appellate court reversed, specifying that whether or not the paperbacks were obscene would have to be determined on trial[5]—and after. Whether or not, then, this erotica as marketed violates our obscenity laws seems unresolved, although a May 1967 decision of the nation's highest Court casts doubts on the obscenity of at least some of this pulp. In reversing the conviction of a Times Square salesclerk for selling two paperbacks, *Lust Pool* and *Shame Agent,* the Supreme Court found the items not obscene. In so doing, however, not only did the high Court duck the scienter issue upon which the particular appeal had been argued, but it failed to discuss their content or to spell out reasons for overruling the state courts' finding that the books were actionably obscene.[6]

This pulp erotica is, however, of great concern to substantial segments of the community. Indeed, the concern exceeds that expressed over many of the more clearly hard-core items. The low retail cost of these books, their fairly broad distribution, and their occasional display alongside legitimate paperbacks (that also use provocative covers as come-ons) render them readily available to the young, to the curious, and to those with erotic but incredibly monotonous reading interests.

13. "Pornographic Classics," Old and New

The descriptions of love are so zoological, the narrator is so intent on making a safari through the bedroom with gun and microscope, that we find he is preserving only the stuffed and mounted hides of his love affairs; what has disappeared is simply their passion, the breadth of their life. And the reader feels like those children in a very progressive school who went to their teacher with a question, "We know all about how babies come to be born," they said, "but what we can't understand is why people like to do it."

—Malcolm Cowley, "Limbo-by-the-Sea" (a review of *Memoirs of Hecate County*), March 25, 1946 *New Republic*, p. 418

The robust animal sport shared at hearthside, in the fields, and in bed by Mellors, the gamekeeper, with Lady Constance Chatterley, his employer's wife, eroded both the American and British barricades that had theretofore banned open circulation of obscene materials, including so-called "pornographic classics." The term is loosely used. Today the books that it embraces are, for the most part, neither legally "pornographic," nor of such first literary rank as to be otherwise deemed "classics." They are publications, most of which have ultimately been held not to be obscene. Yet they would be less well remembered were it not for the notoriety that they had at one time attained as at least questionably pornographic books.

LADY CHATTERLEY'S LOVER

In 1959, Grove Press, known either for its courage or for its taste in pornography (depending upon one's point of view), first published in America the more than thirty years' old *Lady Chat-*

terley's Lover, by D. H. Lawrence. Using directly the four-letter words of the gamekeeper's argot, and expressively picturing the lovers' physical encounters, the novel draws its scenes of adultery with frankness—to those who had banned or shunned *Lady Chatterley* for three decades, with alarmingly obscene frankness. The love scenes are vital to the story and, unlike those found in the pseudonymously authored paperback erotic novels, are not its entire bulk and sole purpose. Indeed, a wry reviewer for the outdoorsy magazine *Field and Stream* took dead aim at the periodical's readers, ignoring all else, in his comment:

> Although written many years ago, *Lady Chatterley's Lover* has just been reissued by Grove Press, and this fictional account of the day-by-day life of an English gamekeeper is still of considerable interest to outdoor-minded readers, as it contains many passages on pheasant raising, the apprehending of poachers, ways to control vermin, and other chores and duties of the professional gamekeeper. Unfortunately one is obliged to wade through many pages of extraneous material in order to discover and savor these sidelights on the management of a Midlands shooting estate, and in this reviewer's opinion this book can not take the place of J. R. Miller's *Practical Gamekeeping*.[1]

Promptly after *Lady Chatterley's* American republication, the United States Postmaster General sought to ban it from the mails. And, as promptly, he was stymied, when the federal court sitting in New York, applying the *Roth* standard, held that the book had clear literary merit, and that when taken as a whole and judged according to contemporary community standards it was not prurient in appeal,[2] a finding affirmed by the intermediate appellate bench.[3] In that court, however, one of the three judges, Leonard P. Moore, concurred reluctantly, feeling compelled to do so by "contemporary *judicial* standards." "As to 'prurient interest,'" remarked this iconclastic jurist, "one can scarcely be so naive as to believe the avalanche of sales came about as a result of a sudden desire on the part of the American public to become acquainted with the problems of a professional gamekeeper in the management of an English estate."

In England, in 1960, the Director of Public Prosecutions ordered the filing of criminal charges against Penguin Books, Ltd., the publisher that had that year publicly issued the first unexpurgated British edition of Lady Chatterley's story. The law of England, the Obscene Publications Act of 1959, provided that "The book is to be deemed to be obscene if its effect . . . if taken as a whole, [is] such as to tend to deprave and corrupt persons who are likely, having regard to all relevant circumstances, to read the matter contained . . . in it." The case was tried before a jury in London's famed criminal court, the Old Bailey. Reflecting more horror than tact, the prosecutor, distinguished senior Treasury Counsel Mervyn Griffith-Jones, in his opening remarks to the jurors, had suggested that they could themselves test the book's obscenity:

> You may think that one of the ways in which you can test this book, and test it from the most liberal outlook, is to ask yourselves the question, when you have read it through, would you approve of your young sons, young daughters—because girls can read as well as boys—reading this book. Is it a book that you would have lying around your house? Is it a book that you would even wish your wife *or your servants* to read?[4]

The jurors were to hear thirty-five expert witnesses, *all called by the defense,* testifying as to the book's merits. After less than three hours of deliberations they returned; "not guilty" was their verdict. (Thereafter, when England's House of Lords chose to level its hindsights on this prosecution, one lord defending Lawrence's book when asked the question "Would you want your wife to read it?" was heard to respond, "I would not object to my wife reading it, but I don't know about my gamekeeper."[5])

TROPIC OF CANCER

Lady Chatterley's Lover, its rebirth thus successfully bihemispherically attended, proved a bestseller; in America Grove Press was off and running in the field of the popularly marketed, possibly literary and possibly lewd, but clearly far-out fictional and autobigraphical. In 1961, it declared its intention to publish Henry Miller's *Tropic of Cancer*. The announcement served its purpose. As has been described, a plethora of legal actions greeted the book throughout America, serving to halt sales temporarily in those places in which court proceedings had been instituted, while simultaneously whetting the waiting public's appetite. Grove's office, the control center for publishing and marketing *Tropic,* was in Manhattan (New York County), one of the five counties that together constitute New York City. The city's five prosecutors after reading the book, met together to agree upon unified action—or inaction. The latter was their choice. Although agreeing that much of the Miller imagery was loathsome and sickening stuff, even for long inured prosecution stomachs, the five district attorneys were convinced that its bona fide literary acclaim precluded effective prosecution. Miller's mastery of language, and the phalanx of critical admiration that this had engendered, was such that the courts would, appropriately, be *certain* to find "redeeming social importance" in *Tropic.* So thought the city's prosecutors.

In another part of the state, however, criminal charges were brought, and in July of 1963 New York's highest court, split four to three, found *Tropic of Cancer* obscene, greatly surprising New York City's district attorneys. In so doing, the court majority rejected the contention that *Tropic's* "substantial literary merit" redeemed it:

It does not follow, then, that because an alleged work of literature does not appeal to the prurient interest of a small group of intellectuals that it is not obscene under the prurient interest, or for that matter any other legal test of obscenity. This would permit the substitution of the opinions of authors and critics for those of the average person in the contemporary community. The fact that a few literary figures have commented favorably on this book and have lent it their prestige does not expunge from its pages the flagrantly obscene and patently offensive matter which dominates the book as a whole.[6]

We in New York City had thought that the artistry, the literary impact, of *Tropic of Cancer* rested on a much broader base than one that might, with a modicum of fairness, be brushed aside as the favorable comments of "a few literary figures." Another year was to pass before the United States Supreme Court, on June 22, 1964, was—in its own review of the book—to *seem* to overrule the New York majority's notion that *Tropic* lacked true literary worth. (Whether in fact it did overrule this notion, or whether it deemed the book not of prurient appeal, is uncertain; the high Court issued only a brief memorandum reversing, but not analyzing any of *Tropic's* pros and cons.) In any event, in vacating Florida's finding that *Tropic* was obscene, the Supreme Court overruled New York's holding that the book was pornographic. Once again, Grove Press had a best seller.

Meanwhile, in England, in April of 1963, the government determined not to risk duplicating its *Lady Chatterley's Lover* fiasco. It announced that it would not interfere with the publication there of *Tropic of Cancer.*[7]

FANNY HILL, OR MEMOIRS OF A WOMAN OF PLEASURE

Fanny Hill was written in the middle of the eighteenth century by John Cleland, an Englishman then in debtor's prison; for it, he received twenty guineas. Thereafter, it was consistently suppressed by the interaction of a number of prosecutions and threats of others. The book is largely the story of the sexual experiences—witnessed or shared—of an orphaned country lass who moved to London in her fifteenth year. There she was given employment by a brothel keeper and was launched on the career on which Fanny's fame has since rested. The work has all the credentials that any "pornographic classic" might possibly acquire. In the more than two centuries of its clandestine existence, before its 1963 American republication under its original title, *Memoirs of a Woman of Pleasure,* it had run through a host of secret editions. Most were in English, some were in other tongues, some with splendid illustrations, some expurgated, others proudly not, some even with added escapades spuriously created. No four-letter words were used, its language being decorous, ornate, metaphorical. In his intimate vignettes of sexual arousal and fulfillment, Cleland's repeated references to genitalia were through euphemisms such as "machine," "engine," and "champion," and "the tender small part framed to receive it," the "pit," and the "wound." About thirty separate acts were depicted, of lesbianism, female masturbation, rape, defloration, seduction, flagellation, and sexual intercourse, over and over and over again, in a variety of positions, occasionally with others looking on, and under a diversity of circumstances. Although termed a novel, *Fanny Hill* is essentially a guidebook to erotic variations, draped in the thinnest of plots. Cleland has left no mark upon literature, other than through this work. As a social document, of and about the first half of eighteenth century England, *Fanny Hill* is far outdistanced by Richardson's *Pamela*, Smollett's *Roderick Random*, and as motion pictures have recently demonstrated both by Henry Fielding's *Tom Jones* and Daniel Defoe's *Moll Flanders*. *Fanny Hill's* indestructibility is attributed largely, if not solely, to eroticism.

New York *Herald Tribune* book critic John K. Hutchens, reviewing *Memoirs of a Woman of Pleasure*, and its introduction by an eminent English student of the eighteenth century, Peter Quennell, commented:

Mr. Quennell makes a game try as he goes about attributing to Cleland's erotic classic a degree of "elegance and energy," "undoubted historical value," and even "a definite literary appeal." The publisher, too, offers a prefatory note, pointing out how far in advance of his time were Cleland's insights into the psychology of sex.

There is a little something in this, though if you could get a subsidy from one of those rich foundations you might enjoy a long, profitable career before you found anyone who ever read Fanny Hill's memoirs for any of the above-noted reasons.[8]

John Chandos, British editor and author, foe of censorship and champion of a free press, considering *Fanny Hill*, noted:

Despite the circumstances in which it was written there is no sign in the book of haste or carelessness. It moves with a racy yet elegant confidence, and a polished felicity of phrase which occasionally, as if to show what the author could do if he would, makes a sally across the border and into the climate of literature. Such excursions, however, are tantalizingly brief; *Fanny Hill* is predominantly an erotic work from start to finish. The narrative sketches introducing each new character or situation are consummately skillful but they are never developed. We are stimulatingly told what people are like, but never shown them being or becoming anything for longer than a fleeting moment other than protagonists in a succession of venereal contests.[9]

Add to all of this that *Memoirs of a Woman of Pleasure* appears to have been the contraband in America's first reported obscenity prosecution of booksellers, dating back almost a century and a half; in 1825 in Massachusetts, two merchants who had offered *Fanny Hill* for sale were convicted, and one of them was jailed.[10] In short, *Fanny Hill's* pedigree was so extensive and so single-tracked that its republication in New York City in 1963 could not possibly have been ignored by the authorities.

In the spring of that year, G. P. Putnam's Sons, reputably engaged in publishing for one hundred and twenty-five years, moved into the profitable arena previously dominated by Grove; it announced its imminent issuance of an unexpurgated edition of *Fanny Hill*.[11] Once again, the five New York City prosecutors met after reading the novel (Putnam's had placed it in the hands of booksellers weeks before the officially announced publication date). After discussions with New York City's corporation counsel, Leo A. Larkin (the city's attorney), all determined upon a joint legal action. That *Fanny Hill* was pornographic had had the uninterrupted concurrence of history. The book's only possible redemption, it seemed, was its extremely facile, highly ornamental, mode of expression. The outcome of this case, it was hoped, would either keep *Fanny Hill* from broad public circulation, as the law seemed to require (and similarly discourage those other books that would be certain to follow were action not taken), or it would tell law enforcement that polished writing alone redeemed an otherwise pornographic work. Either way, the contest seemed well advised.

Putnam's had long been a responsible firm, and among its retail outlets were many of New York City's largest bookstores. These were not stores that had ever engaged in the business of "dirt for money's sake." The city officials determined, therefore, not to act by way of arrests and criminal charges, but to utilize the state's injunctive procedure that the United States Supreme Court had sustained six years earlier in the *Nights of Horror* case. That procedure permitted the court, after preliminarily hearing both sides, to order the listing of inventories and the freezing of stocks, thus preventing further sales until the outcome of the litigation had been determined. This immobility would speed the action; defendants, restrained from selling warehoused stocks, would be eager for prompt adjudication. Moreover, as the injuctive method was not criminal, at least arguably the state's burden of proving that the book was pornographic might only need to be established by a preponderance of the evidence, the measure of proof required in civil cases, rather than by proof beyond a reasonable doubt, the heavier quantum that the criminal courts required.

In July 1963 the corporation counsel sought the injunction. Justice Charles Marks, having read briefs and affidavits submitted by both sides, issued an order temporarily restraining *Fanny Hill's* distribution until a trial could be held. "Neither the quality of the writing," ruled Justice Marks, "nor the so-called literary worth of the book prevents the book from being adjudged obscene as it meets the tests as enunciated in Roth, Richmond County News, and Fritch [New York's *Tropic of Cancer* case]."[12]

Within a month, the case was tried without a jury before

Justice Arthur G. Klein, a colleague of Justice Marks on the state supreme court (*not*, in New York, an appellate court). A number of defense witnesses testified to the literary merit of Cleland's book. Venerable poet, critic, and anthologist, Louis Untermeyer said:

. . . what is interesting to me in the book is not merely the description of the sexual act, which I have read before, but the reaction of the people toward it, and the variations which are played upon this central theme which, to me, sum up, come to, a work of art, of literature.[13]

Among others testifying for Putnam's was John Hollander, a book reviewer and assistant professor of English at Yale. He stated that the book had other values as well as its literary merit: Hollander urged that Fanny's male "benefactor" (who had died leaving her financially well-off), and one of the bawdy-house madams (for whom Fanny had worked), were both examples of "modern industrial capitalism . . . the entrepreneurial man, the self-made man"; he further suggested that Fanny's own use of her intelligence to "heighten" her feelings—she being "not of the aristocracy but rather of the bourgeoisie"—was "in a sense . . . a very democratic possibility as well as being a very sentimental and sweet one."[14]

Norman Podhoretz, American critic and editor, himself a combatant in the war against censorship, was to observe, at another time and place, that ". . . it is a measure of the extent to which the law has forced criticism into hypocrisy that, in order to defend freedom of expression, one must always be exaggerating the literary merits of any piece of erotica that happens to get published."[15]

Seymour B. Quel, the assistant corporation counsel who represented the city in the case (and who has since been named to the bench), called no literary experts. On cross-examination of the defense's experts he had made highly effective use of *Tribune* reviewer John Hutchen's previously quoted comment, and one by the *Saturday Review's* John Ciardi (expressing the strongest antipathy to all anti-obscenity statutes, Ciardi stated that *Fanny Hill* was, historically, "an overt piece of pornography," and opined that time had not changed its nature, "it is today and will be to the dark end of time's last bookshelf"[16]).

Noting that the city had not met its burden of showing that the novel exceeded "customary limits of candor" and was lacking in "social value," Justice Klein, in late August, directed the entry of judgment for the defense.[17]

Word in America that Putnam's was publishing *Memoirs of a Woman of Pleasure* had preceded by some weeks a British sex-and-spy scandal that was to rock, although not to topple, Britain's Conservative government. On June 4, 1963, a month before New York was to institute its action, Prime Minister Harold Macmillan's War Minister, John Dennis Profumo, wrote "confessing" his prior deceit and resigning from the House of Commons and from the Cabinet. His letter was promptly followed by the arrest of Dr. Stephen Ward, artist and osteopath to the rich and influential, charged with living off the earnings of party girls, including Christine Keeler and Mandy Rice-Davies. Involving a British Cabinet minister's private trespasses and, more shocking, his willful and blatant lie *to his colleagues* in Parliament *and to the British people;* involving also the security of Britain (Captain Yevgeni Ivanov, naval attaché of the Soviet Embassy in London was part of the Profumo-Ward-Keller sexual circle); and involving sex uninhibitedly flaunted at nude and near-nude parties, flagellation, voyeurism and copulation *á quatre*, these revelations titillated newspaper readers in Britain and the United States at the very moment that the fictional Fanny Hill was taking her lumps in New York's courtrooms. On July 22, just two days before Justice Marks's restraining order was issued, the Ward trial had commenced at the Old Bailey. (The prosecutor was the same Treasury Counsel, Mervyn Griffith-Jones, who had prosecuted in the *Lady Chatterley* case, and was early the next year to handle London's own *Fanny Hill* case.) And on the last day of July, three weeks prior to the start of New York's *Fanny Hill* trial before Justice Arthur Klein, Dr. Ward took a fatal dose of Nembutal. Rushed to the hospital, he lingered in coma while the jury deliberated his fate, dying within a few days of the verdict of "guilty."[18]

This British scandal not only featured contemporary reruns of a number of Fanny Hill's earlier sexual adventures, but it was to bear directly on the New York litigation. In his opinion dissolving the restraining order, and dismissing the city's action, Justice Klein had taken note:

> If the standards of the community are to be gauged by what it is permitted to read in its daily newspapers, then Fanny Hill's experiences contain little more than what the community has already encounted on the front pages of many of its newspapers in the reporting of the recent "Profumo" and other sensational cases involving sex.

Although seeming to show the law's dynamism by linking it to current events, Justice Klein was clearly wrong: Fanny Hill's memoirs contained a great deal more than what the community had encountered in the reporting of the Profumo affair. True, in outline, some of the incidents were similar. But the contention that *Memoirs of a Woman of Pleasure* was obscene was not based on any suggestion that it was wrong to state, simply and straightforwardly, that sexual intercourse, flagellation, voyeurism, and the like took place in Mrs. Brown's and Mrs. Cole's bawdy houses. Rather, the charge of prurience arose from Cleland's techniques in conveying this information: his sparing of no details, his moment-to-moment animated pictures of the incidents, and his word-creations of the sensual reactions of the participants. *Fanny Hill* abounds in all of the how-to-do-it factors—appearance, coloring, sensitivity, movement, feelings, size, timing, conversations, exclamations—specifics painted to heighten eroticism, and (if it exists) prurience. These pulsating details were not present in the reporting of the Profumo scandal.

The distinction is important; it is one between full and proper reporting and straining after erotic impact.

On appeal from Justice Klein's order, the case against Putnam's seesawed once more. Split three to two, in February 1964 New York State's intermediate appeals court vacated Justice Klein's action, and enjoined Putnam's from the further selling of *Memoirs of a Woman of Pleasure* within the state.[19] (The response, at this point, of a Brooklyn camp follower in the anticensorship battle, one of those ever ready to bask in publicity by attacking law enforcement, was not surprising. The Reverend William Glenesk, momentarily seeing himself as a champion of freedom of the press, a latter-day John Peter Zenger, castigated "organized moral policemen" and proclaimed to his Brooklyn congregation—and to the press—his bold intent to distribute *Fanny Hill* during his church's worship on the following sabbath. Putnam's, with one eye on publicity, sent a carton of books over. When informed by the then Brooklyn District Attorney, Edward S. Silver, that, pastor or no pastor, he would promptly be arrested if he attempted any such giveaway, Sunday soldier Glenesk, intoning that "Book-burning and witch hunting are alien to the open American way of life," divorced his words from his action and just as promptly cancelled his distribution plans.[20])

Putnam's carried the case to the state's highest court. On July 10, 1964, two and a half weeks after the United States Supreme Court had come down with its multiple *Jacobellis* and *Tropic of Cancer* opinions, New York's Court of Appeals, split four to three, once more reversed, thus granting *Fanny Hill* final judicial amnesty in New York. (In all, fourteen of the state's judges had passed on the book; tallied, the score was seven to seven on the question of its legality.) The state's high court majority hedged, however, affording no clear answer to the important query of whether mere graceful writing, as contrasted with *true literary importance*, could be the basis of this, or any, book's salvation. Its opinion, written by Judge Francis Bergan, unlike Fanny herself, was weak and uncertain:

It is an erotic book, concerned principally with sexual experiences, largely normal, but some abnormal.

It has a slight literary value and it affords some insight into the life and manners of mid-18th Century London. It is unlikely "Fanny Hill" can have any adverse affect on the sophisticated values of our century. Some critics, writers, and teachers of stature testified at the trial that the book has merit, and the testimony as a whole showed reasonable differences of opinion as to its value. It does not warrant suppression.[21]

But, apparently not pleased with suggesting that "a slight literary value," or "reasonable differences of opinion as to . . . value" might be sufficient to redeem a pornographic work, the opinion hastened to add that the book's sexual imagery was not pornographic, as a matter of law, under United States Supreme Court standards.

New York's dissenting justices, in two opinions, stingingly rebuked the majority:

The court's reasons for reversal are as unclear as its description of the book is inadequate. "It is an erotic book," blandly admits the opinion, "concerned principally with sexual experiences, largely normal, but some abnormal," surely a euphemistic labeling of this journal of brothel life . . . . Hereafter, pornography no matter how gross . . . is immune and safe so long as critics praise its writing style and discover "social significance,'" whatever that may mean.

• • •

It is today's fashion to find literary values in any sexy writing and to ridicule as blue-nosed prying Puritans and enemies of art and literature all those who try to preserve a modicum of public decency in our society.

and

If this classic example of pornography is not obscene, then I doubt if any written matter can ever be found to be obscene.

But angered dissents supply only injudicious authority as to the scope to be given a court's opinion. Protesting judges are well known for broadly overstating the evils they see in their colleagues' writings. (So common is this practice that it almost seems a perquisite of judicial courtesy.) It is, however, still the court *majority* that makes the law. And neither in New York nor in Washington have a *majority* of the appellate judges yet said "pornography . . . is immune and safe so long as critics praise its writing style," nor have majorities expressed their "doubt if any written matter can ever be found to be obscene."

Counsel for Putnam's, at both trial and appellate level, was the extremely able and honorable Charles Rembar, a New York attorney who had well served the defense in both the earlier *Lady Chatterley's Lover* litigation and in New York's *Tropic of Cancer* case. In his opening remarks on the trial before Justice Arthur Klein, Rembar, seemingly anticipating that pandering standard that the Supreme Court's majority was to promulgate almost three years later, had been careful to point out:

We have a book here that is sold for $6 at all the best bookstores. It is not sold on the newsstands. It is not sold at drugstores. It is sold through bookstores, through the normal channels of the trade book publication. The people that buy this book are the people who are interested in it for what it is. They are not the salacious few who can find much better material with which to stimulate their appetites.[22]

That, of course, was accurate at the time of the trial, and at the time Justice Klein held the book not to be obscene. A lawyer can rarely, however, guaranty his client's later actions. Justice Klein cleared the book in August 1963. Within a month, in September, Putnam's had its own paperback edition on sale, for ninety-five cents, on those newsstands, drug counters, and other outlets that Rembar had truthfully represented as not handling it. Whether or not the paperback was directed at "the salacious few" and the many curious and adolescent, or at literary and historical scholars profoundly interested in the eighteenth century, may be judged from the paper edition's front cover blurbs. Bold type declared, "This and Only This Is the Complete $6 Putnam Edition *Making Today's Headlines.*" Smaller print reminded browsers, "after 214 years *of suppression.*" Putnam's reverted to the well-known name *Fanny Hill* as the paperback's front cover title (*Memoirs of a Woman of Pleasure,* reduced to sub-title level, was shown far less prominently). Clearance had been obtained, and that clearance—as the law then seemed to be— drew no distinction between paperback and hard cover; no reason existed any longer against letting out all the stops.

The contrast between the New York outcome of the *Memoirs of a Woman of Pleasure* and that of a case of seventeen years earlier, also involving fictional memoirs, sharply etches the changes that time had wrought in the obscenity field. In 1947, New York's highest court unanimously had affirmed the conviction of another publishing house of high standing, Doubleday & Co., for selling *Memoirs of Hecate County,* by Edmund Wilson, then and today one of America's foremost men of letters. The book consisted of five short stories and a novella, *The Princess with the Golden Hair.* This last was the troublemaker. In it the protagonist got his princess after almost two years of intermittent courtship, his ultimate victory involving about two pages of lyric praise for her unclad beauty, described from toenails on up—including movements and effusions—with appropriate pauses and paeans at her underbelly and breasts. There were several other lesser scenes of lovemaking, but none sufficiently sustained to begin to place the work in erotic rivalry with those pervading *Fanny Hill.* Moreover, *The Princess with the Golden Hair* tells a story of strange beauty and strong contrasts; one more of compassion than of passion. Comparing the possible obscenity content of *Hecate County* and *A Woman of Pleasure* is comparing the gentlest breezes of evening with hurricane gales. Today, obviously, the Wilson book would not be deemed obscene. Yet between 1947 and 1949 it resulted in Doubleday's conviction, and the unanimous affirmance of that conviction by

New York State's two appellate courts, in each instance without any opinions being written.[23] Carried to the United States Supreme Court, that Tribunal split evenly, four to four (Justice Frankfurter did not participate),[24] also without writing any opinions, and the conviction still stands. Obscenity was then so simple a concept that it was this case in which Whitman Knapp was to give that shortest and boldest of high Court arguments, previously quoted,[25] and it was during Doubleday's argument that the late Justice Robert H. Jackson was to express his later fulfilled premonition that siding with the defense might turn the Supreme Court into the nation's "High Court of Obscenity."[26]

In 1965, *Memoirs of Hecate County* was reputably republished in New York City, in paperback, without the tiniest of ripples disturbing the city's calm.

As has been seen, New York's efforts were not the whole of *Fanny Hill's* contemporary American troubles. Although the book had been issued by a New York publishing house, it had nationwide distribution. Indeed, a second publisher shortly appeared, eager to share in the profits through his own version of the same work. (Whether or not barred to the reading public because of obscenity, the book had long since passed into the public domain, as available to publishers as Shakespeare or the Bible, providing they were ready to venture their own edition— and to pick up their own legal tabs.) In the states of Illinois, Massachusetts, New Jersey, and Rhode Island, trial courts were to pass on *Memoirs of a Woman of Pleasure,* and all were to find it taboo. In Massachusetts, the state's top court, which by a four to three division had found *Tropic of Cancer not* obscene, split four to three again on *Memoirs of a Woman of Pleasure,* this time the majority deeming that the eighteenth century work *was* pornographic.[27] (New York's highest appellate court, having divided four to three *against Tropic of Cancer,* and by the same score *for Fanny Hill,* had produced exactly the same count as had Massachusetts in each case, but had split in precisely the opposite directions.)

In November 1965, the United States Supreme Court agreed to review the Massachusetts action, and heard argument in early December, along with that in the *Mishkin* appeal, and the appeal of Ralph Ginzburg, publisher of *Eros*. In reversing Massachusett's decision, the Justices remarked that evidence as to the manner of *Fanny Hill's* publication there, and its advertisement and distribution, had not been introduced in the Bay State trial. The three Justices (Brennan, Warren, and Fortas) who concurred in the prevailing opinion noted, as has been seen, that expert testimony had established some literary value for the book. The separate dissents of Justices Clark, Harlan, and White were strong ones. ("I have," said Justice Clark, " 'stomached' past cases for almost 10 years without much outcry. Though I am not known to be a purist—or a shrinking violet—this is too much even for me.") And they differed with the Brennan-Warren-Fortas opinion on the impact to be given the book's literary value. So the New York City prosecutor's early question of whether polished writing alone will "redeem" a book remains unanswered, with the nation's highest Court divided in three parts on it—one third, yes; one third, no; and one third resting their opinions on other grounds.

Meanwhile, in London, Fanny Hill's two-hundred-year-old amatory adventures remained suspect. Her exploits, published in unexpurgated paperbacks in November 1963, were soon before the court. The Director of Public Prosecutions secured a seizure order for all copies of the book possessed by a small shop on the fringes of London's Soho. That shop had too eagerly displayed in its window a sign proclaiming "Banned in America." Not only was this incorrect at the time, but the placard placed the emphasis on the wrong values; it did nothing to suggest the book's courtroom-touted literary or historic contributions. One hundred and seventy-one copies were seized. Early in 1964, after four days trial in Bow Street court before London's Chief Magistrate, Sir Robert Blondell, during which a number of defense witnesses testified to its merits, *Fanny Hill* was duly held to be obscene and the previously seized copies were condemned to destruction. Before the seizure had taken place, however, the publisher had distributed some 82,000 copies of the book, and although the firm offered to take them back, it was little wonder, even among the generally law-abiding British, that only a handful had been recovered. The balance, apparently, had been selling briskly under the counter. Meanwhile, a rival hard-cover publisher had issued a more expensive but partly expurgated edition. Reflecting solid British reserve, he had shied away from some of the more salacious descriptions as "too meaty," and Fanny's seduction of the idiot boy he deemed "in bad taste." Even this partially bowdlerized edition, thereafter reprinted as a cheaper paperback, continued in great demand.[28]

A PLETHORA OF "PORNOGRAPHIC CLASSICS"

The bestowal of New York's blessings on *Memoirs of a Woman of Pleasure,* preceded only a few weeks by the Supreme Court's clearance of *Tropic of Cancer,* brought to a standstill New York action against openly distributed and dubiously pornographic "serious" works. The prior trickle of these volumes, hard-cover and paperback, and that of increasingly detailed sex in essentially non-sexual novels, became a cascade. In *Harper's,* in the fall of 1965, Katherine Anne Porter commented:

We are being sluiced at present with a plague of filth in words and in acts, almost unbelievable abominations, a love of foulness for its own sake, with not a trace of wit or low comedy to clear the fetid air. There is a crowd with headquarters in New York that is gulping down the wretched stuff spilled by William Burroughs and Norman Mailer and John Hawkes—the sort of revolting upchuck that makes the old or Paris-days Henry Miller's work look like plain, rather tepid, but clean and well-boiled tripe. There is a stylish sort of mob promoting these writers, a clique apparently determined to have an Establishment such as their colleagues run in London. It's perfect nonsense, but it can be sinister nonsense, too.[29]

Grove's presses had accelerated. Its imprimatur was to be seen on such widely distributed "pornographic classics" as Frank Harris's *My Life and Loves,* the collected writings of the Marquis de Sade (an anthology of luridly depicted group sex of every imaginable variation, only pallidly intimated by the word "sadism"), more of Henry Miller's work, and the Victorian era's contribution to pornographic literature, the anonymously authored *My Secret Life.* It also published an assortment of that rancid contemporary writing that seems indigenous to these years of Western culture: writing that ranged from the savage, eloquent, *Our Lady of the Flowers* of Jean Genet, through Selby's *Last Exit to Brooklyn* and Burroughs's *Naked Lunch,* to the monotonous scribblings in John Rechy's *City of Night,* the fictional autobiography of a male prostitute. Ultimately, in 1966, it produced an American edition of the novel, printed originally in Paris, of sexual deviation and degradation that out-saded de Sade, the *Story of O.* Putnam's followed its successful *Memoirs of a Woman of Pleasure* with an up-to-date distaff sexual odyssey, *Candy,* a best-selling mélange of satire and satiety. (As with *Memoirs of a Woman of Pleasure,* another American publisher, benefiting from copyright ambiguities, soon had its own paperback in print, thus joining Putnam's, and together taking booty from two *Candys.*) Current editions of ancient Eastern eroticism, the *Kama Sutra* and the *Perfumed Garden,* were to be seen in bookstores and heralded in newspaper mail-order ads. A pair of publishers, almost simultaneously, released separate new editions of Krafft-Ebing's *Psychopathia Sexualis.* Other works, with diverse permutations lavished on the erotic, abnormal or excretory, were to be freely publicized, displayed, and sold, with no New York interference, and little elsewhere in America. Maurice Girodias, founder of Olympia Press of Paris, which had been Europe's major source of banned or shunned English language books, now pursued by bourgeois de Gaullist French censorship, talked of reopening in the artistically free air of Manhattan.[30] Girodias's own *Olympia Reader,* a patched-together time saving collection of excerpts (the pre-selected choice parts) from the books he had issued during the Paris years, had been published by Grove in America in 1965, selling to the cognoscenti at $12.50 per copy.

Some, disagreeing with Miss Porter, may find this a vibrant, new, and long overdue freedom, although that conclusion may more readily be reached *before* a sampling of the books that give rise to it than *after*. Little more than a decade ago, the climate for the author or publisher who ventured into the realm of the obscene was hostile. In 1954, Minnesota's Dean William B. Lockhart and Professor Robert C. McClure wrote:

. . . The publisher's fears are likely to be transmitted in even greater degree to the author. For the author is ordinarily less able to bear the financial risk involved in a book that might be suppressed as obscene . . . . The inevitable tendency is to make the serious author timid, to cramp his mind so that the books he is not afraid to write will fall below the level of his abilities.[31]

But a decade later precisely the opposite was true. In March 1965, reporting on discussions between publishers, writers, and critics held in New York City during National Book Awards Week, *The New York Times* reported:

One view expressed by authors was that publishers were responsible for the number of books that dealt with such themes as sexual deviation. The publishers let writers know that was the way to make money, it was said.[32]

14. The Girlie Magazines

Alice was beginning to get very tired of sitting by her sister on the bank, and of having nothing to do: once or twice she had peeped into the book her sister was reading, but it had no pictures or conversations in it, "and what is the use of a book," thought Alice, "without pictures or conversations?"

—Lewis Carroll, *Alice's Adventures in Wonderland*

ON TUESDAY MORNING, December 6, 1960, the New York City newspapers headlined "Joint City Drive on Smut Opens; Court Cites 140 in 5 Boroughs" *(Times);* "City Launches Smut Drive, Bars Sale of 50 Magazines" *(Herald Tribune);* and "Cops Move in on Smut Sellers" *(News).* New York City's entire enforcement armada, the district attorneys, the police and license commissioners, and the city attorney (the corporation counsel), acting jointly, had launched the first stage of an injunctive campaign against most of the largest local girlie magazine publishers, distributors, and newsstand vendors. Commenting to the press, New York's mayor, Robert F. Wagner, said the intention was:

. . . to rid our city of those publications which in my opinion have contributed significantly towards juvenile delinquency and have played a major part in encouraging criminal acts and the increase of crime.[1]

The crudest of these magazines, those driven off the stands, consisted, for the most part, of provocatively posed female nudes.

These were supplemented, for those with the patience to read the simplest English, by tawdry fiction and sex-centered non-fiction, all embellished with advertisements for erotica. The injunctive drive was to come close to ridding America's most populous city of these publications, until its success was enervated by judicial action.

The drive was no belated reprise of the thinking that, more than fifteen years previously, had temporarily cancelled *Esquire's* second class mailing privileges. The magazines involved were not *Esquire, Playboy,* or *Gent.* There were vast differences between the girlie publications that the city had attacked and the so-called magazines for men. Or at least the officials who had joined in bringing the injunctive actions thought so.

The seeming differences are best crystallized by comparing the two types of magazine, matching some of the girlie variety against, as an example, *Gent.* Long before the girlie magazine drive had started, and quite independent of it, the April 1957 issue of *Gent* had been earmarked as contraband in an obscenity prosecution against the Richmond County News Company, one of its distributors. That case was to reach New York's top court six months after the start of the girlie magazine injunctive effort, and *Gent* was there cleared by a split decision.[2] Although not precisely a breath of cool night air, that particular issue of *Gent* reflected a rollicking sexiness and a polish not to be found in the banned magazines. *Gent's* tone was sophisticated; that of the girlie magazines was unrelievedly coarse. *Gent* had wit, artistry, elegance; the others were cheap, obvious, crude. *Gent* was bawdy, ribald, suggestive; the girlie magazines were morbid. The particular issue of *Gent* featured short fiction by Irwin Shaw and Budd Schulberg; the schoolboy writing in the girlie magazines was largely anonymously or pseudonymously authored. And no wonder. The girlie magazine near-nude picture of a busty British movie newcomer, for instance, was captioned, "This big girl from Britain has a problem—ah, *two* problems— the same two that earned her stardom"; and another nude in the same magazine bore the legend, "We vote her the sort of girl we'd most like to end up with—or is it the sort we'd like to up-end with?" Zsa Zsa Gabor, in scalloped-below-the-breast Las Vegas finery stood posed against the desert sands in a *Gent* pictorial spread; girls, known only by such pet names as "Bubbles," "Bobbie Daring," and "Tootie Flutey" were pictured in the enjoined magazines. In them, the girls, the props, and the poses tended to be reminiscent of the striptease nudes, with models chosen not for grace or beauty, but seemingly for breasts and buttocks that tended to wildly "o'erstep the modesty of nature."

Although, as court decisions stemming from the city-wide drive were to show, this dichotomy between the magazines for men and the girlie magazines may, in part, be subjective, and the dividing lines may be obscured by some of the same uncertainties that curse the entire obscenity area, some obvious distinctions, quite apart from the quality and the artistry of the materials, impart a different over-all flavor to the two types of magazines. *Gent* (and like it, today's *Playboy, Cavalier*, etc.) regularly features *some* writing on fashions for men, foreign policy, folk-singing, and other departures from the themes of sex and nudity. In doing so, these magazines suggest that their male readers may, at least in moments of fatigue, entertain some non-sensual thoughts, and may reflect some diversity of interests. This was not so in the unrelievedly single-track magazines that were the objects of the 1960–61 New York City campaigns. Their morbid prurience remained unwavering, uninterrupted by the semblance of anything asexual.

The magazine titles themselves signified this singleness of purpose. The December injunctive effort sought to ban the sale of fifty-four publications with titles ranging from *Adam* through *Venus*, and including along the way: *Bare, Black Garter, Boudoir, Consort, Fling Festival, Follies, Gala, Kuties, Minx, Ogle, Scamp, Sizzle*, and *Torrid*.

Few of these publications carried advertising. Those that did ran ads of a piece with the rest of the magazines' contents:

"*Peaches,* from the Southland. Lazy, voluptuous gals, who'd rather pose than work. Revealing shots of young things."
"Movies—Some were taken on location at plush nudist resorts."
"Unretouched, uncensored photos released from a private collection."
"Sex harmony. If you, like most virile men, cannot 'wait' for your wife —if your climax comes too fast, leaving her unsatisfied and frustrated —then you should read . . . ."

And one ad, illustrated, and repeated in a number of the magazines, was for an electric gadget:

"Vibrafinger (full length) Novel Design.
Allows localized massage in needed areas!"

Most of these magazines, like "*Touch,* vol. 1, no. 7," and "*Tonight,* vol. 1, no. 5," were undated; they were identified only by title and by number. Thus elasticity was built-in, and danger of obsolescence eliminated. Although this datelessness itself could not render these magazines pornographic, it did suggest a certain fly-by-night insubstantiality, a preparedness to stay two steps ahead of the law, a readiness to be hurriedly bundled up in the event trouble threatened, and preserved for re-offer once the air had cleared, or sold later in another community. These self-doubts as to legality, this willful evanescence, were underscored by the unavailability of most of them on a subscription basis. Both historically and realistically postal inspectors tend to be less tolerant than many local law enforcement officials; use of the mails would be the only feasible way of serving subscribers, and postal action that might then ensue might also serve to prod napping members of the local constabulary. Hence, the safer course was to stay away from the mails, although it meant foregoing the dividends of subscriptions. (Bulk deliveries to distributors, made by private carriers, required no postal intervention.) Moreover, the number of annual issues under any single title was uncertain; if one title failed to catch fire, it could simply be discontinued (no complications being caused by obligations to subscribers), and hopefully more combustible magazine names could be sparked into life. (We were to learn the extent to which these magazines were known by their covers: *Taboo*, banned from the stands in February 1961, was to reappear in April in a reincarnation identical with the original, except that it was concealed within a changed set of covers retitled *Sirens on Parade!*)

A small band of publishers, utilizing a mixed bag of corporate names, and centered in Los Angeles and New York City, deluged America with these "girlie" magazines. One of their number, named a defendant in the injunctive campaigns, rated an "A" for apparent candor—or for advertising. It did business under the descriptive title of "Synmag Publishing Company."

THE INJUNCTIVE EFFORT

The unheard prelude to the early December 1960 kickoff had included a long session at the Manhattan prosecutor's office in late November. Representatives of each of the city's district attorneys, the corporation counsel, and the license and police commissioners spent the day reviewing, issue by issue, the piles of recent publications the police had purchased. (Although in reasonable dosages, these magazines may serve to titillate, by day's end all echoed the sentiments of that wise Massachusetts trial judge who, weighing the bulky novel, *Forever Amber*, had observed, "While conducive to sleep it is not conducive to a desire to sleep with a member of the opposite sex."[3]) Magazines with any arguably "redeeming social importance" were promptly screened out: nudist magazines, espousing the uninhibited sun-drenched life, so-called photography magazines that specified appropriate exposure information while emphasizing nudes (not always in the most artistic poses) to the near exclusion of other less photogenic subject matter, magazines picturing male nudes for homosexual tastes but camouflaged with body-building veneer, and the sophisticated magazines, such as *Gent* and *Play-*

boy. A publication ended on the "condemned" list only if, after a separate review by each of the officials, *all* agreed that it was obscene. And each sought to apply the *Roth* standards with minimal interference from his own personal predilections, views that varied among the assembled "censors." The design was to play it safe, to pick out only those magazines that appeared to be most clearly offensive and irredeemable. Doubtful cases could be litigated later, but not until these earlier rounds had provided a solid foundation and until the most clearly pornographic had been knocked out of New York City.

Fifty-four different magazines met the test. They had been purchased from a large number of newsstands and stores, and stemmed initially from a variety of distributors and publishers. The injunctive campaign named the one hundred and forty responsible magazine dealers, distributors, and publishers as defendants.

The city's corporation counsel, Charles E. Tenney (since appointed to the federal bench), handled the case; one of Tenney's assistants, a dedicated and sound lawyer, Murray Rudman, did much of the legal work. The affidavits that Rudman collected to initiate the action were strong. New York City's police commissioner, Stephen P. Kennedy, an intelligent, courageous, and outspoken former policeman, who had walked a beat and risen through the ranks in a non-political police department, earning on the way a college and law degree at night, stated:

I have been informed by members of my Department that there has been a great increase in recent years in the dissemination of vile and obscene literature. I can say without hesitation that the publications referred to in the annexed papers come within this category. It is the considered opinion of police officials whose professional lives have been dedicated to the fight against crime that one of the causes for an increase in crimes of sex and violence is the availability to the youth of literature of the kind that are the subject of this proceeding.

And corporation counsel Tenney's own moving affidavit had pointed out:

These "Girlie" magazines deride the value and meaning of marriage and love, emphasize the pleasure of sex for sex's sake, glorify promiscuity and present the female as the constant provoker to sex passion, whose sole reason for living is the gratification which illicit love and passion bring . . . . In those individuals who subconsciously have immoral tendencies, these tendencies are reinforced and crystallized and given form by the reading of these magazines . . . .

On Rudman's application, after inspecting all of the girlie publications and reading the affidavits, Justice Arthur Markewich of the state supreme court signed an order temporarily staying the defendants from further trafficking in the magazines, authorizing the police to take inventory of the stocks that each defendant possessed, and setting the entire matter down for a hearing, at which both sides could be fully represented, one week thereafter.

Armed with copies of Justice Markewich's order, and the affidavits supporting it, with inventory forms and instructions, and cautioned to inform dealers that they were *not* being arrested or *criminally* summoned, that they were in no trouble providing the enjoined magazines were not sold pending the litigation's outcome, the police fanned out through the city. The press was to carry the estimate that one million magazines would be immobilized pending court action. During the pre-injunctive survey of newsstands and distributors, however, there had been a leak (not uncommon when many persons, be they police, other public officials, or housewives are in on a "secret"). That leak had sent magazine reserves packing out of the city. When the orders were served, distributors were found to have sparse supplies on hand; over-all, the police inventories revealed a tie-up of less than thirty-thousand copies of the fifty-four publications.

The late state supreme court justice Henry Epstein, after listening to all of those defendants who wished to be heard, on December 29, 1960, ordered Justice Markewich's stay to remain in effect until the case could be tried. In so doing, he stated:

These publications, each and every one of them, open the gates to the presentation of lust and unfaithfulness. To call the photograph illustrations "art" is evidence of a concupiscent mind.[4]

There was no prompt trial, however. Most of the defendants chose not to contest the city's suit and refrained from selling the contraband issues of the named publications—in New York. Those few that did take issue with the city occupied themselves, as well as the courts and the corporation counsel, with a series of legal attacks and appeals that served to delay trying the issue of whether or not the magazines were obscene.

Meanwhile, back at the stands new issues of the magazines were beginning to appear. These copies were not affected by the temporary restraining order. The United States Supreme Court, thirty years earlier in the *Near* case, had barred "prior restraints"; it had held that unborn issues of existing publications could not be aborted injunctively on the assumption that their contents would be on a par with that of their predecessors.[5] And so, on February 16, 1961, the injunctive process was repeated. "Smut Raiders Ride Again and Claim 100 Casualties," was the *Daily News* headline the next morning. (A number of dealers, not wishing the nuisance of future court actions, and some having had their consciences tweaked by the litigation, had discontinued stocking the magazines.) This time, thirty-nine magazines were involved. Although some of them bore new titles, the melody remained the same: *Bachelor, Black Lace, Brunette, Demoiselle, Flame, French Frills, Les Girls, Satin and Silk,* and *Tempest* were a few of the "new" ones.

Two months later, on April 10, 1961, the third and final round was launched. This time only twenty-seven magazines were involved, just half the number that had been attacked by the first injunction. The campaign, at this point, showed clear signs of success. The magazines no longer decked the stands in anything approaching their profusion at the campaign's birth.

THE CAMPAIGN'S GOALS

The time and energies expended in the campaign had been considerable. Had it been appropriate for all of New York City's law enforcement to have banded together, to have created a massive multi-party, multi-stage juggernaut, in order to crush these publications? Or had the city used a sledge hammer in an attempt to annihilate an annoying swarm of fleas?

If the girlie magazines were indeed pornographic and were a real danger or at least a nuisance, there was no lesser way, no easier path, for *effectively* ridding the city's busy magazine racks and eyecatching newsstand displays of the worst of them. So many girlie magazines had become available so rapidly, through so many outlets, so widely scattered throughout the city, that were a particular issue to draw police or judicial fire in one place only, it would generally remain available elsewhere, and dozens of similar magazines would be likely to arise phoenix-like from the conflagration, ready to profit from any public curiosity that news stories had stimulated. A drive in only one of the busier of New York City's clustering five counties would nicely serve to spur sales in its neighbors.

Furthermore the girlie magazines did seem worth getting rid of. Not only were they utterly lacking in positive values, but they were, clearly, the single greatest irritant to adults agitated by the spread of pornography in our neighborhoods. Street corner newsstands displayed their covers in rows; racks at candy, stationery, and cigar stores dedicated shelves of space to them. Their covers not only featured boldly decolletaged girls (*not*, for most householders, the girl next door), but heralded by title the photo-stories or brief fiction to be found inside: "How to Go to Bed," "Big Big Girl, Tight Tight Fit," "Nude Mood," "Are You Doing It Now?" "The 32½ Hour Seduction," "Make Out With Big Girls," or "Shenanigans at Madam Bikini's." The prices of these girlie magazines put them at the command of all who had lunch or movie money; many sold for as little as thirty-five cents (less expensive than paperback erotica); the most expensive were a dollar. They were the most available and cheapest kind of seeming pornography on the market. And they were the most effortlessly consumed, consisting for the most part of photographs augmented with sensational drawings and crude cartoons. Their textual materials were so scanty that even illiterates couldn't miss their flavor. Describing their impact, the affidavit of the corporation counsel said:

They glamorize and glorify indecency, lewdness, sex and promiscuity and ridicule the accepted standards of social behavior. Read by the youth, they interfere with normal development of decent sex habits and impede the proper moral and ethical development of children. They teach children everything that is immoral and horrible in regard to their relationship with the opposite sex. They glorify illicitness and promiscuity and sex and make a mockery of democratic living and respect for law and order. Youth, being highly imitative and prone to experimentation, the malevolent influence of these magazines, would in many cases drastically effect his sex attitudes.

A substantial number of New York City's leading clergymen, Catholic, Protestant, and Jewish, urged action. By the late 1950s, the clergy had drawn up their interfaith battle lines against pornography. A Committee of Religious Leaders had been formed, pitting righteous wrath against "dirt for money's sake," hoping thereby to drive the pornographers, and particularly the magazines, from the city's streets. Angered sermons, however, proved to be words whispered on the winds. Publishers, distributors, and dealers heard few of them and heeded them not at all. And the city's most garish displays tended to be at some of the most convenient newsstands, at the city's crossroads—Wall Street, Greenwich Village, Times Square, the Grand Central Station neighborhood—where the parish's sabbath anger was likely to have puny impact. The religious leaders, priests, ministers, rabbis, and lay congregants, sought the mayor's assistance. In 1959, Mayor Wagner met with them and with all the city's law enforcement to see what officialdom (The Law) could do to protect Morality. Learning immediately of the multitude of obscurities and frustrations that plagued obscenity enforcement, the religious leaders then ventured a different tack. A meeting with magazine publishers was arranged. The strong talk from one side met with doubletalk from the other, and it became obvious that present profits outweighed any earthly damnation; voluntary self-restraints would not eventuate.

It was apparent that legal steps only, on a large scale—even if uncertain in outcome—might be effective. A memorandum was prepared by the district attorney's office that was eventually to serve as a blueprint for the campaign, finally launched after the situation had steadily worsened. "I am uncertain," cautioned the memorandum's concluding paragraphs, after originating and detailing the massive multi-defendant injunctive program, "whether the goal of driving these magazines off the stands justifies this effort." In 1960 the memorandum was circulated to the city's district attorneys, corporation counsel, and police and license commissioners, and the decision was made to launch the injunctive effort it had charted.

THE CAMPAIGN'S ULTIMATE FRUSTRATION

In mid-September 1961, nine months after the campaign had commenced, one of the defendants, G. I. Distributors, was finally brought to trial. In the interim, the defendants had been successful in obtaining an order severing them from each other, and mandating separate trials for each.[6] The trial was to determine whether the thirteen magazines G. I. had been temporarily enjoined from distributing during the campaign's second round (in February 1961) were so "obscene, lewd, lascivious, filthy, indecent or disgusting" that they were to be surrendered and destroyed. The outcome was of little real consequence to the particular magazines, but it would serve to guide the future conduct of distributors and publishers, at least in New York, perhaps their busiest and most fertile territory. None of the scores of other defendants who had been involved in December 1960 and in the February and April 1961 phases of the campaign had previously sought trials on any of the ten dozen magazines that had been temporarily damned, although the injunctive statute provided that the defendant "sought to be enjoined [was] entitled to a trial of the issues within one day"[7] after its filing of an answer to the obscenity charges.

The defendant, distributors of *Boudoir, Brunette, Cocktail, French Frills, Sir Knight, Mr. Cool, Nightcap, Rapture Showcase, Snap, Tempest, Tonight,* and *Touch,* had shrewdly chosen as counsel one of the patriarchs of the civil liberties bar, Osmond K. Fraenkel, distinguished and venerable general counsel to the American Civil Liberties Union. Although the United States Supreme Court had held obscenity to be without constitutional protection, the choice of Fraenkel was certain to prompt some instinctive identification of the defendant's cause with civil liberties.

Dr. Hugo C. Beigel was the sole expert witness called by Fraenkel for the defense. A Viennese psychologist, replete with authentic accent and academic aura, author of *Sex From A to Z* and other volumes, his specialized study, he stated, was "sexology." He was called to testify that the girlie magazines were not repugnant to the community standards of the 1960s. ("Our concept about sexual behavior," Dr. Beigel ponderously expounded, "have changed in comparison to what it was in the 18th and 17th Century.") To support his contention that these particular magazines did not affront community standards, Dr. Beigel brought with him some that he had purchased at several of the city's newsstands shortly before testifying. *Lark, Lithe, Magnifique,* and *Paree* were among the titles. They had been drifting back to some of the newsstands during the lull between the last injunctive round of April 1961 and the start of the trial five months later. (The city, lulled into relaxing its injunctive pressures for an overlong summer, had the fruits of that relaxation served up to it as proof of lowered community standards!) Under assistant corporation counsel Rudman's quiet cross-examination Dr. Beigel conceded that the magazines were "erotic" and "aroused erotic thoughts," and recognized that they were not realistic. Rudman referred to the strongly anti-censorship husband-wife team of psychologists, Drs. Eberhard and Phyllis Kronhausen, and used the term "erotic realism" (of which *Lady Chatterley's Lover* is an excellent example), by which the Kronhausens distinguished items of value from those that they deemed hard-core pornography;[8] Dr. Beigel conceded that the girlie magazines did not constitute valued "erotic realism." He had no quarrel with the contention posed to him that magazines like these were used by males in provoking fantasies that accompanied masturbation.[9]

Had the trial started six months sooner, had it taken place within a few weeks of the issuance of even the last of the three temporary restraining orders, it would have preceded New York's top court's ruling in the *Richmond County News* case, the case involving *Gent*. Once again delay and the ever-changing pornography picture had damaged the state's case. The May 1961 decision concerning *Gent* was to add substantially to the city's burden at the trial in September. The burden had, courtesy of the *Gent* case, become one of convincing the trial judge that *all* magazines featuring nude photographs and sex stories did not stand alike before the law; that although neither nudity nor sex nor the combination of the two in magazine form were *per se* obscene, they might be—depending upon the nature of their presentation—and that there were legally significant differences in their presentation in *Gent* and in the girlie magazines.

Three months after the trial, in December, Acting State Supreme Court Justice Samuel C. Coleman (since retired) ruled that the city had not convinced him. Dismissing the city's suit and dissolving the temporary restraining order, the judge leaned squarely and effortlessly on the *Richmond County News* case. He said that the state appellate court's

. . . description of "Gent" is a description of the magazines in question. Not all of them may contain "short stories of apparent literary merit," but the absence of such stories will not make an otherwise obscene publication any less so [sic]. And nothing is gained by attempting qualitative differentiation among them, as though there were degrees of obscenity.[10]

The city's efforts to distinguish the offending magazines from *Gent* were thus fobbed off with the bare conclusion that "nothing is gained by attempting a *qualitative* differentiation . . . *as though there were degrees of obscenity.*" By 1961, four years after the *Roth* decision, judges should have known that the law of obscenity had not been computerized; they should have learned not to expect that lights would flash and bells would ring when the pornography laws were violated. *Questions of quality and of degree were precisely what was involved,* more in the law of obscenity, under then existing statutes and interpretations, than in any other phase of the criminal law.

With Judge Coleman's decision, what remained of the impact of the 1960-61 injunctive drive evaporated. In New York City, looking back on the campaign it seemed an unreal if troubled dream, something that had never truly been ventured. Newsstands promptly resumed their displays.

Yet in other American states during the same years, the courts were sustaining drives against the girlie magazines. In August 1961, Maryland's highest court (split four to one) upheld the conviction of several retailers for selling some of the same publications (possibly not the same issues) that had been involved in the New York litigation.[11] (As to one title, *Black Garter,* and one set of striptease nudes, the Maryland court reversed the conviction, finding the particular items insufficiently offensive to constitute obscenity. Here was a court not afraid to attempt "qualitative differentiation.") New Jersey's intermediate appellate court unanimously ruled that particular issues of *Exotic Adventures, High, Mermaid, Sir Knight,* and *Spree* were pornographic:

We find these magazines to be obscene, not because they deal with nudity and sex, but rather because of the nature of the treatment of these subjects and the manifest intent and purpose behind such treatment.[12]

(While stating that the magazines could properly have been found obscene, New Jersey's highest court reversed the conviction, ruling that the search that produced them was unlawful, and hence that the magazines should not have been considered by the trial court.[13]) The appellate courts of Connecticut[14] and Wisconsin[15] have found magazines of similar content obscene.

On June 10, 1964, three and a half years after the first injunctive papers had been served, on review New York's highest court, by the margin of a single judge (split four to three), affirmed Judge Coleman's action.[16] Neither the majority nor the dissenters explained their views of the law. In this failing, the New York court was to foreshadow similar non-communicativeness by the Supreme Court in the same area. On May 8, 1967, that high Court reversed Kentucky and Arkansas findings that particular issues of *High Heels, Spree, Gent, Swank, Bachelor, Modern Man, Cavalcade, Gentleman, Ace* and *Sir* were obscene.[17] Some of these magazines may not have been as unrelievedly coarse as were the girlie publications that New York had—briefly—enjoined, but the Washington Tribunal, in its opinions (the Court split, 7 to 2) provided no direct analysis of the magazines' contents that might, in the future, provide guidance for law enforcement and for publishers.

The actions of New York's highest judges, however, require little explanation. Almost a score of years earlier, United States Supreme Court Justice Felix Frankfurther had written:

. . . the judge, if he is worth his salt, must be above the battle. We must assume in him not only personal impartiality but intellecual disinterestedness. In matters of statutory construction also it makes a great deal of difference whether you start with an answer or with a problem.[18]

Most of New York's highest judges, when confronted with alleged obscenity, and the application to it of the state's anti-obscenity laws, seemed to "start with an answer," one dictated by their own pro- or anti-censorship philosophy, and not by discerning judgment brought to bear on the pornographic content of the particular item before them. Those anticipatory answers go further in explaining their votes than would reams of rationalizations, solemnly issued and printed as majority, concurring, and dissenting opinions. This nose-count method of legal analysis, and some strong doubts as to whether ours is truly a system of laws and not of men (in the obscenity area), have previously been considered. Nowhere is the method more applicable, or the doubts more appropriate, than with reference to the seven high judges constituting New York's highest bench. The names of the judges little matter, other than as labels through which to identify their almost perfect consistency. The tabulation that follows suggests the near futility of briefing and of arguing the obscenity law before judges whose actions demonstrate the degree to which their views are fixed. And it illustrates the frightening impact, in a state of more than seventeen million people, of the preconceptions held by a single man, should he happen to be the swing judge on the state's highest bench. This tabulation reflects the votes of the New York judges in difficult cases in which, on essentially the same facts, other jurisdictions have moved in varying directions. The cases are those involving *Gent* decided in May 1961, *Tropic of Cancer* in July 1963, the girlie magazines in June 1964, and *Fanny Hill* in July of the same year:

	Gent	*Tropic*	*Girlie Mags.*	*Fanny Hill*
Judges ruling item *not obscene.*	Dye Fuld VanVoorhis Desmond	Dye Fuld VanVoorhis ——	Dye Fuld VanVoorhis Bergan*	Dye Fuld VanVoorhis Bergan*
Judges ruling item *obscene.*	—— Burke Froessel** Foster*	Desmond Burke Scileppi** Foster*	Desmond Burke Scileppi**	Desmond Burke Scileppi**

With the exception of the then Chief Judge, Charles S. Desmond, who drew a distinction between *Gent,* on the one hand, and the girlie magazines, *Tropic of Cancer,* and *Fanny Hill* on the other, the judicial lineup reflects each judge's unwavering

*On December 31, 1963, Judge Sidney Foster retired to be succeeded by Judge Francis Bergan; their obscenity views were opposite.

**On December 31, 1962, Judge Charles Froessel retired, to be succeeded by Judge John Scileppi; their obscenity views were kindred.

personal pro- or anti-censorship predilections, views that precluded each from recognizing distinctions in the differing materials to have come before them.[19]

The line drawn by Judge Desmond tended to redeem New York City law enforcement's stubborn failure to throw in the towel completely on the girlie magazine campaign when, six months after its start, the state's highest court handed down its *Gent* decision. The city's delay, however, of more than two years in getting Justice Coleman's December 1961 decision reviewed by the state's high court, was fatal. Had the girlie magazine case reached New York's top tribunal, and been there decided six months sooner—before Judge Foster's retirement, and succession by Judge Bergan—it is almost certain that these publications would have been held to have been unlawful (the four to three split seesawing the other way). When the law that governs millions of the citizenry hinges on the happenstance of the birthday, and hence the retirement date of a single judge, something seems radically amiss. Almost a quarter of a century ago, in writing a dissent in one of the so-called "flag salute cases," in which the United States Supreme Court invalidated a state board of education's requirement that students salute and pledge allegiance to the American flag, Justice Felix Frankfurter had noted:

As a member of this Court I am not justified in writing my private notions of policy into the Constitution, no matter how deeply I may cherish them or how mischievous I may deem their disregard. . . . It can never be emphasized too much that one's own opinion about the wisdom or evil of a law should be excluded altogether when one is doing one's duty on the bench. The only opinion of our own even looking in that direction that is material is our opinon whether legislators could in reason have enacted such a law.[20]

When it comes to "the wisdom or evil" of the laws touching on the censorship of obscenity, Justice Frankfurter's strong reminder of the proper judicial responsibility has, it would seem, not been sufficiently emphasized.

15. Sophisticated Sexuality: *Eros*

Was ever book containing such vile matter
So fairly bound? O, that deceit should dwell
In such a gorgeous palace!
　　　　　　　　—William Shakespeare,
　　　　　　　　Romeo and Juliet, Act III, sc. ii.

NEW YORK CITY had shared with the Los Angeles area the dubious distinction of leadership in supplying girlie magazines for the nation's true or simulated adolescents. It stood alone, however, as the source of America's single most elaborate and extravagant adult sex periodical, Ralph Ginzburg's quarterly, *Eros*. Mailmen, trudging their appointed rounds during the winter of 1961-62, may well have been warmed by both the text and the weight of the mailing pieces they were carrying for Ginzburg. In content, *Eros's* pre-publication flyers heralded it as "a new quarterly on the joys of love." But the joys pictured were not those suggested in the sonnets of Elizabeth Barrett Browning.

Ginzburg's earliest *Eros* mass mailer blazoned that it would be "the magazine of sexual candor," featuring among its writing and illustrations discussions of "The Devil as a Phallic Symbol," "Manhood Restoratives," "U.S. Patent #587,994" (for a male chastity belt), "The Love Lives of Pirates" ("describes the fates of noblewomen kidnapped on the high seas"), "The Contraceptive Industry," and other similar fare. Ginzburg knew intimately both erotica and promotion, and his direct mail campaign was as formidable in volume as it was in content. He had been *Look* magazine's circulation promotion director at the age of twenty-three, and after a stint as *Esquire's* articles editor had published and sold more than a hundred and fifty thousand copies of his own work, *An Unhurried View of Erotica,* largely through mail order. Launching *Eros,* he ultimately directed about nine million mailing pieces at hoped-for-subscribers. For $19.50 annually (upon publication, the price would be $10 per issue), Ginzburg pledged an advertising-free, graphically rich, daringly written, beautifully printed, hard-cover quarterly, "devoted to love in its every aspect." After federal action had compelled the suspension of *Eros,* Ginzburg was to claim that his pre- and post-publication campaign had produced some 150,000 subscribers, and revenue in the neighborhood of three million dollars.[1]

With a provocative mail campaign of such mammoth proportions listing a return address in New York County, it was to be expected that long before the first issue had appeared the New York County prosecutor's office was to be deluged with complaining mail from points of origin scattered from coast to coast. As the second issue of *Eros* was to remark, Ginzburg himself received several thousand letters—many of them, he noted ruefully, in his own pre-paid postal return envelopes—presenting, as he called it, "a candid view of present-day puritanism in the United States." (Others might have deemed it an outpouring of evidence of contemporary community standards.) A selection of those missiles, reproduced in *Eros,* tended to be more candid and colorful than those that had been addressed to the prosecutor. Among the milder ones were some returning Ginzburg's subscription cards anonymously marked, "You filthy, lousy sex maniac, "FILTH," "Father, Forgive them: for they know not what they do," "REPENT," "Boy! Would I like to be invited to your office parties!" and one, in shaky scrawl, "Sorry, I can't subscribe. I have a severe heart condition and know what is best for me." The New York County prosecutor's office, mindful of the *Near* case, took no action other than to subscribe, using a detective and his home address as a "mail drop." The mailing pieces alone were clearly not violative of the *Roth* standard. Whether or not *Eros* itself would be, only examination *after* it had been published might show.

Eros's first issue appeared early in 1962. (Promotion conscious Ginzburg has variously set the date as Valentine's Day and as the first day of spring!) Thereafter, each new season was to bring a new issue, until interrupted by the United States government before the year's end. The magazine was as eye-appealing as had been promised. Ginzburg, at his mildest anything but reticent, was understandably proud of the graphic art laurels that *Eros* received. In content, in its maiden issue, *Eros* was *not* titillatingly erotic. Volume one, number one was far more learned than licentious. "One quick trip through the newcomer's 80 pages," reported *Time* magazine, "should have been enough for even the basest appetite to discover that *Eros* is a four-letter word spelled 'bore.' "[2] Indeed, cataloguing its contents suggests that the party-loving anonymous card-writer might, were he invited, expect to find the office parties to be no more orgiastic than those held at the British Museum. The first issue of *Eros* began with a half dozen full-page, full-color reproductions of classical paintings showing the child-god, Eros (Cupid), with Aphrodite, Hermes, Ares, Adonis, and Psyche. An essay by jazz critic Nat Hentoff followed, comparing the watery lyrics of popular love songs with the moving, more direct and robust language of the blues. A two-page spread was devoted to a Rabelaisian cartoon of goings-on on the Place Pigalle. Next was an updated version of an eighteenth century *Classical Dictionary of the Vulgar Tongue*, the work of a distinguished contemporary etymologist. Then, following in order, came a devil's advocate's *Plea for Polygamy*, by psychotherapist Albert Ellis; multicolor reproductions of the picture cards and aces in a uniquely embellished deck, picturing Florentine Renaissance costumes and feminine nudity; *The Agonies and Ecstasies of a Stripper*, a sympathetic interview with a

Brooklyn-born exotic dancer who had learned that on-stage bareness brought, if not happiness, at least money; several pages of pictured nineteenth century ads for virility restoratives; a serious study of the philology of the word "bastard," naming some of history's most renowned; some seventeenth century bawdy poems by the Earl of Rochester, reprinted in facsimile from an early edition, using words, both four-letter and longer, both out of date and current; a humorous short piece on *Why Bachelors Stay Single,* and a candid photo essay, *Love in the Subway,* revealing kissing—and less. Maupassant's classic short story, *Madame Tellier's Brothel,* printed in its entirety, was the issue's longest item, illustrated with Degas drawings. The issue closed with a report on heart attacks during coitus, telling far more about the former than the latter; a text-accompanied color photo story on *The Male Prostitutes of Bombay;* and a brief essay by Dr. Theodor Reik on *Erotomania,* the delusion that somebody loves you. There is no way of knowing for certain whether those who had sent in their $19.50 were pleased with the intellectual and artistic stimulation, or disappointed in the lack of the promised erotic provocation; the magazine was to be cut off in its infancy, just as subscription renewal time was upon it.

Whether the *Time* review had stung Ginzburg, whether Ginzburg, who seemed to thrive on the publicity of controversy, felt that his first issue had created an inadequate stir, whether he willfully sought martyrdom on the altar of press freedom, or whether the infusion of fresh subscriptions threatened to abate is not clear. What is clear is that with later issues *Eros* became more erotic and increasingly perverse. "The first issue was only so-so," Ginzburg is quoted as saying, "After that it got progressively better. The fifth—which never got printed—was the best." When the fourth issue appeared in late 1962, its content seemed to require presentation to a New York County grand jury.

"*Eros* is the result of recent court decisions that have realistically interpreted America's obscenity laws and that have given to this country a new breadth of freedom of expression," the magazine's earliest mailing piece had proclaimed, *"Eros* takes *full advantage* of this new freedom of expression." It seemed possible, however, that by the winter issue of 1962, Ralph Ginzburg, in two respects, might well have taken unfair—or, more important, unlawful—advantage of this new freedom.

First, in that issue of *Eros,* Ginzburg had used classical oddments, ranging from verses snipped from the Bible, through a rather free-swinging translation of ancient Greek comedy, to isolated lines taken from Shakespeare's sonnets. He had also drawn on portions of Frank Harris's autobiographical writings of almost a half-century earlier. Censor-fashion, Ginzburg had gone leapfrogging through these works, hunting for passages dealing with sex and sensuality, substituting, however, the anthologist's shears and pastepot for the censor's blue pencil. (With similar tools and skills he had made a small fortune on his *An Unhurried View of Erotica,* combining in it a goodly helping of Ginzburg with substantial sensuality and bawdiness culled from centuries of both banned and shunned books.) This patch-quilt method of composition was not, however, entirely free of jeopardy. In *Roth* the Supreme Court, developing the lead that Judge Woolsey had provided in the *Ulysses* case (". . . reading 'Ulysses' *in its entirety, as a book must be read* on such a test as this . . ."), had stated that in judging obscenity the prurient appeal of the material *"taken as a whole"* had to be considered. Ginzburg did not, however, take his source materials as a whole. One reason that the bits and patches that *Eros* had used had not been obscene (legally) in their *original* form was the very fact that they were in that form: each was an integral part of a non-obscene artistic whole. *Eros's* surgery, however, had severed that relationship. In throwing out the redemptive portions, and saving only the sexual or erotic allusions, all that Ginzburg had kept might—depending upon its content—have been the pornographic.

Second, and quite possibly more significant, Ginzburg's "anthology," his collection of the erotic, the abnormal, and the coarse, might be deemed *more* offensive than were any of its parts. In the foreword to his own book, *An Unhurried View of Erotica*, Ginzburg, commenting on his grouping of "erotic samples," had written, "Hopefully, in this book the whole will be greater than the sum of its parts."[3] And so it was in *Eros*. Each item, even though when taken alone was not legally pornographic, might when added to its fellows snowball to prurient proportions. The morbidity, the perversity, and the bizarrerie might build as vulgarity was heaped upon vulgarity. The Supreme Court had not said so, but neither had it previously dealt with anthologies such as *Eros*.

The winter 1962 issue embodied Ginzburg's mastery of reverse bowdlerizing. The fragments in it that had been culled from literature led off with *Love in the Bible*. Illustrated with old woodcuts and etchings, it quoted briefly and pointedly from biblical chapters telling of the Sodomites and recounting Lot's incest with his daughters, of Potiphar's wife's attempt to seduce Joseph, of Judah's sexual liaison with his daughter-in-law, and of Amnon's rape of his sister. In *Was Shakespeare a Homosexual?*, *Eros* pulled together lines and half lines pried loose from the sonnets, and through such use suggested the bard's deviancy. For example, omitting a line and a half from the opening of the 144th sonnet ("Two loves I have *of comfort and despair,/Which like two spirits do suggest me still:/*The better angel . . ."), *Eros* urged Shakespeare's love was an "irresistibly beauteous boy," by quoting just this much,

Two loves have I . . .
The better angel is a man right fair
The worser spirit is a woman, colour'd ill.

Clearly, neither Ginzburg's biblical nor Shakespearean choppings were pornographic. Yet, shelving legal definitions momentarily, both constituted *a different sort* of obscenity. One dictionary definition of the "obscene" is that which is "offensive to taste; foul; loathsome." Wrenching source material of uncommon beauty so out of its proper context, and placing it in a new and hostile setting, would—certainly to many—understandably evoke this use of the epithet, "obscene."

Eleven pages devoted to Frank Harris included the Ralph Ginzburg brand of "instant" Harris: a drastically abridged version of the first volume of *My Life and Loves,* that in the Grove Press paperback edition ran to two hundred and thirty-six pages. (At the time, the Harris autobiography had not been published or openly circulated in America.) Brief as was this condensation, it consisted in large part of Harris's moment-to-moment experiences as a child witnessing coitus, the particulars of his early knowledge of female anatomy gleaned from his sisters as willing instructresses, his extensive petting experiences at puberty, and his debut at intercourse—along with several encores. By all existing standards, the Harris extract would seem to have been, at least arguably, pornographic. Not being published in *Eros* as simply one phase of a *completely candid* self-history, its descriptions went unredeemed. *Eros* had wrested them from that possibly safe-conduct background. The volume ended with a prose re-creation of Aristophanes' *Lysistrata.* While catching the bawdiness the play must have provided for its audiences more than two thousand years earlier, the *Eros* version all but eliminated the ancient classic's anti-war theme and so busily used street language that the exaltation that had had a hand in keeping the comedy alive through the ages was not even remotely suggested.

Amongst these clippings from the classics, *Eros* sprinkled its own more current creations. A brief tally of some of them cannot adequately convey the tone that cumulatively they produced in a magazine ostensibly dedicated to creation, to Love. The issue's crudest item was an unexpurgated collection of *Bawdy Limericks,* extremely explicit, and in the tradition of latrine limericks, quite gymnastic in some of the sexual accomplishments they described. (Testifying *for* Ginzburg at his Philadelphia trial, *Esquire* movie critic Dwight Macdonald *volunteered* " 'Bawdy Limericks' I don't think are terribly funny, and I think quite vul-

gar, but again I don't think they are obscene or pornographic."[4]
The federal trial judge who found Ginzburg guilty, went further:
" 'Bawdy Limericks' consists of the grossest terminology describing unnatural, offensive, disgusting and exaggerated sexual behavior."[5])An article by Phyllis and Eberhard Kronhausen, *The
Natural Superiority of Women as Eroticists,* consisted largely of
an unnamed lady novelist's descriptions (taken, allegedly, from
an unpublished erotic novel) of foreplay, the movements of love,
and the experiences and joys of both female and male orgasm.
Brief running commentary by the Kronhausens wove in and out
of the generously quoted erotic prose contrasting it with Henry
Miller's more abrupt treatment of the same experiences. A photographic essay on *The Jewel Box Revue,* a musical variety show,
featured chorus girls and strippers (pictured on and off stage,
candidly, in various degrees of undress)—the entire cast being
female impersonators. Also included were a set of color photographs, several of which showed the two nude subjects, this time
man and woman, pressed so closely in face-to-face embrace as to
suggest that genital contact might be taking place; a prose letter
to Editor Ralph Ginzburg from avant-garde poet Allen Ginsberg
railing, with explicit sexual imagery and hyperbole, against the
laws directed at certain sex practices; and a short story of an ambulance trip to the morgue with the body of a young girl suicide
—who turned out to be a male transvestite.

ACTION AGAINST GINZBURG

Judged by today's criteria, most of these items, standing alone,
would *not* be deemed pornographic. But cumulatively the unrelieved dedication of the issue to the erotic, the deviant, the shocking, the perverse, tinged the entire volume with prurience.
Whether, however, it was sufficient to constitute pornography, to
affront contemporary community standards, was something upon
which reasonable men might, and subsequent history was to
show in fact did, differ.

As had been done two years earlier with Kozy Books, and as was to be done about a year later with Lenny Bruce, after some preliminary investigation the proof against Ralph Ginzburg was presented to a grand jury in New York County in April 1963. And, as in those other instances, care was taken to present the case to the jurors "down the middle." The decision as to whether or not criminal charges were to be brought was one the grand jurors, the "conscience of the community," would be asked to make themselves, unpricked by prosecutorial thinking. Copies of the fourth issue of *Eros* and of the mailing pieces were distributed for study by the jurors, along with the Supreme Court's *Roth* majority opinion. Ralph Ginzburg appeared and testified. (Prospective defendants cannot be *summoned* before a grand jury in New York, but should they request a hearing, as Ginzburg did, they have a *right* to testify.) In his early 30s, of below average height, balding, owlish in horn-rimmed glasses, Ginzburg gave evidence with precisely the degree of humility, but none of the polish, of a William H. Buckley or a Robert Moses. He was smart, but excessively volatile, and had the unerring instinct for insulting most of his auditors. The grand jurors, in New York County, men and women of extremely high caliber and, generally, considerable maturity and tolerance, listened carefully, scrutinized *Eros*, read and reread the guidance that *Roth* offered, and voted to file "no bill." So doing, in effect they declared that a majority of their number had *not* found *Eros* repugnant to community standards, or at least to their own sophisticated standards, and that the few advertising flyers that happened to get addressed to youngsters had been sent unintentionally, inevitably incidental to *Eros's* mail campaign, a campaign that, obviously, was meant to reach only those who were likely to have had checkbooks handy and $19.50 to spare.

Although in April 1963, the New York County grand jurors declared *Eros* not obscene, a federal grand jury sitting only ninety miles away in a quite different city, Philadelphia, had the previous month indicted Ginzburg and his several alter-ego corporations for sending the fourth issue of *Eros* through the mails, and for distributing other allegedly pornographic publications. This division between the two sets of grand jurors, each differently evaluating contemporary community standards, spotlighted the need—debated but not resolved in the *Jacobellis* opinions—for determining the nature of the community involved. If it is to be those wholly theoretical standards of our *national* community, are they better known to jurors in sophisticated New York or in more orthodox Philadelphia? Or is the problem best resolved by not seeking the reactions of such a wholly theoretical community, but letting each locale separately bar that which it finds repugnant, as Justice Harlan has repeatedly urged? And even should this last be our chosen mode of action, is a jury that has been impaneled as an adjunct to a *federal* court in a particular part of America to have its views given national impact because it is weighing federal crime? (Harlan would minimize this potential by giving the states wide latitude, but only permitting federal action against clear hard-core; Ginzburg's materials he found not in this forbidden category.)

The Philadelphia federal grand jury charged Ginzburg (and his companies) not only with criminal conduct arising from the mailing of *Eros,* but with similar crimes for sending out a bi-weekly newsletter, called *Liaison* (dealing with biology, sexology, philology, and scatology, emphasizing freedom in sexual discussion, and urging it in sexual action), and a book distributed by Ginzburg and described by its title, the *Housewife's Handbook on Selective Promiscuity.*

In June 1963, at the end of a five day trial before federal Judge Ralph C. Body, Ginzburg (who had waived a jury, fearing in Philadelphia lay hostility toward possible pornography and pornographers) was convicted. Months later when trial Judge Body's opinion was delivered, it was to note that Ginzburg and his publishing corporations, "in order that the postmarks on mailed material would further defendants' general scheme and purpose," had first tried to mail the publications from Blue Ball, Pennsylvania, and when that had failed, from Intercourse, Pennsylvania; ultimately they were in fact mailed from Middlesex, New Jersey. (Ginzburg, clearly, thought of everything!) The judge found as fact that *Eros, Liaison,* and the *Handbook* were all within the *Roth* definition of obscenity. In the course of his opinion he commented:

It is one thing to create an integrated work of art containing what would be obscenity standing alone, and another thing to create an integrated work of obscenity containing excerpts from recognized works of art.

On December 19, 1963, Ginzburg was sentenced to five years' imprisonment, and he and his corporations were fined a total of $28,000.

Having finally earned his martyrdom Ginzburg with customary modesty, commented:

Today's sentencing marks not only the end of a trial, but the beginning of one of the great free-speech battles of the century. It is not merely one man who has been condemned today, but everyone who values the right of freedom of speech with regard to love and sex . . . . Important ideas and great literature invariably survive the best efforts of censors and smut-hunters.[6]

There are times when Kahlil Gibran's statement, "He who wears his morality but as his best garment were better naked,"[7] seems made to measure for Ginzburg.

Almost a year later, five months after the Justices of the Supreme Court had hammered out their six separate opinions in *Jacobellis,* the intermediate federal appellate court, resting on that and the *Roth* case, unanimously affirmed Ginzburg's conviction.[8] "The censor's heavy hand has won judicial sanction in this case," said the American Civil Liberties Union urging the Supreme Court to review the action. And, continuing with the non-sequitur (considering the unique anthological and snipped-up nature of *Eros),* the A.C.L.U. averred, "the conviction and affirmance below pose *such a serious danger to literary freedom* in the

United States that it is imperative certiorari [Supreme Court review] be granted."[9] In April 1965, the nation's highest Court, at the same time that it agreed to review Edward Mishkin's 1960 New York conviction, decided also to review that of Ginzburg, later completing the bill by granting review also of *Fanny Hill.* Thus these two men, Mishkin and Ginzburg, both adjudicated pornographers (one in the state courts and the other federally, as in the *Roth-Alberts* doubleheader), both operating profitable professional publishing ventures, both with nationwide markets, one catering with some veneer of style to interested eggheads, the other with unalloyed crudity—but "nicer" language—to offbeats, were to have America's "High Court of Obscenity" review their convictions. Side-by-side, on March 21, 1966, these convictions were affirmed, in one *(Mishkin)* the Court tally being six to three, in the other *(Ginzburg),* five to four.

Finding that Ginzburg's marketing methods pandered to prurient interests, and " 'the leer of the sensualist' also permeates the advertising," and that, *seen against that background,* Ginzburg's publications were violative of the federal obscenity statute, the high Court majority expressly *avoided* ruling whether the materials themselves, seen out of the advertising-marketing context Ginzburg imparted, were obscene. As to the materials themselves, the Court noted repeatedly:

We agree that the question of obscenity may include consideration of the setting in which the publications were presented as an aid to determining the question of obscenity, and assume *without deciding* that the prosecution could not have succeeded otherwise.

• • •

Thus we do not decide whether particular articles, for example, in EROS, although identified by the trial judge as offensive, should be condemned as obscene whatever their setting.

• • •

But the trial judge found that "[t]he deliberate and studied arrangement of EROS is editorialized for the purpose of appealing predominantly to prurient interest . . . ." However erroneous such a conclusion might be if unsupported by the evidence of pandering, the record here supports it.

Thus the high Court, in articulating the pandering test, neatly avoided branding Ginzburg's materials obscene *per se*. And the fallacy of the Civil Liberties Union avowal that Ginzburg's conviction represented "a serious danger to literary freedom in the United States" was exposed: it was not literary freedom that was here in danger, but only willful pandering to *non-literary* prurient interests.

In recent years, the New York County prosecutor has not taken major action against other varieties of possibly pornographic periodicals—magazines other than *Eros* and the girlie magazines —although there have been others that cause degrees of community annoyance.

The "body building" periodicals, directed largely at a homosexual audience, and far more insidiously at a groping teen-age group, using physical culture as a cover for picturing nude and near-nude males, have been effectively immunized by the Supreme Court's *Manual Enterprises* decision.[10]

Nudist magazines, sold largely on sooty city newsstands to those whose visual kicks far exceed their pleasures in crisp air and woodland nooks, had been given clearance in the late 1950s, both by the United States Supreme Court and by New York State's highest court.[11] Clearly mere nudity was not obscene and the magazines' advocacy of the tonic value in unimpeded sunshine and the abolition of shame by the return to an Eden (possibly somewhere just off a main highway in Pennsylvania), constituted redeeming social importance, even though those were not the pitches that drew the customers. Manhattan's neighboring county, Queens, in 1958 had arrested one Herbert C. Cohen for selling a special "annual edition" of a nudist magazine, *Sunshine and Health*. In 1960, County Judge John F. Scileppi (since elevated to the state's highest appellate court) had denied a motion to dismiss Cohen's indictment,[12] distinguishing the magazine from the much earlier issue of the same nudist periodical that had gone to the United States Supreme Court three years before. Justice Scileppi pointed out that the magazine before him featured more sunbathers' photos, many picturing genitalia clearly, and seeming to invite attention to them, while in the earlier magazine genitals tended to be in shadow, photographed from a distance, or concealed. (Today's nudist magazines often feature full-color dual page center spreads of handpicked nubile nudists, viewed with less coyness and less camouflage than those found in like position in *Playboy, Gent,* and the other male magazines.) After a jury trial, Cohen was convicted. But in an appeal that was not to reach the intermediate appellate court for years, and was not to be there decided until December 1964, that court, expressing its distaste and its regrets ("The findings of fact implicit in the verdict are affirmed . . . . If we were not required as a matter of law to reach such conclusion, we would have affirmed the judgement"), reversed, holding that the state and federal highest courts' cases governed.[13]

Before leaving written pornography, and local law enforcement's problems with it, a few words are to be said about its international repercussions. In late September 1964, the New York prosecutor's office received an informal visit from a member of the British Embassy staff in Washington, deferentially making enquiry about American police and prosecution practices regarding paperback erotica and the girlie and other magazines. Part of the informal memorandum, originating with the Home Office, that had sparked our guest's visit, had noted:

In 1960, a price restriction on the importation into this country [the United Kingdom] of cheap printed matter, originally imposed during the war for economic reasons, was removed. Shortly afterwards, there began a flow of cheap pornographic magazines and paper back novels from the U.S.A. and this has grown to very large proportions. Action has been taken by our Customs authorities under their statutory powers to seize this material, and since the beginning of 1961 they have seized and condemned over one million copies of novels and magazines bearing over 1,000 different titles. A certain amount of material has slipped through the net and there have been seizures of this from retailers and distributors' premises under police powers. The courts have ordered the destruction of over 360,000 novels and magazines of U.S. origin seized in this way in 1961 and 1962 . . . . Our understanding is that these magazines and novels are freely available in some States of the U.S., and that the copies exported to the U.K. are surplus to the home requirements [sic!]. The fact that the surplus would otherwise be sent for pulp enables them to be sold to the U.K. distributors very cheaply, and this means that it is still economically worthwhile to send consignments even though a considerable proportion is seized by the U.K. authorities . . . . [T]he British Embassy has been asked to ascertain informally from the appropriate United States authorities whether it would be possible for the latter to take action to prevent the export of this material from the United States.

All we could do was to commiserate together. Ours was an ungrateful way—or was it?—of repaying Britain for its own bestselling sex symbol, Agent 007, James Bond!

16. Live Entertainment

His good has no nuances. He
　Doubts or believes with total passion.
Heretics choose for heresy
　Whatever's the prevailing fashion.
Those wearing Tolerance for a label
Call other views intolerable.
　　　—Phyllis McGinley,
　　　　In Praise of Diversity

UNTIL HIS DEATH IN 1966, aged forty, apparently from "acute
morphine poisoning caused by an injection of an overdose,"
Lenny Bruce was a nightclub entertainer billed as "the dirty-talk-
ing comic," and author of an autobiography, *how to talk dirty
and influence people*. His influence on the nation's police, however, had netted him a half dozen or so arrests in less than three
years—in Philadelphia, Chicago, San Francisco, Los Angeles, and
New York—both on narcotics and on obscenity charges. In the
courts and among a dedicated following his impact had been
more propitious: most of these arrests had ended in dismissals
or acquittals, and with each new one Bruce's claque, lauding
both his and their own iconoclasm had chanted swelling
choruses of "persecution" at those with the temerity to have regarded their idol as subject to mortal laws.

This once effective panjandrum of social protest, whose
pointed satire had increasingly lost its way in the mounting obscenity and the evermore perverse shock of his club routines,
was arrested in Greenwich Village's Café Au Go Go on Friday

evening, April 3, 1964, shortly before he was to begin the first of that evening's twice nightly performances. The police had acted, executing an arrest warrant, after a New York County grand jury had leveled criminal charges. Along with Bruce, the cafe's proprietor, Howard Solomon, a pleasant, low-pressure, young stockbroker turned impresario, had been arrested. Both were charged with presenting obscene and indecent performances, in violation of New York State's penal statutes. Seduced by the gate receipts the post-arrest publicity had stimulated, Solomon extended Bruce's all-but-expired week-long New York engagement at three thousand dollars per week, *raised* his admission prices appreciably, and continued to herd in the faithful and the not-so-faithful, including the police. At the conclusion of another show, on April 7, Bruce was rearrested.

Emitting howls of protest, brigades of absolutists in the war on censorship joined the avant-garde, who the month before had been outraged by Jonas Mekas' Village arrest for exhibiting the film *Flaming Creatures.* This time their battle for the public mind seemed an easy one. Bruce had appeared on television, and recordings of his monologues had sold briskly. Here was proof positive, available to all, that his satire was both brilliant and biting, that his material violated no "contemporary community standards," and that his arrests constituted both harassment of the arts, and bluenose-ism at its most virulent. It was not until *after* Bruce's trial that one articulate Bruce partisan, who long before the New York arrests had written lauding Bruce's raw power, was to concede that the 1964 Lenny Bruce was *not* the Bruce of yore. "In the last year," wrote Professor Albert Goldman of Columbia University's English Department, "he has suffered a loss of inspiration—partly attributable to ill health and emotional distress—and his use of obscenity has begun to resemble the twitching of a damaged muscle."[1]

That Bruce, an "artist," could do no wrong proved to be Bruce's main line of defense, both on trial, and outside the courtroom, before the court of public opinion. Ephraim London, an attorney experienced in defending obscenity cases and in appealing the convictions that resulted, in moving unsuccessfully that Bruce's New York trial be before a jury, laid stress on Bruce's eminence as a performer on television and in recordings. He pointed out that "Among [Bruce's] most articulate disciples are British social satirists currently performing in New York in 'The Establishment' and 'Beyond the Fringe' who have acknowledged his influence." (Surprisingly, the content of London's motion papers, seeking an order for a jury trial, were the subject of press coverage *before they had been shown to the prosecution*. Here was a criminal charge that the defense was consistently to seek to pre-try in the press.) In meeting these defense contentions, the district attorney's office sought to get the court to focus on the *relevant* facts:

This Court is, I am certain, concerned not with Bruce's success, or with his recorded or televised satire; it is concerned with specific criminal charges now pending against him . . . . I can state without hesitation that much of what I heard in both these performances [that led to the arrests] was such that I cannot conceive of it being permitted on any television show, nor does it bear even the most superficial resemblance to the performances seen in "The Establishment" or "Beyond the Fringe" mentioned in the London affidavit.

THE "MANIFESTO"

Lenny Bruce's principal ploy for popular support was a "manifesto" publicized by a release to the papers for use on Sunday, June 14, 1964.[2] (The trial was scheduled to start two days later before a bench of three judges.) The document declared what its signatories deemed the law *should* be, not bothering to note what it, in fact, was. And, in accord with the temper of the times, it chose to level the weight of its attack upon the police. In full, the manifesto said:

We the undersigned are agreed that the recent arrests of nightclub entertainer Lenny Bruce by the New York police department on charges of indecent performance constitute a violation of civil liberties as guaranteed by the first and fourteenth amendments to the United States Constitution.

Lenny Bruce is a popular and controversial performer in the field of social satire in the tradition of Swift, Rabelais and Twain. Although Bruce makes use of the vernacular in his night club performances, he does so within the context of his satirical intent and not to arouse the prurient interests of his listeners. It is up to the audience to determine what is offensive to them; it is not a function of the police department of New York or any other city to decide what adult private citizens may or may not hear.

Whether we regard Bruce as a moral spokesman or simply as an entertainer, we believe he should be allowed to perform free from censorship or harassment.

Writers, artists, poets, professors, and theater people were among the hundred signers: James Baldwin, Lillian Hellman, Norman Mailer, Robert Rauschenberg, Allen Ginsberg, Robert Lowell, Louis Untermeyer, Eric Bentley, Albert Goldman, Lionel Trilling, Ben Gazarra, Rip Torn, and Rudy Vallee were just a few, not here listed in order of importance. There were some with vested interests and personal experiences in the battle against censorship: Jonas Mekas (*Flaming Creatures*), Henry Miller (*Tropic of Cancer*), John Rechy (*City of Night*), Terry Southern (*Candy*), and Barney Rossett (president of Grove Press). Latecomers to have their names added to the list were those firmly established authorities on our contemporary community standards, Elizabeth Taylor and Richard Burton. A handful of persons later to testify for Bruce at the trial as expert witnesses had also signed. Their subscription to the manifesto was to prove one of the follies of litigation by press release: the objectivity of each, the purity of his critical judgments, was slightly soiled (at the very least) by the fact that each had, through the manifesto, declared four-square for Bruce and against the arrests *before* ever having seen or heard the particular monologues about which he was later to testify at the trials.

The press release that had accompanied the Bruce manifesto led off:

Theologian Reinhold Niebuhr, Columbia University Professor Lionel Trilling [then followed eight other names] headed a list of persons demanding today that the New York City Police Department cease "censorship and harassment" of this "popular and controversial" nightclub personality.

Niebuhr's was a name to conjure with. And conjure, truly conjure, the defense did. During the trial's course the Niebuhr name was interjected (despite contrary hearsay rules) by defense experts and defense counsel to bolster their own opinions. The fact that the press had previously revealed that the world-renowned theologian, reached by telephone, had stated that he had never seen or heard or read about Bruce, but only had word of the case from friends, did not seem to faze the defense. But prompted by the facts the press had supplied, the district attorney's office got in touch with Dr. Niebuhr. Ill and at home in Stockbridge, Massachusetts, that modest, candid man wrote:

July 4th

Dear Mr. Kuh:

I should like to communicate with you in regard to the petition I signed in behalf of Lenny Bruce. I want to confess that my signature to that petition was ill advised. It was prompted by conversations with friends who knew Bruce and who had competence to judge the merits of social satire.

But I should not have signed the petition at all because I had no first hand knowledge of Bruce's performances; and therefore my witness about the charge of obscenity was useless; and it may have led other signers of the petition astray. Incidentally, I violated the habit of a lifetime in signing a petition which had to do with some issue about which I had no personal knowledge. I will make no charge against Bruce; but also I will not say anything in his defense.

I am writing you this note in order to correct an error of judgment, of which I was guilty.

Sincerely yours,
Reinhold Niebuhr

When, during trial, this letter was tendered by the prosecution, solely to meet the defense tactic of having wrung his name into the testimony as a sort of absent and exalted witness, the objections could have been heard clear to Stockbridge. The letter was excluded. But this attempt at correction did not prevent post-trial newspaper stories from perpetuating the picture of Reinhold Niebuhr as a Bruce supporter.[3]

The manifesto had been the work of the letter-writing poet Allen Ginsberg (he had written that pungent note to publisher Ralph Ginzburg that had appeared in the controversial fourth issue of *Eros*—"Who cares if people want to copulate in public on TV? Why not? The controllers can always turn off the screen. . . ."). Expressive laureate to the beat generation, bearded, balding, and sometimes sandaled, Ginsberg, a thirty-eight year old mystic from Newark, New Jersey, was also leader of LEMAR, a committee seeking the legalization of the sale and use of marijuana. Before the trial finally started, Ginsberg had appeared in the courtroom several times. Bruce had drawn a beat audience to the Criminal Courts Building, but poet Ginsberg—intense eyes peering through horn-rimmed glasses above the heavy beard— stood out among the rooting section of the carefully unregimented. Although Ginsberg had introduced himself (at times, the Philistines and some of the literati were almost cordial, off the record of the court proceedings), on the opening day of the trial he was almost unrecognizable, being for some reason clean-shaven. The next day's mail brought a syrupy, old-fashionedly ornate, commercial friendship card, headed in curlicued script, "From Your Secret Pal," replete with a stanza of distinctly non-Ginsbergian, greeting-card poetry ("Your Secret Pal just wants to say/You're nice as you can be. . . ."). Between the card's double folds were two locks of dark curly hair—preserved from the beard of the avant-garde's prophet. "Please accept the enclosed offering of my shorn locks," Ginsberg had written round the card's margins, "as a sort of spiritual bribe that you look with friendlier kindlier heart on the earnest strivings of the artists of N.Y. to

communicate with all man, including my self and your self. . . .
Meanwhile accept and guard this part of my head which I have
cut off in your honor, as a devotional offering to the God in you."

This "offering," and the card accompanying it, crystallized the
vacuum in two-way communication existing between the avant-
garde on one side, and law enforcement on the other. The Mekas
and Bruce prosecutions had not been anti-artist or anti-avant-
garde, they were not, as some had charged, politically or sectarian
inspired retaliation for political or religious irreverence. They
were simply an inevitable reflex at what seemed to be a sudden
effort to push too far too fast. Although, along with our sexual
mores, standards of obscenity were obviously changing and
changing rapidly, existing unrepealed and uninvited statutes still
banned certain public "entertainments." Ginsberg's card had referred to "the earnest strivings of the artists of N.Y. to communicate with all man." Assuming, with Ginsberg, that they were
"artists" and were "earnest" (as well as, prospectively, highly
profitable in the case of Bruce and his New York impresario,
Howard Solomon), if these strivings chose as their channel of
expression sexual imagery that stripped all privacy from sex and
distorted it and made it ugly, whether this was done on film
(Mekas), or in words and gestures (Bruce), such "strivings"
could not be blithely ignored by those charged with enforcing
existing law. It was for law enforcement to start the processes
that would determine whether or not they accorded with our
"contemporary community standards," and whether or not they
were redeemed by any—or by adequate—"social importance."

Moreover, the timing of Ginsberg's "spiritual bribe," his shear-
ing, reflected on its sincerity. It came less than a week after the
bearded Ginsberg had, by manifesto, attacked the New York City
police department for its arrest of Bruce. The attack had reflected
no efforts toward achieving a "friendlier kindlier heart." Quite
the contrary. The attack was harsh in its condemnation, stating
unequivocally that the police had violated the Constitution in ar-
bitrarily exercising a censoring function that was not theirs; and

it was brash in its choice of "facts." It chose to ignore that the first Bruce arrest was made, not by police acting upon their own judgment but pursuant to court-ordered warrants, *after a grand jury had acted,* charging violations of a statute that declared that "any person who . . . presents or particpates in, any obscene, indecent, immoral or impure . . . show or entertainment . . . shall be guilty of a misdemeanor." Approximately one hundred prominent Americans chose to accept Ginsberg's leadership and spoke in a public manifesto, completely ignoring the existence of the statute; they chose to overlook completely the grand jury's action; and, from the security of their artistic and intellectual eminence, they chose to lash out at the police, and by so doing did their best to further foment those anti-police feelings that were already too active in too many areas. The chasm was broad between the olive branch of Ginsberg the beard-shaving mystic, and the anti-police attack of Ginsberg the authority-bearding organizer.

If the Bruce manifesto's signers were driven in part by their ingrained hostility to all censorship, if the experts testifying for Bruce during the trial shaded their critical objectivity for the same reasons, if the defense efforts were to divert attention from Bruce at the Café Au Go Go in favor of focusing upon him as a recorded and televised pace-setting satirist, if the public was being misled into believing that what one could say autobiographically, before TV cameras and on phonograph records, should be passable in a night spot, just what was it—what were the obscene words or filthy concepts—that Bruce gave voice to in early springtime at the Café Au Go Go?

THE NEW YORK CONVICTION

On November 4, 1965, after a trial of ten court days spaced throughout six weeks of early summer, and after the balance of the summer and early fall had provided respite and time to study the law memoranda submitted by both sides, the bench of three judges—Justice John M. Murtagh (administrative judge of the New York City Criminal Court) presiding, and Associate Justices J. Randall Creel and Kenneth M. Phipps—announced its verdict. "Guilty," held the majority of Justices Murtagh and Phipps. Dissenting, Justice Creel stated that Bruce had "made a studiedly offensive and deliberately insulting use of a mass of the most vulgar and erotic words," and that he had "made a calculated use of vulgarity for vulgarity's sake alone," but, the judge believed, the "confusing contradictions" in the law concerning obscenity required him to vote as he did.

The hush that publicly cloaked the majority's opinion mirrored the one-sided publicity that had preceded it, keeping the community from any real perception as to what the trial had actually involved. Justice Creel's dissenting opinion was reported, in some detail, in newspaper comment. The majority's views, explaining Bruce's conviction with specific strong references to the content of his monologues, although officially a matter of public record, remained all but unnoticed. *The New York Times,* for instance, having devoted seven paragraphs to the dissent, gave only one to the majority opinion.[4]

Even the bar was kept in the dark, despite the fact that the trial had aroused considerable professional interest. Although opinions of the trial courts are not always printed, they commonly are when likely to be of particular interest to the bar. The *Bruce* opinions were clearly such. Yet the public official charged with compiling New York's reports decided against their publication. New York City has a daily legal newspaper, the New York *Law Journal,* widely subscribed to, and regularly scanned, by the city's bench and bar. Anyone who has ever seen its daily eight-column almost pictureless format, bulging with court calendars and official pronouncements, its reprinted judicial speeches and lawyers' serious writings, its plethora of court orders and opinions, its simple and uninspired column captions, would know that it is hardly a source to which any but the weirdest fetishist might turn in search of prurience. A month after the *Bruce* opinions were rendered, in front-page space the *Law Journal* announced that it had decided against their publication:

The majority opinion, of necessity, cited in detail the language used by Bruce in his nightclub act, and also described gestures and routines which the majority found to be obscene and indecent. The *Law Journal* decided against publication, even edited, on the grounds that deletions would destroy the opinion, and without the deletions publication was impossible within *Law Journal* standards.[5]

This adolescent shyness about publishing the trial court's strong, but thin distillation of the monologues, may itself bear witness to the patency with which the monologues violated our contemporary community standards. But such bowdlerizing of the law completely ignored common sense. The *Roth* standard, in demanding that inspection of alleged obscenity take it "as a whole," expresses some awareness of context. Although monologues performed for a fun-seeking café audience may be obscene, court-prepared summaries of them, written primarily for persons seriously interested in how the law draws obscenity lines, and that must therefore give at least the gist of that being judged, are not.

In convicting Lenny Bruce and Howard Solomon, the trial court majority (drawing substantially from the prosecution's memorandum) had this to say:

All three performances of the defendant, Lenny Bruce, were obscene, indecent, immoral and impure within the meaning of Section 1140-a of the Penal Law. While no tape is available as to the first performance [past midnight, March 31-April 1], this monologue, according to the testimony, was essentially the same as that of the second [April 1, after 10:00 p.m.] and third [April 7, after 10:00 p.m.] performances. In the latter two performances, words such as "ass," "balls," "cock-sucker," "cunt," "fuck," "mother-fucker," "piss," "screw," "shit," and "tits" were used about one hundred times in utter obscenity. The monologues also contained anecdotes and reflections that were similarly obscene.

For example:

1. Eleanor Roosevelt and her display of "tits." (1st performance; transcript of 3rd performance at p. 27)

2. Jacqueline Kennedy "hauling ass" at the moment of the late President's assassination. (Transcript of 2nd performance at p. 22; transcript of 3rd performance at p. 13)

3. St. Paul giving up "fucking." (1st performance; transcript of 2nd performance at p. 12; transcript of 3rd performance at p. 19)

4. An accident victim—who lost a foot in the accident—who made sexual advances to a nurse, while in the ambulance taking him to the hospital. (1st performance; transcript of 2nd performance at p. 25)

5. "Uncle Willie" discussing the "apples" of a 12-year old girl. (transcript of 2nd performance at p. 20; transcript of 3rd performance at p. 12)

6. Seemingly sexual intimacy with a chicken. (transcript of 2nd performance at p. 25)

7. "Pissing in the sink" and "pissing" from a building's ledge. (transcript of 2nd performance at p. 24; transcript of 3rd performance at p. 15)

8. The verb "to come," with its obvious reference to sexual orgasm. (1st performance)

9. The reunited couple discussing adulteries committed during their separation, and the suggestion of a wife's denial of infidelity, even when discovered by her husband. (1st performance; transcript of 2nd performance at p. 29)

10. "Shoving" a funnel of hot lead "up one's ass." (transcript of 2nd performance at p. 22; transcript of 3rd performance at p. 13)

11. The story dealing with the masked man, Tonto, and an unnatural sex act. (1st performance)

12. Mildred Babe Zaharias and the "dyke profile of 1939." (transcript of 3rd performance at p. 27)

During the first performance Bruce fondled the microphone stand in a masturbatory fashion. In the second performance, while telling of an act of exposure, Bruce turned his back to the audience and moved his hand outward and upward from below his waist in an obvious and crude pantomime of an act of exposure and masturbation.

The dominant theme of the performances appealed to the prurient interest and was patently offensive to the average person in the community, as judged by present day standards. The performances were lacking in "redeeming social importance."

The monologues were not erotic. They were not lust-inciting, but, while they did not arouse sex, they insulted sex and debased it. [A discussion of the legal authorities, sustaining such debasement as pornography, followed here.]

• • •

. . . They [the monologues] were obscene, indecent, immoral, and impure. The monologues contained little or no literary or artistic merit. They were merely a device to enable Bruce to exploit the use of obscene language. They were devoid of any cohesiveness. They were a series of unconnected items that contained little of social significance. They were chaotic, haphazard, and inartful.

Convicted, Bruce, acting as his own lawyer, having dropped London during the early fall after all the evidence had been taken and the legal arguments had been made, sought aid from the federal courts, unsuccessfully asking them to enjoin the state judges from imposing a sentence upon him. (In this fashion he nursed the futile hope of leap-frogging the state appellate system, and landing in the lap of the Supreme Court in Washington.) This maneuver having failed,[6] a tired, pallid Lenny Bruce pleaded disjointedly for more than an hour before the bench that had tried him and was to pass sentence. In December 1964, he was given a four month workhouse term; Howard Solomon was fined one thousand dollars. Both were released pending their appeals. Bruce's appeal, ultimately, was to be dismissed after repeated delays on his part, but he never surrendered to serve his sentence—or did he ever reappear publicly in New York State. Solomon's appeal is still pending, but as this goes to press (two and a half years after his conviction), it has not yet been argued in the state's *intermediate* appellate court.

ADULT FREEDOM TO ELECT THEIR OWN ENTERTAINMENT

Should Bruce have been convicted, or was the manifesto sound contending that it was not for the police—or, more accurately, grand jurors—"to decide what adult private citizens may or may not hear"? In the face of New York's statute barring lewd and indecent shows, this was a proclamation that legislative bodies *could not* declare obscene shows out-of-bounds to those who were ready with the price of admission. That inhibition on our lawmakers was to be urged in the press with some regularity during the Bruce excitement. "Nobody forced patrons into the Café Au Go Go to hear Bruce," editorialized New York's *World-Telegram*, "They *even* paid. And the privilege, *if any*, was reserved for adults only."[7] Columnist Dick Schaap, writing in the *Herald Tribune*, noted that the Bruce performances were such that "people are perfectly entitled to be offended, honestly, sincerely offended. . . . I think these people should stay away from the Au Go Go, or any place where Mr. Bruce is appearing, and I think they do."[8]

Were this thinking to prevail, were adults free to enjoy any and all entertainments they were ready to pay for, the "beat" in each of our larger cities might be able to provide home-grown duplicates of that "happening" that Parisians, and Americans in Paris, were exposed to in the late spring of 1965. Of this Parisian Festival of Free Expression, *Time* magazine was to report, a "girl stood by beatifically as a grave-faced artist shaved her groin. Later, beat poet Lawrence Ferlinghetti [one of the manifesto's signatories] intoned his latest work while a naked couple made love vertically in a burlap bag, black light playing on their shoulders." And, lest this was not enough, the two thousand "in" on-lookers were assured by the Festival's promoter that with sufficient funds the following year, they could "*really* have a happening that could say things. A real happening *without all these restrictions*."[9]

Obviously, such "happenings," whether they took place in New York City or in Neodesha, Kansas, would *not* torpedo our Western culture. Most Americans having survived without ever having witnessed as much as a single Lenny Bruce monologue are likely to remain untouched, and probably untempted, by the lure of such "happenings," or of more prurient fare. Why not, then, let adults, those with both the admission price and the requisite desire, patronize whatever public entertainments each may wish to choose?

Answering that question requires a long look at anti-obscenity legislation generally, and in so doing probing for a workable and reasonably predictable way of reconciling the benefits of unimpeded freedom of expression with at least a significant degree of protection from *such harms as pornography inflicts.* For present purposes, accepting the law as it is, not necessarily as it should be, the *Roth* case tells us that adults may *not* buy or read anything or everything that they wish. (Ability to pay seems to have nothing to do with the matter.) Does *Roth* also apply to obscene entertainments? The Supreme Court has said that it does.

More than a quarter of a century ago, several New Jersey communities, just across the Hudson River from New York City, gained—after a fashion—when New York City's colorful mayor, Fiorello H. LaGuardia, banished burlesque from his municipal domain. New Yorkers and their visitors, eager to goggle at the strippers, trouped over to Newark in neighboring New Jersey. Finally, in the mid-1950s, Newark clamped down. Amending its own ordinances, Newark sought to bar "lewd" performances. To minimize escape routes created by vague adjectives, the revised laws specified a ban on obscene shows involving "The exposure by a female performer in the presence of the audience, or the giving of the illusion of nudeness in the presence of the audience, of the lower abdomen, genital organs, buttocks or breasts"; the ordinances also prohibited "The use by a performer of profane, lewd, lascivious, indecent or disgusting language." The targets were obviously the burlesque strippers and overly unrestrained burlesque comics, along with those who brought them before the public. Owners of Newark bump-and-grind emporiums hurried into court, demanding that these new ordinances be struck down as unconstitutional. Although the theater owners were successful initially, like their artistes the early promise exceeded the performance. On appeal, New Jersey's top court reversed, and by so doing sustained the local provisions.[10] The United States Supreme Court, in a short opinion issued on the same day that it handed down its *Roth-Alberts* opinions, affirmed New Jersey's action.[11] Clearly, then, the high Court's obscenity standards apply not only to the written word and to the pictured form, but apply equally to perverse performances, including live acts that obscenely use "profane, lewd, lascivious, indecent or disgusting language."

It is particularly appropriate that live shows, whether or not restricted to an admission-paying audience, are as subject to obscenity restrictions as are books. Most judges, although they may talk of "*contemporary* community standards," are likely to have one eye on tomorrow. Accustomed to long drawn-out criminal appeals and knowing that today's mores may well be next year's prudery, most judges neither relish prospects of reversal, nor wish to have (at some time in the future) the citizenry scoff at their seeming puritanism. This particularly applies to books, or even magazines. But live performances, *being wholly for a present audience,* should—in reality as well as in theory—be judged wholly by our *contemporary* standards, without any anchor to tomorrow's windward.

In fact, the appealing conclusion of the manifesto's signers, and of some of the journalists, that a pornographic entertainment is wholly without impact on those not attending it, is somewhat out of touch with reality. In this age of public relations, those who are successful entertainers become our folk-heroes. They are canonized by annual incomes vying with the riches of Genghis Khan, by hoopla beyond the dreams of Barnum, by appearances and gossip and pictured imagery that rivals that of the

Caesars. Lenny Bruce, "the dirty talking comic," was still a far distance from the pinnacle, but had sufficient acclaim to have inspired the plaudits of the Committee of 100, a number of whose prominent members had never personally seen or heard him or read a transcription of his performances, and to boast an annual income in excess of one hundred thousand dollars. When pornography has provided the path to this prosperity, and filth has fostered this adulation, whether or not the young are permitted to witness a specific performance, they are certain to learn something of how the entertainer's success was grasped. The very act of barring teen-agers from an entertainment to which their elders flock serves to telegraph its nature generally to all blessed with the inquisitiveness of being young. What each man does, and does in a public show presented with legal sanction, will not be without impact upon his neighbors and his neighbor's children.

BRUCE'S PERFORMANCES

To return, then, to the question of whether the grand jury should have leveled criminal charges against Lenny Bruce for presenting monologues seen and heard only by those adults who had paid the Café Au Go Go's tariff. Neither the admission price nor the consent inevitably accompanying its payment, it is clear, *now* immunize obscene entertainments from the force of the anti-obscenity laws. New York had had a half-century-old statute banning obscene shows, and the statute had, on at least two occasions, made the trip to the state's highest court, presenting ample opportunity—never seized—for that tribunal to have ruled the law invalid had it been so inclined.[12] And, if any shows could be within the statute's ban, Bruce's surely seemed to be: his cumulatively nauseating word pictures were interspersed with all the three- and four-letter words and the far more acrid ten- and twelve-letter hyphenated ones, spewed directly at his audience; his pornographic content, the trial court had found, he underscored through his use of the crudest of gestures.

As to the words and gestures, even Bruce's prime "expert" witness, the late Dorothy Kilgallen, longtime newspaper feature writer and columnist, conceded their immorality and community repugnance to them. On the witness stand, she was hostile to all who were hostile to "Lenny"; she was—as in print and on TV— adept with words, and she was quick to evade and reluctant to yield an inch. Tensely prim in the courtroom, as on the home screen, Miss Kilgallen initially testified that in her opinion Bruce's Café Au Go Go monologues were not obscene, that they were chock-full of "redeeming social importance." On her direct examination by Martin Garbus, Ephraim London's able, intense, younger associate, she volunteered that Bruce ". . . is a very brilliant man and that he has great social awareness, and basic- ally he's an extremely moral man and is trying to improve the world and trying to make his audience think, which, I think, is a very good thing and very moral and to be applauded."[13] On cross-examination, this took place:

Mr. Kuh: Turning to the April 1st transcript, page 21 of the April 1st transcript, may I ask you to look about six lines down, where the transcript starts: "Because my aunt—my mother—came home every day telling me stories about some guy took it out in the park, went "yoo hoo, lady," and she hit him with the pocketbook, and so—"

Miss Kilgallen: Yes, I have it.

Q. Now, you mentioned that in judging Bruce's performance it was very difficult, if not impossible, to judge solely by reading the script, that one had to hear his voice and had to see what he did. If I tell you in that portion of the performance he turned partly away from the audience, put his hands together, and moved the hands, from the region of his pubic area, up and down, would you tell me what artistic value was in that per- formance? [There was testimony to this effect; and in its opinion, the court's majority was to find this the fact.]

A. I couldn't tell you.

Q. Can you tell me what morality on the part of Bruce that that demonstrated?

A. I don't think it would demonstrate morality.

Q. Indeed, it would contradict morality?

A. I think so.

Q. Did you say you *think* so?

A. I say I think it would not reflect morality.

Q. Would it contradict, contravene, be the opposite of morality? Indeed, represent immorality?

A. I think it might.

Q. Might?

A. Yes.

Q. Is there any question in your mind about that?

A. I didn't see it; I'm just taking your—

Q. Assuming I pose a hypothetical—

A. Hypothetically, I think it would not be moral.

Q. Hypothetically, do you think it would be immoral?

A. Yes.

Q. Do you think, hypothetically, it could be completely without any redeeming social purpose?

A. I think that's going too far, I cannot say that.

Q. If you think there might be some redeeming social purpose, would you tell me what social purpose might possibly exist?

A. Sometimes, when we see something on the stage that is bad, there's a moral in it that we can draw. It very often happens.

Q. Can you tell me, reading the script and assuming the action that I described to you, what moral you would draw, or what moral your readers would draw, or what moral you think anyone who saw the show would draw?

A. Well, I would not describe that to my readers; I work for a family newspaper.

Q. In fact, would you, in terms of your readers, reprint any of the Bruce dialogue that you have presently before you?

A. I would not reprint any of the phrases that you have pointed out, as being unacceptable to some people, because they don't belong in a newspaper.

Q. Why?

A. Because a newspaper has a wide circulation, it's read by children, it's not like a place of entertainment where people go knowing fully well what they are going to see and pay for it.

Q. Well, the newspapers do report divorces, and sometimes juicy divorces, sometimes other sexual incidents, and they are read by children. Is there any particular reason why you would not reproduce the Bruce dialogue, other than the children affected?

A. It's simply not newspaper style, when you are working for a newspaper with a mass audience. It might be all right in an esthetic publication read by intellectuals, but it's not proper form in a newspaper and it's certainly not my style, as a woman, to reproduce these.

Q. Are you suggesting to us that the overwhelming majority of the community—the American community—would find this highly offensive, and repugnant, if it appeared in the newspaper?

A. I think that in print, the majority of the American people would object to it.[14]

Lenny Bruce's prosecution, and his conviction, did not rest solely on his gestures and on the heavy barrage of obscenities, short and long, hyphenated and simple, he so insatiably employed. A prime requisite of the *Roth* rule was that the materials under judgment be viewed, *"taken as a whole."* And grossness of language was only one aspect of the Bruce monologues. Clearly, obscenities have established a place in today's vivid theater when used to achieve verisimilitude. One of America's keenest exploders of pomposity, Marya Mannes, known for her barbed and wholly independent satire, was called as a witness against Bruce. Miss Mannes deemed Bruce's Café Au Go Go monologues offensive and vulgar, his audiences jolted into shock-laughter by the unbelievable smut. This use of obscenities for laugh-getting, she found, was "the last resort of the comedian." Her reaction was no outcropping of prudery. As a drama critic, she had warmly praised Edward Albee's play, *Who's Afraid of Virginia Woolf?* and as a witness she noted that *vulgarity in a proper framework,* such as that provided in the lacerating Albee drama, served a valid function in terms of providing realism, dramatic impact, and insight into character and its development. Lenny Bruce hurling words at an audience, however, was of a quite different species.

And as the dozen illustrations summarized in the trial court's opinion demonstrate, apart from Bruce's vocabulary, the stand-up comic's "bits," with which he regaled his café audiences, were themselves innately obscene.

Some of the defense "experts" stated, as their opinions, that neither Bruce's language nor his concepts were obscene. But the patent offensiveness of both were such—the words, for example, called "obscenities" in everyday language—that this only served to cloak with further doubts the experts' objectivity. Candor might better have compelled recognition that the words and concepts *were* obscene, and have gone on to suggest, as had been recognized thirty years earlier, that their obscenity might nevertheless not be criminally actionable. In the *Ulysses* case, in 1934, federal appellate Judge Augustus Hand had stated:

> *That numerous long passages in Ulysses contain matter that is obscene under any fair definition of the word cannot be gainsaid;* yet they are relevant to the purpose of depicting the thoughts of the characters and are introduced to give meaning to the whole rather than to promote lust or portray filth for its own sake.[15]

Despite Bruce's pungent vocabulary and distinctive concepts, had his performances been redeemed by their social importance, under the *Roth* and *Jacobellis* cases, he should not have been convicted. That is and was the law, whether or not, as an observation of columnist Inez Robb's has suggested, it made much sense when applied to the Bruce "entertainments":

What makes Bruce's obscenity so great in the eyes of his admirers is that his is the thinking man's obscenity. It's good for you! That was patiently explained to me by one of Bruce's idolators.

"He's a great social critic. A great social critic," this man kept repeating, "You ought to hear him on the Catholic Church, the Pope, marriage and motherhood! Great! Just great!"

When I ventured that American homes and schools have always taught that anyone forced to use obscenity is (1) illiterate and (2) consequently wholly ignorant of the usages of his mother tongue, my friend said, "My God, what ——!"[16]

Whether the Bruce performances were redeemed by any artistry of form or by any cogent social criticism, or whether they were utterly without redeeming social importance, was at the eye of the conflict in Bruce's New York trial.

The conclusion of the trial court had been that "The monologues contained little or no literary or artistic merit." This finding was made although the defense had produced a half score of expert witnesses who had professed that Bruce was skillfully articulate. (Concerning them, Professor Albert Goldman commented, "To a man, defense witnesses asserted that Bruce is a brilliant social satirist, and then struggled to prove it from the crude and unfunny 'bits' mercilessly laid out in the transcript. The inflation of values was bizarre: Bruce was compared to Rabelais, Swift, Twain, Joyce, Henry Miller and Hosea."[17]) Bruce himself, in a letter he was to write to his attorney, Ephraim London, in August 1964, said:

As Gilman [Richard Gilman, *Newsweek* theater editor and Bruce expert witness] said, I do move quite rapidly, my work is compressed—and he's seen me work many times. And you, my own attorney, refused to put me on the stand because I was inarticulate. *That is just the way I speak on the stage.*

(The letter was part of befuddled sheaves of documents sent to the prosecutor and to the trial court by Bruce in the process of discharging London as his counsel.)

This very *inarticulateness* of Bruce in the spring of 1964 caused some double-talking among the defense experts. Rather than calling upon their own well-honed critical faculties to explain just how, and why, and where they found Bruce's artistry in the early April monologues, they began with an assumption that such artistry existed and resolutely avoided inspecting that assumption. They declared that whatever Bruce said, being in his own style, was necessarily said artistically. Happily, the rules of evidence permit a so-called expert to be cross-examined, after he has given his opinion, as to the reasoning, the logic—if any exists—to support that viewpoint. If the expert's reasoning inadequately justifies the expert's conclusions, the trier-of-fact (jury or judge) is free to discard completely the expert's opinions. This question-and-answer interlude took place with Dorothy Kilgallen:

Mr. Kuh: Now, can you tell me, Miss Kilgallen, how the use of this language, not in Mr. Bruce's eyes, but in your eyes, as a critic, a person who was qualified here as an expert witness, will you tell us how the use of this sentence that I read, is necessary to the artistic unity, if you will, of the Jackie Kennedy story?

Miss Kilgallen: I think that the necessity comes from the writer or the performer of the material. I believe Mr. Bruce is both his own writer and performer and if he feels it's necessary, I do not object to it.

Q. Well, are you saying then, that in your eyes Mr. Bruce can do no wrong?

A. No.

Q. Can you tell me, apart from the fact that if Mr. Bruce feels it's necessary, you are satisfied, as a critic, that it's necessary, can you tell me specifically your own personal critical appraisal of how that is necessary to the artistic unity of the Jackie Kennedy story?

A. I do not underwrite everything that Mr. Bruce may have said; I'm just saying that what I have read does not offend me.

Q. Then you concede, as a critic and as an expert in criticism, that these words may be unnecessary to this story, that you personally cannot find a justification for them, although you personally do not object, is that what you are telling us?

A. I believe that if Mr. Bruce in his routine felt it was necessary, then it was necessary.

Q. Although you personally would not use them in your own vocabulary?

• • •

A. As a critic, I have only to tell what I think about an act, I don't have to justify every word in it.

> Judge Murtagh: But you are being asked now to justify it. In other words, to testify on the soundness of your meaning.

A. Well, I feel it is in Mr. Bruce's style, just as "Blues for Mister Charlie" is in James Baldwin's style, and "Tropic of Cancer" is in Henry Miller's style. He has the right to use the words he feels are fitting and pertinent and perhaps dramatic.

• • •

Q. Isn't one of the skills of a critic—of an expert, if you will, in the field of criticism—an ability to articulate for persons who cannot articulate?

A. Yes.

Q. Now, will you do your best, in light of your years of experience as a critic, to articulate to us what is the artistry in the Bruce performance that can be seen by anyone reading the cold script?

A. I think the artistry is his reflection of reality.[18]

After the trial, Bruce's attorney, Ephraim London, was to translate Miss Kilgallen's evaluation of Bruce into legalese. London was quoted in the press, while the case was *sub judice* (fully tried, but with its results undetermined, and still under judicial consideration), as asserting the "constitutional right of the artist to express himself in his own way. . . . An artist should be given complete freedom."[19] The London phrases were nice, but as long as censorship laws existed and were sustained, they would mean that once the label of "artist" had been pinned on, the "artist" would have an immunity far beyond that granted to the more earthbound. If artistry is to redeem, and the *Ulysses* case taught that it may, it must be artistry discernible and definable *in the very item under judicial scrutiny.*

Some of the defense "experts" conceded, with seeming understatement, that Bruce was *not* at his best in the monologues upon which the New York prosecution was based. This tack was taken by defense witnesses Richard Gilman, cartoonist-satirist Jules Feiffer, and publisher and leader in New York's "intellectual establishment" Jason Epstein, all Bruce long-term fans, friends, and manifesto-signers. Epstein, remarking that monologues might, and sometimes did, have literary value, acknowledged that those of Bruce were not thus blessed. In the opposing camp, experienced critics called by the prosecution, persons of the highest professional stature whose disinterestedness was underscored by their conscientious *opposition* to censorship laws, found Bruce's effusions "confused," "incoherent," and generally "incomprehensible." Witnesses so testifying included former theatrical critic and New York *Daily News* columnist ("Dream Street") Robert Sylvester, *Harper's* magazine editor-in-chief John Fischer (who, in an essay famous in the annals of American free speech, *The Harm Good People Do,* eight years earlier had attacked vigilante citizen action as a "shocking" form of "literary lynching"[20]), and Marya Mannes. After Fischer had so opined, this interchange, focusing on a particular segment of one of the monologues, took place on cross-examination:

Mr. London: Do you see in that statement an indication to white people, of the injustice of having white jurors judging a negro?

Mr. Fischer: That might be an implication in it, yes. You stated it much more clearly than the transcript does.[21]

In all, if Bruce's obscenities of word and of concept were to be redeemed, their redemption would not spring from the form or language into which they were woven. Did Bruce, then, regardless of absent artistry, provide such cogent social criticism as to redeem otherwise objectionable performances?

The weight to be given Bruce's social criticism had twice been considered by the highest court of the State of Illinois. That court did a somersault, with its final legal conclusion running counter to that of the New York trial bench.

In late 1962, Bruce had been arrested in Chicago on an obscenity charge; convicted, he had been fined $1,000 and sentenced to a year's imprisonment. In the Illinois high court this action was affirmed unanimously on the same date that same court affirmed a *Tropic of Cancer* conviction, June 18, 1965. "[W]e do not agree that *Roth* has eliminated the rule heretofore prevailing in this State of balancing the obscene aspects against the affirmative values," the Illinois justices had said as they affirmed Bruce's conviction.[22]

The United States Supreme Court's *Jacobellis* and *Tropic* decisions, however, led the Illinois bench to withdraw its own *Bruce* and *Tropic* opinions, and in November, 1964, the state court said:

While we would not have thought that constitutional guarantees necessitate the subjection of society to the gradual deterioration of its moral fabric which this type of presentation promotes, we must concede that some of the topics commented on by defendant are of social importance. Under *Jacobellis* the entire performance is thereby immunized, and we are constrained to hold that the judgment of the circuit court of Cook County must be reversed and defendant discharged.[23]

In writing this second opinion, the Illinois judges appeared to have been pricked into anger possibly by the overturning of their *Tropic* affirmance, and possibly by the rejection in the Supreme Court's prevailing *Jacobellis* opinion of their "balancing" test. For whatever reasons, in their second *Bruce* opinion, the Illinois court went far further than the *Jacobellis* case compelled. *First,* that Supreme Court case's language, focusing on the phrase "utterly without redeeming social importance," and stating that *any* value redeemed, was only found in the opinion of *two* of the Justices. (In March 1966, three Justices were to share this interpretation, another three expressly taking issue with it.) *Second,* even had a majority of the Justices expressly rejected the "balancing test," the word "importance," as has been noted, embraces some qualitative considerations: not every *mention* of a socially significant topic is, necessarily, a socially "important" comment. *Third,* even had much of Bruce's Illinois commentary been socially "important," *if* any of his objectionable passages were *completely* unrelated to such comments, nothing in the Brennan-Goldberg *Jacobellis* opinion barred a finding of obscenity.

Whether Bruce provided serious social commentary for his merry-making night-spot audiences, and whether, if so, his criticisms were of such "social importance" as to redeem him from charges of obscenity, proved the focus of expert testimony in the

New York trial. On this point, the conflict was substantial. The state's experts, besides Marya Mannes, John Fischer, and Robert Sylvester, were Dr. Ernest van den Haag (psychoanalyst, sociologist, and author), and the Reverend Dan Potter (Executive Director of the Protestant Council of New York City). Their evaluation of the Bruce shows as "incoherent," anticipating Bruce's own later comment that Ephraim London had deemed him "inarticulate," precluded for them any serious likelihood of his tendering social criticisms that audiences might find enlightening.

A long tradition exists of straining in order to claim social values for items that appear to lack them completely. Ralph Ginzburg, personally vastly experienced, has suggested that this reaching goes back at least two centuries. Discussing the legal troubles experienced by the author of *Fanny Hill,* Ginzburg noted that, charged with writing an "excessively sexual" book,

Cleland's reply was that he had written it as a work of crusading journalism to expose the degradation of the underworld of sexual vice in his day. If the brothels, bagnios and procuresses in Fanny Hill seemed unbelievably crude, argued Cleland, it was only because that's the way they were in real life.[24]

And more than half a century ago, in 1914, in one of the earliest New York cases to consider the question of obscene entertainments (under the forerunner of the statute involved in the *Bruce* case), a movie company sought to enjoin New York City's police commissioner from interfering with the showing of a picture called *The Inside of the White Slave Traffic.* The New York justice before whom the injunction application was argued refused to grant it. In his opinion, written the year before D. W. Griffith's *Birth of a Nation* was to make early motion picture history, the judge—in rejecting the claims of social values—noted:

The performance as conducted by the plaintiff in said theater is one consisting of moving picture films cast upon canvas by a moving picture machine and depicting what is alleged to be a play known as "The Inside of the White Slave Traffic," describing the working of prostitutes . . . . It is contended by the plaintiff, in affidavits furnished by distinterested individuals whose motives it is not within the province of this court to question, that the pictures contain a great moral lesson to fathers and mothers, calculated to impress upon their minds the urgent need of protecting their daughters from the influence of evil associations . . . .[25]

Similarly, defense witnesses heaped praises upon the Bruce shows. Many of the values they posted to Bruce's accounts seemed, however, to be more of their own contrivance than of that of their idol. For example Bruce had referred to the "tits" of the late Eleanor Roosevelt. Critic Gilman believed this significant in that it showed Mrs. Roosevelt as, to all, "the mother of us," an interpretation seeing her as someone *greater* than the rest of us. The Reverend Forrest Johnson, Bruce fan and pastor of a Bronx church, saw in it quite the opposite: to him, it was "an attack upon our making idols of anyone," it showed Mrs. Roosevelt as just another person, built—and equipped—as were all other women. One or two defense experts deemed the Bruce story of a man embracing a chicken to be an original commentary on American marital customs. Dorothy Kilgallen found social merit in it—somehow—as the Bible too dealt with sodomy. And so on. Defense witnesses in those obscenity cases in which "social importance" is likely to provide the only colorable defense, often require the most free-swinging imaginations in order to transmogrify the words they hear. When so equipped, like the citizenry in *The Emperor's New Clothes,* they see only garments of their own imaginings, not the nudity that is obvious to less artful thinkers.

A half dozen years ago, after *Lady Chatterley's Lover* had received American judicial clearance, Katherine Anne Porter wrote of those who had praised the book:

The critics who have been carried away by a generous desire to promote freedom of speech, and give a black eye to prudes and nannies overlook sometimes—and in a work of literature this should not be overlooked, at least not by men whose profession is to criticise literature—that purity, nobility of intention, and apostolic fervour are good in themselves at times, but at others they depend on content, and in this instance they are simply not enough. Whoever says they are, and tries to persuade the public to accept a book for what it is not, a work of good art, is making a grave mistake, if he means to go on writing criticism.[26]

Even assuming some social importance in the monologues, such assumption would not finally dispose of the charges against Bruce. The high Court had not mandated clearance for materials containing pornographic portions that, unlike the obscene references in Joyce's *Ulysses*, were not a vital part of the mosaic, contributing to the whole. One of New York State's most consistently anti-censorship judges, Stanley H. Fuld, had noted:

If any single item, considered as a whole, were pornographic, the circumstances that it was included *in a collection* otherwise without taint would not save it from criminal prosecution.[27]

The Bruce monologues were a loose sort of "collection." They consisted of a performer's "bits," each often without relevance to or bearing on the others, with sequence, substance, and word selection shifting from show to show. That some, or many, of the Bruce "bits" may have had some value would not have served to redeem such other *unconnected* items as may have been clearly obscene. Once again, examination of Bruce's witness, the late Dorothy Kilgallen, showed that there were no redeemingly important themes, no subtle schematic build-up, providing common strains that ran through all of the Bruce materials. Sex—indeed, abnormal sex—was all that bound the "bits" together; this, clearly, was "the dominant theme of the material taken as a whole." After some probing for social importance in Bruce's routine about a wife finding her husband in bed with a chicken, these questions-and-answers followed:

Mr. Kuh: You said something in your last answer about I "have taken it out of context." I'm asking you to tell me how it ties into the context at that point. What is the lead, what is the flow, from a story about the accident, and then this sodomy piece, if you will, the chicken-in-bed piece, and then some comment on Italians, Jews, and Anglo-Saxons. Will you tell me what the order, or symmetry, is of these three stories?

Miss Kilgallen: I think I can answer this, sir. He starts with the man who is amorous to the nurse, and then he goes on to give his opinion on the amorous proclivities of racial groups, and he does so, so they are connected.

Q. And that is the connection?

A. I think.

Q. And so the connection is a connection having to do with deviant sex, is that correct? I withdraw the word "deviant." The connection has to do with sex with a nurse while severely injured, with a foot just severed, with sex with various animals—

A. No.

Q. —sex possibly with the chicken, and the sex customs of Italians, Jews, and Anglo-Saxons, is that it?

A. Well, it's not quite in that order.

Q. You tell me what the thread is, other than sex, as purveyed in this particular portion of the transcript?

A. Definitely, there's sex in all of it.

Q. This particular portion, is there any thread other than sex, Miss Kilgallen, that is portrayed in this particular portion?

A. I will agree with you, that there is sex throughout.

Q. And is it sex of a type that, at least, has overtones of immorality, indecency, and possibly, possibly, perversion?

A. There's nothing perverted about making a pass at a nurse, there is nothing devious about that.

Q. I gave you several words: indecency, immorality, and possibly perversion. I think you would concede that sex with animals, at least some segments of our community might find perverted?

A. I think almost all would.

Q. And would you find it at least strange and abnormal that a man in an accident, just having had a foot cut off, immediately is making a pass in the ambulance at the nurse?

A. Well, I don't think I know that much about men.[28]

EXPERT WITNESSES

Intolerance of any form of censorship has created another of those paradoxes that strew the field of obscenity. Anti-censorship zeal seals the lips of numbers of academicians and critics, persons clear-eyed enough to recognize that many claims of artistry and social importance advanced on behalf of much that seems pornographic are unadulterated poppycock. Recognizing that all that festers is not gold is one thing; it is quite another—and one requiring courage—to walk the long steps to the witness stand in order to say so publicly under oath. Even one of Lenny Bruce's most ardent partisans, his friend and witness, Nat Hentoff, recognized this. Discussing the state's experts, Hentoff conceded (in an article appearing the day before Bruce was to be sentenced):

I grudgingly admitted to myself that it took some courage for them to declare themselves squares—or so they would be regarded by many of those in the intellectual community who were supporting Lenny.[29]

A sort of reverse McCarthyism has long been afoot in the censorship-obscenity arena, with the intellectuals doing the name-calling. Those with the courage to stand up and proclaim aloud their honest views that trash *is* trash are apt to end up being shunned or even castigated by those who most loudly proclaim their own "liberalism." Few critics are courageous enough to court this calumny.

And few seem to have such faith in democracy's methods as to wish to assist the courts with candid testimony. Critics who deem something valueless, but who refuse so to testify because of their convictions that censorship can *never* be proper, substitute their own ideas of what the law should be for what, in fact, it is (as determined by appropriate legislative and judicial action). As long as anti-obscenity statutes exist, and are sustained by the courts, judicial willingness to hear experts is based on the hope that what they say will help in truthfully evaluating the worth, if any, of the alleged obscenity. When, however, defense witnesses, obdurate against censorship, pluck values from the air in order to support their cause, and when others who might be objective refuse to testify for reasons of similar obduracy, or for fear of personal abuse, then the resulting testimony is likely to be so slanted as to be of little real value in the search for the truth.

Consider, for example, some few of those who refused to testify in the *Bruce* case. The Sunday after Lenny Bruce's New York trial had started, *The New York Times's* outspoken motion picture critic, Bosley Crowther, writing about a film then playing, said:

The critic must speak out boldly and let his anxieties fall where they may.

• • •

What is irresponsible about it [the motion picture then under discussion]—what is downright dangerous, indeed—is that it tends to become a sheer projection of sadism and violence for violence's sake.[30]

New York County's universally respected, eminently fair-minded, marathon district attorney, America's leading prosecutor, Frank S. Hogan, promptly telephoned critic Crowther: would he read the Bruce monologue transcripts and consider testifying in the Bruce trial? The transcript was sent off. Several days later, by letter, Mr. Crowther responded:

Although I find the material distasteful and disgusting in the extreme, I feel it would be inconsistent with my concepts of free speech to participate . . . . I deplore the fact that there are people who will listen to such stuff, but I don't feel it would help matters—or be consistent with our democratic principles—to lock up Mr. Bruce.

The district attorney's office had hoped for Mr. Crowther's testimony solely as a critic. (This was not, of course, a legislative hearing on the advisability or inadvisibility of anti-obscenity legislation.) In a telephone conversation the prosecutor's office

explained this, pointing out that, wise or unwise, legislation existed that banned obscene performances, and that every effort
would be made to see that he was not inhibited in expressing
his discontent with our existing laws. (As with several of the
State's witnesses, the harboring of strong feelings *against* censorship was actually helpful; it served as a barometer of the
witness's objectivity and candor.) Crowther, however, was firm
in his refusal.

Professor Lionel Trilling of Columbia University was one of
the Bruce manifesto's notable signers. The newspaper account
had indicated, however, that he had never attended a Bruce
performance. A phone call to Trilling, followed with a mailed
copy of the monologue, produced his reaction that it was "filthy,"
and "shocking." He stated further that possibly, in some fashion,
this shock value had added to its impact. He was invited to appear, but explained that his interest in freedom of speech would
prevent his giving his critical opinion.

Abel Green, editor of the hip show business weekly *Variety*,
some years earlier had commented concerning the then milder
Bruce show, "The ugliest of phrases applying to minorities are
interjected to no good purpose. . . . He is undisciplined and
unfunny."[31] In a telephone conversation in which he was asked
to consider appearing as a witness, Green replied that he
strongly preferred not to get involved.

And so on, down through a long list who found they were
too busy, who felt so strongly against censorship that they would
not testify in an anti-obscenity trial, or who simply wished to
be excused. Unlike eyewitnesses to a crime or others who can
testify to facts, expert witnesses, whose knowledge is not first
hand and who only give their opinions, cannot be subpoenaed to
appear against their will. With this in mind, courts—both trial
and appellate—must be wary of surrendering their own common sense judgments out of deference to experts' testimony.
If that testimony stands up well under cross-examination, it is
entitled to be credited. If, however, the thinking behind critical

judgments cannot be clearly articulated, if opinions remain unsustained by cogent logic, courts should not use witness nosecounts (no matter how eminent the faces behind the noses) in determining whether an item may be redeemed by some artistic or other social values. Yet even Supreme Court Justices have reflected homage for experts in numbers. In the *Fanny Hill* case, Justices as polarized as William O. Douglas (for reversal) and Tom C. Clark (for affirmance) commented on the paucity of prosecution witnesses, as contrasted with the plentitude of those for the defense. Said Douglas:

The prosecution made virtually no effort to prove that this book is "utterly without redeeming social importance." The defense, on the other hand, introduced considerable and impressive testimony to the effect that this was a work of literary, historical and social importance.

And Clark noted:

While unfortunately the state offered little testimony, the defense called several experts to attest that the book has literary merit and historical value. A careful reading of testimony, however, reveals that it has no substance.

EVIDENCE OF LIVE SHOWS

Live entertainments pose one further problem in the courtroom, a problem not without its moments in the *Bruce* case. How is a live performance to be duplicated so that, "taken as a whole," it can be inspected and judged? Quite apart from the Fifth Amendment (the privilege against self-incrimination) ban against compelling a defendant to perform in a courtroom, such re-creations would, inevitably, tend to exculpate, not to duplicate the original. When, as in the *Bruce* case, the performance is largely verbal, a hidden wire or tape recorder is one answer. But recordings are often unavailable. The public's jittery impression that "bugging" is child's play is a false one. Concealed recorders and transmitters, often employed under conditions inhospitable to their use, are at best a gamble, as the *Bruce* experience shows.

Initially, the D.A.'s office simply wanted to hear what Lenny Bruce was all about; to learn whether his performances seemed so obscene that the best available evidence of them ought to be collected for grand jury presentation. At that preliminary stage the use of recording equipment seemed premature. And so a city license department investigator, Herbert Ruhe, who had cultivated a phenomenally well-developed memory, was sent to attend. Cued by notes he made at his stageside table during the Bruce delivery, his own Bruce performance proved better-than-fair mimicry. On the basis of Ruhe's narrative, police equipped with a tiny concealed recording device were sent to a later Bruce show. The device caught most of it. The show of a week thereafter, the one to have resulted in Bruce's New York *re*-arrest, was later similarly audited. This time, however, something went awry, and only some electronic squawks were recorded.

Once again the prosecution was to be aided, this time materially, by the Bruce fondness for trying the case in the press.

The day following Bruce's second arrest, a local Greenwich Village weekly apeared on downtown New York City newsstands with a four-column spread detailing some hours spent by its reporter in Lenny Bruce's company. The story described their visit "to the Fifth Avenue apartment of a prominent civil libertarian, for whom *they play the tapes of the shows for which Bruce was arrested.*"[32] This was welcome news. (The attorney, not then named, proved to be one of America's most ardent, able advocates of free speech, the dynamic Morris Ernst. Ernst did not take the case, and according to the story, lectured Bruce "on the history of the good fight against censorship in this country and explained that Bruce's language stems from an anal fixation.") Happily, the Café Au Go Go, where Bruce had been arrested, was owned by a corporation. Although individuals may claim the protection of the Fifth Amendment, and refuse to produce self-incriminatory items, corporations may not, and although they may be-one man closely held businesses they may be compelled to produce documents that deeply implicate their sole owners and agents.[33] The prosecution subpoenaed the corporation to produce the tapes.

It quickly became apparent that Bruce the iconoclast's iconoclast, Bruce the martyr at hypocrisy's altar, Bruce the brave, was to present a far more pallid picture as Bruce the accused. Proclaiming publicly that the arrests were witch hunts and that the monologues were legally guiltless, indeed, that they were matchless satire, the defense went down the line battling against the prosecution's efforts to get the best possible versions of them before the trial court. Clearly, the defense was well within its rights in so doing. A defendant need never waive his right of putting the state to its burden of proving guilt. But the gulf seemed broad between Bruce's courtroom trepidation and the public intrepidity his friends sought to counterfeit for him.

Almost forty years earlier, Boston's blue-nosed Watch and Ward Society, the Bostonians who were to make "banned in Boston" a prime sales slogan, had pressured newsdealers to remove an issue of *The American Mercury* from their stands. (The issue had carried the tale of a small-town prostitute who plied her trade in the town's cemetery, and then, each Sunday, sought forgiveness in church.) The magazine's editor, Baltimore's sage, H. L. Mencken, combined a well-known flair for publicity with genuine moral courage. Mencken rushed to Boston. There, on the historic Boston Common, he personally sold a copy of the magazine to the Watch and Ward's agent. Promptly arrested, with equal alacrity he was aquitted.[34] In the *Bruce* case, although the defense's publicity flair was evident throughout, little of the Mencken bravery could be sighted.

Resisting the subpoena, the Café Au Go Go Corporation failed to produce the tapes, and counsel for both Solomon and Bruce argued that to compel their production would be to compel the individual defendants to incriminate themselves. After a long day of some argument, much bickering, and the necessary testimony, criminal court Judge Frederick L. Strong ruled that the corporation:

> . . . owned and controlled the tape recordings . . . . They were made on corporate premises, by an employee on the corporate payroll, under the supervision of a corporate officer, on equipment used in the corporate business, with tapes . . . kept in the custody of a corporate officer. Recordings on tapes were made . . . of the entire shows presented to a paying audience by the corporate owner of the Café. The tapes represented an asset of the corporation of potential value either for commercial reproduction or as defensive material in a possible civil, criminal or administrative proceeding . . . . The Court finds, specifically, a failure to establish ownership and control of the tapes in Mr. Howard Solomon . . . or in Mr. Lenny Bruce . . . . In this connection, it is immaterial that the tape recordings may have been made at the suggestion or request of Mr. Bruce in the absence of any persuasive evidence that they were to be or become his personal property.[35]

The judge ordered the tapes turned over to the prosecution.

"Sitting in on Lenny Bruce's current New York 'obscenity' trial," reporter Stephanie Gervis Harrington commented, "one gets the feeling of being present at an historical event—the birth of the courtroom of the absurd."[36] The spectacle of three judges and five attorneys, deeply involved day after day, trying to unravel the intricacies of what was and what was not unlawfully obscene in an area, verbal live shows, that had previously been little litigated—and knowing that their conclusions would be tentative at best, depending for survival upon the vicissitudes of time and appellate manpower—was part of the absurdity. Part was the testimony of decent, honorable, critics and clergymen, passionate believers in freedom, learnedly finding values (whether or not such values might, with study, be discernible) in a rapidly intoned oral patter—values that even the most quick-minded audience could not possibly have gleaned on the instant, before the monologuist was deeply into the next "bit"—the witnesses engaging in this dubiously ingenuine charade largely because of their deep convictions that speech must remain wholly free. Part was that Bruce's principal lure—assuming momentarily that his monologues *were* prurient—was neither for dirty old men nor for hunters of erotic fantasies and scatalogical kicks; an appreciable portion of the clamor for Bruce was from young adults (men *and* women), and the no-longer-so-young intellectuals, the sensitive (some genuinely, some of the follow-the-leader variety), and the dissatisfied. For them, Bruce, and the sex and scatology of his monologues, crystallized rebellion. In four-letter words and in brutally obscene word pictures, the very shock of these "entertainments" screamed out with the old, and in with the new. "Community standards have to be changed," testified a defense witness. "Lenny Bruce is in the process of helping that change."[37] And so the straining after prurience of some in Bruce's audiences was likely to be completely non-pruriently intended. Their end was not drooling sensuality, but the discovery of new and stronger means for expressing their utter freedom from traditional restraints, and for identifying with others similarly shackled with compulsions toward unshacklement. Familiarity with and empathy for Lenny Bruce supplied a common bond. They were "safe-conducts" of sorts for those who wished to be counted as part of the "in" group. The cruder and more shocking the pornography, the greater the scorn it expressed for the established. Lenny Bruce provided not only bone-searing talk, but fanfare and a rallying point. Pornography had become a phase of pop culture; it was pop culture gone putrescent.

PART IV

Proposed Action—
Why and How

17. The Easy Course—Anything Goes!

I'd have joined a Trappist order rather than take more. All those ghastly novels—sex is an obsession with the Americans.
—Malcolm Muggeridge, quoted in *Time*, April 16, 1965

SOME GLIMPSE has been given of the uncertainties that hedge obscenity in the courts, the wasted though prodigious efforts of police, prosecutors, and judges, and the developing permissiveness of the highest tribunals.

And some glimpse it is!

All the busy confusion of a Mack Sennett comedy is there, with black-robed judges—Keystone Cop-fashion—dashing off simultaneously in all directions. When ruling on obscenity, state and federal appellate benches do not split, they splinter. Trial judges' rulings, and the reasoning they express, provide no inkling as to what may happen on appeal. Indeed, justices of like rank vitiate each other's decisions before the divided higher courts successively reinstate and vacate them in a now-you-see it, now-you-don't unmagical performance. Traditional criminal law requirements of certainty in legislative enactments are invoked when convenient and, at other times, are rejected as without application. In toto, applying the law to specific questioned materials has been a labor as frustratingly impossible as is nailing custard pies to trees.

Yet the anti-pornography statutes do exist, and the challenges to them continue to appear in print, photograph, sketch, film, phonograph record, and live performance. A question is inevitable: would the community do well to try to ignore the whole amorphous business of obscenity, to turn its collective back on the pornographers, rather than continue to battle their never ending effusions?

Perhaps.

The idea of banishing all censorship, of removing that dubious task from officialdom's duties, has great appeal, not only for civil libertarians, but for law enforcers. "Censor" is a dirty word, one that adds to the other onerous burdens that police and prosecutors shoulder in these days when their public image is rarely the best. Ending all censorship has been touted as an indirect method, a psychologically sophisticated one, of curtailing the obscene. Repression, it is suggested, only makes the pornographic profitable and colors the obscene with the allure of the forbidden. Once the prohibitions go, obscenity, it is suggested, will taper off. Clearly, legal bans have advertising value, once they have evaporated. *Lady Chatterley's Lover* is Lawrence's best-known but certainly not his best work. "Banned in Boston" became a selling slogan long years ago. The film, *The Lovers,* litigated in the *Jacobellis* case, thereafter used its own prior troubles as the theme of its advertising campaign. "By order of the United States Supreme Court," heralded a large come-on for the post-*Jacobellis* New York premiere of the uncensored picture, "on June 22, 1964, the U.S. Supreme Court ruled the prize-winning film 'The Lovers' is *not obscene!*" The ad stressed that the version being exhibited was "original and uncut."[1] When, in March 1965, the nation's highest Court narrowly restricted film licensing,[2] a dull melodrama that had brought the issue to a head in New York State, *A Stranger Knocks,* scored substantial box office success with nearly full-page newspaper space invoking the same simple formula: "By action of the U.S. Supreme

Court—now you can see 'A Stranger Knocks' uncut and uncensored!"[3]

Disputes with the censors can mushroom profits, once the risks, expenses, and uncertainties of litigation have been amortized. But it is specious to urge seriously that censorship *benefits* the obscenity trade. Today's flood of dubious literature, in the wake of *Lady Chatterley* and *Tropic of Cancer*, shows the folly of arguing that increased permissiveness *reduces* the production of borderline and over-the-border materials. Moreover, the idea that ignoring something will curtail it more effectively than would its outlawry runs contrary to the basic approach of criminal law; were it sound, all of the law's "Thou shalt nots" would now be out of date. It is also at odds with the full stream of American experience. Nevada, our one state in which gambling is legal, has more gambling, more gamblers, and more hangers-on matched against state population than the rest of the nation. New York City, with sanctions on prostitution that, at least until recently were enforced, had less prostitution proportionately than cities that tolerate and profit from it. Maurice Girodias of Olympia Press did a brisk business as a publisher of borderline pornography in Paris as long as that city was safer than America. Now he has announced his intention of heading for New York. Although there may be sound reasons for ending all bans on the obscene, the suggestion that unimpeded freedom will *minimize* both the public's interest in the obscene and the profiteer's circulation of it is hardly one of them.

In addition to the so far unsurmounted difficulties and frustrations involved in banning or regulating obscenity, there are two principal lines of contentions ranged against all anti-pornography legislation. One is that no matter how carefully circumscribed it may be, it will encroach upon the constitutional prohibition against any law "abridging the freedom of speech, or of the press." The other is that our American community today is so steeped in generally approved eroticism that stamping out those proportionately few items that are completely lacking in social importance can accomplish nothing significant, and is thus considered realistically, an exercise in futility.

Neither of these contentions can be hastily written off.

THE CONSTITUTIONAL ARGUMENT

The constitutional argument is most often made. The express wording of the First Amendment, that provides that "Congress shall make no law . . . abridging the freedom of speech, or of the press," according to its arch-advocates means just that. It means *"no law,"* not "no law, *except for anti-obscenity legislation."* And, they urge, the "due process" clause of the Fourteenth Amendment, that constitutional catch-all that provides that no state shall "deprive any person of life, liberty, or property, without due process of law," encompasses these First Amendment prohibitions, enjoining the *states* from any interference with freedom of expression in the same manner as the First Amendment enjoins *federal* meddling.

This argument has a simple directness, a surface appeal, unmatched by any of the other contentions that are ranged against state and federal anti-pornography statutes. The absolutist position gains fervor from reactions its rallying cries engender. "Constitution," "Bill of Rights," and "Free Speech" are all *good* words, words that create a Spirit of '76 feeling. Words such as "Censorship" and "Bluenose" are quite the opposite; they afford appropriate targets for hissing and hooting. Justice Oliver Wendell Holmes and his talismanic phrase, "clear and present danger"— in the absence of which no incursion upon the First Amendment's guarantees is to be permitted—although initially advanced as a limitation on anti-sedition enforcement not on the anti-obscenity laws, provides both a saint and a rallying cry.

The constitutional attack upon any and all censorship is in fact extremely practical. Drawing meaningful lines in the obscenity area, recent history proves, has seemed impossible. By barring *any* censorship, by enjoining *any* anti-obscenity enforcement, these difficulties are instantaneously eliminated. James Reston, discussing (in another context) American fondness for oversimplification, has noted,

> The more complicated life becomes, the more people are attracted by simple solutions; the more irrational the world seems, the more they long for rational answers; and the more diverse everything is, the more they want it all reduced to identity.[4]

Ending all censorship is simple, apparently rational, and—by hypothesis—produces a uniformity of non-interference that would apply alike to the seemingly obscene in James Joyce, Ralph Ginzburg, stag movies, sado-masochistic books, and Lenny Bruce.

There are, however, serious troubles connected with this absolutist position.

Of course, the Supreme Court ever since its *Roth* holding has consistently rejected the idea that obscenity is constitutionally protected free speech. Was this evasion by the Court, meant to preserve censorship, which was clearly repugnant to it? Not at all. Little of the Constitution's seemingly unequivocal language is so unequivocally applied. The Second Amendment, for instance, says in black and white, that "the right of the people to keep and bear Arms shall not be infringed." Yet both the federal government and many of the states have long had legislation subjecting the sale and shipment, and even the possession, of pistols and revolvers to some regulation. (Since the assassination of President Kennedy, pressures have mushroomed for still further congressional and state firearm restrictions. Some of those same civil libertarians who insist that the First Amendment must be deemed an absolute have joined with law enforcement in pressing for such tighter restrictions.) Equally unequivocally, the Fifth Amendment specifies "nor shall any person be subject for the same offence to be twice put in jeopardy of life or limb." Yet, in America, a defendant can be tried again, and again, and again, even in a capital case, if prior convictions have been vacated by the appellate courts. But in England, where no written constitution proclaims any double jeopardy ban, such retrials are taboo; they violate traditional concepts of double jeopardy! Even those who press hardest for broadly interpreting the First Amendment's free speech guaranty concede that it must yield when a "clear and present danger" of some substantive evil is present. Justice Holmes, in articulating the "clear and present danger" test, observed:

The most stringent protection of free speech would not protect a man in falsely shouting fire in a theater and causing a panic.[5]

In determining the scope of constitutional proscriptions, it is often necessary to search behind the words that seem to define them, to see them in their historical setting, and to discover just what it is that they were directed at. Their wording alone rarely precludes this more meaningful inspection. The judicial Olympian who contributed the phrase "clear and present danger" to our free speech vocabulary had earlier cautioned, "It is one of the misfortunes of the law that ideas become encysted in phrases and thereafter for a long time cease to provoke further analysis."[6] The need to plumb phrases in fixing the law's proper scope has long been stressed by legal scholars. Some three centuries before Holmes, Sir Edward Coke appears to have coined an aphorism mouthed today by legal Latin learning law students, "*Cessante ratione legis, cessat et ipsa lex.*" ("The reason for the law ceasing, the law itself also ceases.") What, then, is the *reason* for the constitutional ban on any abridgment of free speech and press?

The free speech and press amendment was *not* designed to express any colonial antipathy toward obscenity statutes. By 1792, when the Bill of Rights had been ratified by fourteen states, as the *Roth* opinion notes,[7] all of them had statutes against blasphemy or profanity. At least one, which was long to lead in the battle against the obscene, the Commonwealth of

Massachusetts, had a then already venerable law declaring it criminal to publish "any filthy, obscene, or profane song, pamphlet, libel or mock sermon." The First Amendment's prohibitions were intended to serve a different purpose. In mind was that freedom of speech and of press needful to protect freedom of political and religious beliefs, not to shield obscenity, or even sexual discussion. The wounds inflicted by royal rule in the colonies had not yet healed. The charges of seditious libel against John Peter Zenger, courageous colonial editor and publisher, arising from his criticisms of Britain's governor and government of New York, were not yet out of mind.[8] The speech and press guarantees were, as *Roth* noted, to protect the free espousal of ideas, "unorthodox ideas, controversial ideas, even ideas hateful to the prevailing climate of opinion."

But recognizing that freedom to express ideas *is* protected by the Constitution, and that obscenity *is not* really determines very little. No ready touchstone exists with which to tell when something is obscene, on the one hand, and when, on the other, it is frankly espousing a possibly unconventional idea about sex. Things that will appear to some persons obscene will be viewed by others as lively embodiments of argument: perhaps an argument for broader tolerance toward deviancy, or for less guilt about sex generally, or for greater, if less conventional, sexual enjoyment, for diminishing personal inhibitions, or for destroying society's taboos. An example may help to drive this home. Two years after *Roth,* in ruling that New York State had improperly denied licensing to a motion picture that had been made of *Lady Chatterley's Lover,* the high Court—*in one of six separate opinions*—commented:

What New York has done, therefore, is to prevent the exhibition of a motion picture because that picture advocates an idea—that adultery under certain circumstances may be proper behavior. Yet the First Amendment's basic guarantee is of freedom to advocate ideas. The State, quite simply, has thus struck at the very heart of constitutionally protected liberty.[9]

The movie, *Lady Chatterley's Lover,* was mild. It merely *suggested* adultery. Today, ideas that were hardly whispered a decade ago—abortion, homosexuality, promiscuity, and a whole range of perversions—are discussed in the parlor by strangers who enter and talk to us via the television screen. What, then, about the book or the movie that takes these reasonably frank television debates a further step forward, going so far as to describe carefully or to picture sexual, or even sadistic, masochistic homosexual, or lesbian acts? In debate such explicitness may be the most effective form of advocacy. *Fanny Hill* may be viewed as an eloquent tract, pressing upon its readers the idea of uninhibited, rollicking, sexual enjoyment; indeed, it is a guidebook crammed full of goodies about it. In reverse, the stark ugly death-and-deviation images of an addict in *Naked Lunch* may, by dramatizing addiction's evils, serve to scare readers away from drug experimentation.

If the Constitution is read as a document safeguarding the right to present *any* idea by using *any* aggregate of words, descriptions, or pictures, regardless of how abhorrent that aggregate may be, if the presentation of any idea thus confers redeeming social importance on the seemingly obscene, the Constitution would then be read as providing that *the end,* complete freedom in the advocacy of ideas, *justifies the means,* the advocate's invocation of even the most squalid and disgusting imagery. On its face, when so phrased, this reading of the Constitution seems preposterous. Morality generally rejects the notion that a proper end can justify immoral or improper means.

This result is not unavoidable. Rejection by the high Court of the proposition that the end justifies the means would require no change in its position. Only Justices Potter Stewart, William J. Brennan, and Chief Justice Earl Warren indirectly *implied* that it did, in their opinion concerning the licensing of the movie *Lady Chatterley's Lover.* Moreover, the court below had found that the movie was not obscene, and so the Stewart opinion did not mean that *obscenity* could be called upon to do battle for ideas. Five years later, in *Jacobellis,* Justice Brennan (this time in an opinion in which former Justice Arthur J. Goldberg joined) again suggested that the manner of expression remained invulnerable as long as ideas were communicated:

It follows that material dealing with sex in a manner that advocates ideas . . . may not be branded as obscenity and denied the constitutional protection.[10]

But this was only the view of two Justices, one of whom is no longer on the Bench, and the other had joined with two colleagues five years earlier to say the same thing. Without rejecting any of its own precedents the Court may still rule that although freedom to advocate unpopular views may be untrammeled, it is *only the unpopular ideas and the right to espouse them* that are shielded; no license exists to utilize pornography as the means of their expression. Conversely phrased, the Court may still hold that the mere presentation of an idea is not in itself necessarily a purgative for otherwise rancid and obscene language or imagery used in its presentation.

Declaring that ideas do, or that they do not, immunize the most depraved of the pornographic should be recognized for what it is, *not* something inherent in the free speech-free press clause, but only a conclusion reflecting the particular preferences and prejudices of the person so declaring. The "anything goes" philosophy has much to recommend it, and much running against it. But, clearly, the Constitution itself does not *require* its acceptance.

THE ARGUMENT THAT ANTI-OBSCENITY ENFORCEMENT IN TODAY'S SOCIETY IS AN EXERCISE IN FUTILITY

Writing in *Esquire* early in 1965, Britain's Malcolm Muggeridge, answering his own question, "What has happened to sex?" had this to say:

The simple answer is that sex has been overplayed. It has become an obsession, a mania, a sickness . . . . In America particularly, but to a greater or lesser extent throughout the Western World, we have all got sex on the brain, which, apart from any other considerations, is a most unseemly and unsatisfactory place to have it. Every poster yells it at us, every popular song is about it, every dance enacts it. Motion pictures and the television drench us with it, novels make it their interminable theme. It permeates every corner and cranny of life, from birth to the grave. Dating begins at nine years old, and even earlier; tiny tots who ought to be reading about Peter Rabbit and the Seven Dwarfs wear padded bras, paint their faces, and howl like randy hyenas at Bobby Kennedy and the Beatles. Young lovers arm themselves with birth pills and the *Kama Sutra,* and engage in erotic exercises which might have seemed excessive in the pages of *Les Liaisons Dangereuses;* middle-aged couples swap partners, bone up on soixante-neuf, and fill quiet suburban nights with love cries that Cleopatra or Madame de Pompadour would have found memorable. Oldsters, male and female, with dentures gleaming, look lecherously round; doze in their bath chairs over *Candy* and *The Tropic of Cancer,* and with gibbering eagerness inform themselves on the sex practises of the young. Even the dead are curled and pomaded and scented for a tumble in the grave should any such possibility arise . . . . The bodies we resume on the Last Day will be in good shape, thanks to Elizabeth Arden and Helena Rubenstein; the trumpet will sound in the manner of some beatific Satchmo, and we shall twist and belly-dance our way into eternity.[11]

Obscenity and sex, happily, are not synonymous. Obscenity's design, largely, is to stimulate desire, or sometimes to exalt, impersonalize, mock, degrade, or negate sex. But the relentless sea of sex that engulfs us serves the same ends. The sexual stimulants, reminders, and energies that Muggeridge has bewailed, mostly non-obscene by present legal standards and constantly proliferating, do far more to set today's moral tone than do the concededly or arguably obscene. Obscenity (borderline and hard-core), massive as is the multi-million dollar commerce it enjoys, pales in proportions when viewed against a backdrop of this legally non-pornographic, impersonal, sexual diet. Muggeridge's listing is only a part of the snowballing sex in which we are steeped. American humorous essayist, William Iverson, contributor to *Playboy* magazine (itself—through its monthly issues, its "bunny" clubs, Caribbean playground, and gamut of bachelor-oriented enterprises—a reflection of depersonalized sex), has chronicled the women's magazines, the homemaking journals, as lively sources of sexually stimulating items.[12] Playing "doctor," as well as marriage counselor, sexologist, and all-knowing big sister, these periodicals feature jottings detailing sex techniques and frequency, extramarital attractions and affairs, venereal disease, male and female physiological disorders, abortion, menstruation, breast-feeding and nipple care, and the timing of orgasms. Although pitched primarily at housewifely leisure, the women's magazines cater as well to the interests and curiosities of adolescent daughters.

Nor are the men and the boys slighted in today's "pop" literature. The parent or youngster who shares in the general zest for Mickey Spillane novels or the James Bond mania finds himself not only on the side of the good guys, steeped in adventure, international intrigue, and crime, but knee-deep in sado-masochistic sex fantasies, involving steely-eyed women who kill determinedly, and just as instinctively head for the nearest couch or hayloft, with softer looks, but with equal composure—and precisely the same initiative.

And if we get away from this world of everyman, and plunge into either the designedly grubby beat society, or into our well-scrubbed best society, sexual preoccupation seems the way of life. A so-called *Festival of the Arts Today,* produced in early 1965 in Buffalo, New York (a town not renowned for its national news since McKinley's assassination there, and never remotely a pacesetter in either arts or fashion), featured a male-female dance team, locked in close face-to-face embrace, wearing naught but a glistening coat of mineral oil. When the same duo repeated the program some three weeks later in the sanctuary of a swinging New York Greenwich Village church, *The New*

York Times reporter was to note that "groans of disappointment were heard from the audience, at least some of whom had come hoping for an adagio or a pirouette that would have taken more advantage of the situation.[13] At a 1966 "happening" in Milwaukee, Wisconsin, a surprised audience walked in on a poised man and girl—imports from the Madison student body—skinnydipping in beer coolers. Whether or not the beer brand had theretofore made Milwaukee famous, it was in "poor taste" conceded the Milwaukee Art Center director.[14] Couturier Rudi Gernreich livened up the summer of 1964 for the private pool set, and even at a few public beaches (until the constabulary intruded), with topless bathing suits, shortly followed by the monokini. Topless dresses too appeared, mostly at private parties, both in America and, according to reports from the mother country, in England. California, home of the Townsend plan, Forest Lawn, and Disneyland, early in 1965 saw the emergence of barebosomed waitresses at dozens of its bars and restaurants; court tests found judges holding the new non-costumes not to be violative of community standards.[15] And a San Francisco judge found "nothing lewd" in the entertainment tendered by a toplessbottomless girl rocking in a velvet swing for a cabaret crowd's enjoyment.[16]

Muggeridge's plethora of sex, *Playboy*, women's journals, Agent 007, accounts of nude dancing and "happenings," topless bathing suits and evening gowns and underdressed cocktail waitresses—we are surrounded by a cornucopia of half-formed daydreams. Our sexual codes are hopscotching through change. Victorian morality has disappeared in much of society; the vestiges that remain are being heavily cannonaded. These changes, the sex around us, are *not* there by courtesy of the United States Supreme Court. The brickbats or the laurels for human conduct today, be it deemed libertine or libertarian, must go to a complex of factors, only one tiny element of which is the present Court-dictated dearth of significant censorship. As censorship, beset by vast uncertainties, currently requires mountains of energies to accomplish molehills with our mores, why not accede to that reading of the Constitution that would bar it completely, thus declaring that as far as the law is concerned "anything goes"?

The idea has appeal. But there are countervailing considerations.

Lawmaking is *not* a process that exists solely for results that can be ticked off on our fingers. Law serves as an expression of morality, of social approval or disapproval, in our communities. Whether or not it succeeds in deterring, it declaims against specified conduct; it spells out what the community deems undesirable. In charging the jury in the British trial involving the book, *Lady Chatterley's Lover*, the trial justice, quoting one of Britain's most highly revered twentieth century judges, Sir Patrick Devlin, pointed out:

. . . just as loyalty is one of the things which is essential to the well-being of a nation, so some sense of morality is something that is essential to the well-being of a nation, and to the healthy life of the community; and, accordingly, anyone who seeks, by his writing to corrupt that fundamental sense of morality is quilty of obscene libel.[17]

Thurman Arnold, who as a federal appellate judge had written an oft-cited and amusing opinion reversing the Post Office's denial of second-class mailing privileges to *Esquire* magazine,[18] as a *defense* attorney (after returning to private practice) was to concede the propriety of obscenity legislation:

It is in its essence a moral declaration on the part of the legislature, a recognition of a taboo which is as old as history. Such laws are passed because most men are stimulated by erotica and at the same time they are ashamed of it. Society requires a public denunciation of this almost universal sin whether or not it leads to positive harmful conduct . . . . The fact that laws against obscenity do not have a rational or scientific basis, but rather symbolize a moral taboo, does not make them any the less necessary. They are important because men feel that without them the state would be lacking in moral standards.[19]

This application of censorship to sexual behavior is not peculiarly Anglo-American. "Every known human society," anthropologist Margaret Mead has noted, "exercises some explicit censorship over behavior relating to the human body, especially as that behavior involves or may involve sex."[20]

We court error if we cavalierly conclude that laws against the obscene are without impact. The differences in our book lists of today from those of a decade or so ago surely are, *in part,* a reflection of the judicially made changes in our laws against obscenity. New York City's short-range experience with its injunctive campaign against the most offensive girlie magazines, and the *temporary* changes that the campaign worked in newsstand displays throughout the city, proved that intensive enforcement is immediate and significant in its impact on the availability of obscene and borderline materials. Conceding that the removal of this pulp does not magically transmute a Peyton Place into an Elysium, at least—visibly—there is a transformation: the *moral tone* of the community *appears* to be improved.

Finally, although the vagueness of our laws renders enforcement uncertain, and excessively energy-consuming when weighed against meager results, common sense does not compel the abandonment of all pornography legislation. We are not forced to throw out the baby with the bath water. There is no need for complete surrender, for the substitution in the place of poor laws of no laws at all. Our search should be, rather, for *increased specificity* in our statutes. By now it is all too obvious that the use of abundant although imprecise synonyms yields no clarity. No osmotic process infuses each word or phrase with precise meaning drawn either from its cluster of neighbors or from the judicial pinnacle from whence it emanates. Suppose, for a moment, that robbery were to be described in the fashion our legislators and our judges use to define crimes of obscenity. Then, rather than defining it as "the unlawful taking of personal property, from the person or in the presence of another, against his will, by means of force, or violence, or fear of injury,"[21] robbery, we might be told, would be the "committing of a vicious, cruel, wicked, iniquitious, or harsh act, selfishly, arrogantly, or inconsiderately, against the person of another." Who would then know just what actions the statute would make criminal? In this as in most areas of crime, thanks to present precise formulations, police and prosecutors, who may or may not have trouble proving who did the deed, can routinely be reasonably certain whether or not a crime has been committed. When obscenity is the charge, proving who did what, generally, is easy; the real riddle, one not solved by stringing out adjectives and phrases and one that makes this area of the law so maddeningly frustrating, is: "But is it criminal?"

Reasonably precise statutes would vitiate the contention that bans on the obscene are necessarily too vague to be sustained. Simultaneously the reliance upon personal judgment that is at the nub of the resentment toward censorship, the idea that many of us may be barred access to items because of some censor's *personal* distastes, would evaporate. Even publishers, those with a professional stake in the battle for untrammeled freedom of expression, would be far better off than they are at present. "When you publish books here," said Barney Rossett, president of Grove Press, "it's like playing roulette. You don't know. You publish a book and a few years later you're told you've done something wrong."[22] Although knowledge of Grove's many lucrative and litigated ventures in the shadow-world of erotica stanch sympathetic tears, it is obvious that the same vagaries that plague courts, prosecutors, and police are likely to run up appreciable legal fees for publishers. And the prospect of these expenses may restrain ventures that might never, had they been launched, run afoul of the obscenity laws. Uncertainty itself thus works a kind of prior restraint, a highly sinister form of censorship.

This discussion, so far, has been largely in the abstract. While suggesting that carefully drawn statutes may save anti-pornography enforcement, it has not come down to cases. Just what might such statutes say? Indeed, is such precision likely to be possible when free speech and free press are in the balance? How can statutes draw lines between one nude and another, between one use of the most repulsive vulgarity and another?

To a large extent, statutes cannot. But such line drawing is not the only possible approach to obscenity. Statutes might focus upon the audiences for whom the alleged contraband is intended.

The sale of obscenity to minors is an area of greatest community concern, and it is one that can be most readily isolated. But there are others. If narrow proposals dealing separately with each are to be weighed by our legislative bodies, the need for legislation as to each will have to be established. Our communities, acting through their legislatures, should have to examine the demands, the dangers, with which each such proposal might cope. In the chapters that follow, several areas for such special legislation are considered, along with the ends that may be served by such new laws, and suggestions are tendered for effectively framing each such statute. The tack taken here is one for which the Supreme Court has foreshadowed approval. In May 1967, in reversing New York, Kentucky, and Arkansas findings that certain paperbacks and magazines were obscene, and in doing so with no weighing—in the opinion—of those aspects of the publications that had led to the state court conclusions that they were pornographic, the high Tribunal noted:

> In none of the cases was there a claim that the statute in question reflected a specific and limited state concern for juveniles . . . . In none was there any suggestion of an assault upon individual privacy by publication in a manner so obtrusive as to make it impossible for an unwilling individual to avoid exposure to it . . . . And in none was there evidence of the sort of "pandering" which the Court found significant in *Ginzburg* v. *United States*.[23]

As will be obvious, the suggestions that follow will not wrap a neat blue ribbon around the unmanageable chore of reconciling freedom and censorship. But they should provide a workable compromise. As such compromise, they are unlikely to satisfy either of the loudly articulate extremist groups whose contributions to the obscenity muddle have been unrelenting: those who insist the First Amendment must be read in absolutist terms, and those who would roll the clock back, at least to pre-*Lady Chatterley* days. But, if they are adopted, they will provide reasonably fixed standards that different police, and different prosecutors, and different judges (assuming that the courts find these new proposals to be constitutional)—and different publishers, wholesalers, and dealers—can, for a refreshing change, all be expected to interpret similarly. Worlds of waste motion should thereby be rooted out of the obscenity-censorship controversy. Applying the obscenity laws will become almost as clear-cut as applying the laws against robbery, or rape, or assault. While achieving a large measure of certainty, these proposals will not eliminate, but should minimize, those hazards to our society that rampant obscenity appears to pose, and should do so without denying the adult public access to materials recommended by literary, artistic, historical, scientific, or other social merit.

What more can obscenity laws be expected to do?

18. Sales to the Young—the Crime Danger

Some 50 million pieces of obscene advertising annually mailed mainly to our teenagers, and a $500 million a year pornographic business in this country certainly contribute a tangible share to the growth of juvenile delinquency, to the too early and too erratic sexual life of the "wild" portion of our youth, and to the cult of cynicism, vandalism, and sterile rebellion of our beatniks.

—Pitirim A. Sorokin, "Demoralization of Youth: Open Germs and Hidden Viruses," *Christianity Today,* p. 3 (July 6, 1959)

THE NEED FOR SPECIAL SAFEGUARDS for the protection of the young and misgivings concerning much of the literature contemporaneously available to them seem almost as ancient as is our Western culture. In *The Republic,* Plato reported this dialogue between Socrates and Adeimantus:

You know . . . that the beginning is the most important part of any work, especially in the case of a young and tender thing; for that is the time at which the character is being formed and the desired impression is more readily taken.

Quite true.

And shall we just carelessly allow our children to hear any casual tales which may be devised by casual persons, and to receive into their minds ideas for the most part the very opposite of those which we should wish them to have when they are grown up?

We cannot.

Then the first thing will be to establish a censorship of the writers of fiction, and let the censors receive any tale of fiction which is good, and reject the bad; and we will desire mothers and nurses to tell their children the authorised ones only. Let them fashion the mind with such tales, even more fondly than they mould the body with their hands; but most of those which are now in use must be discarded.[1] Socrates, Plato tells us, would have "discarded" the poetry of Homer and of Hesiod, not for any sexually obscene content, but because the great poets told false stories concerning the gods, stories that would set poor examples for children. Ultimately, Socrates himself, having given his blessing to such censorship, was forced to drink the fatal cup of hemlock—when charged with corrupting the youth of Athens.

Plato's pupil, Aristotle, urged that special care be taken in protecting the immature from talk, and books, and pictures, for reasons more closely akin to those that worry today's adults:

> In general the legislator ought to banish from the state, as he would any other evil, all unseemly talk; the indecent remark lightly dropped results in conduct of a like kind. Especially therefore it must be kept away from youth; let them not hear or see anything of that kind. . . . And since we exclude all unseemly talk, we must also forbid looking at pictures or literature of the same kind. Let it therefore be a duty of the rulers to see that there shall be nothing at all, statue or painting, that is a representation of unseemly actions . . . . But it should be laid down that younger persons shall not be spectators at comedies or recitals of scurrilous iambics, not, that is to say, until they have reached the age at which they become entitled to recline at banquets, and share in the drinking; by this time their upbringing will have rendered them immune to any harm that might come from such spectacles.[2]

Now, almost twenty-four centuries later, should we continue such efforts at protecting the young against pornography? Adults, generally, hold to the belief that we should, although there is some dissent from the most ardent of the civil libertarians. The reason most strongly and frequently urged for such protection— whether or not it is the most compelling reason—is that the rising tide of pornography accounts, at least in part, for the increasing flood of youthful crime.

This book's opening pages, in commenting on the colliding contentions that have contributed to today's obscenity uncertainties, quoted statements made by a cluster of distinguished persons, including J. Edgar Hoover, Dr. Nicholas G. Frignito, and Norman Thomas; they stood united in their conviction that obscene materials in the hands of the young caused crime. Their observations articulate the experience of tens of thousands of police veterans, long-term prosecutors, judges in criminal cases, court psychiatrists, and other experienced and interested persons who over the years have had massive contact with crime and delinquency. Further support for this point of view comes from hearings held and reports issued from time to time by legislative committees on both state and federal levels.[3] All such observations are not lightly to be brushed aside, although in determining the weight they merit it is appropriate to consider the bias of their authors. Long-term law-enforcement officials when viewing our changing morality often tend toward shocked exclamations and strong statements. They are likely to envision cause-and-effect when only co-existence can be demonstrated.

Legislative committee reports that build on these observations compound with them the politician's wisdom: smart politics require the articulation of what followers hope to hear from their leaders. And attributing causal connection between our growing mountain of obscenity and the growing mountain of crime has a simple and generally popular appeal. My comments are not meant to discredit the conclusion that pornography and crime are *sometimes* causally connected, but I hesitate to apply that conclusion as broadly as some of its advocates might like. "Th' devil," noted the late Sean O'Casey—colorfully stating the case for the other side—"was as often in th' street, an' as intimate in th' home when there was nor film nor play nor book."[4]

In late 1965, after New York City's police commissioner, Vincent L. Broderick, charged that civil libertarians had not "given adequate consideration to the rights of parents to protect their children from harmful literature," a spokesman for the New York Civil Liberties Union, in responding, challenged:

. . . if anybody brings forth any proof that any particular literature is harmful, then we would not oppose efforts to prevent distribution. But until such proof is brought forward, we oppose any form of censorship.[5]

This blithe discounting of all adverse expert opinion is only one more instance of the extremism in pursuit of claimed virtue that has made the whole subject of obscenity such a tangle of hostilities. Concededly, no scientific or statistical surveys have proven obscenity and adolescent criminality to be causally related; *but neither have any disproved any relationship.*[6] Just how such studies might be conducted, in order to weed out the hosts of other variables and to concentrate on pornography in our sex-saturated society, has never been made clear. The libertarians' cries for scientific *proof* of causality, as a prelude to *any* regulation, cynically reflect their knowledge of the practical impossibility of complying with their demands. That delinquent youth are likely to be non-readers, of limited literacy, has been established.[7] But this fails to disprove the impact upon them of pornography. Delinquent-prone youngsters may be unlikely to plod through the pictureless pages of *Lady Chatterley's Lover* or even the more fruitful *Fanny Hill,* but they may take readily to other forms of the obscene. Striptease nude sets, girlie magazines, and sado-masochistic books—the last generally being combinations of the simplest, most unadorned English with pictures in kind—require little learning to spot their eroticism. Indeed, this sort of stuff seems made to order for those whose literacy and abilities to sustain interest during any lulls in the sexual fireworks are low.

Those who see pornography as utterly without impact upon crime, persons arrogantly eager to discount completely the practical experience of others who have earned at least some measure of respect for their views, are equaled in their intolerance by those who see obscenity at the very root of adolescent delinquency. Pornography, it should be obvious, is not the *only* touchstone of today's juvenile crime. Human conduct and particularly crime which is aberrant human conduct cannot be so simply accounted for. Pornography alone is not at its root, nor is ghettoed slum living alone, nor economic privation, nor vast human inequalities both of talent and opportunity, nor non-existent or woefully inadequate family life, nor any one of the whole dismal gamut of personal and social problems that, individually, contribute to delinquency. But *some* cause-and-effect relationship between obscenity and *some* delinquency there is.

In discussing the *Kingsley Books* case, in which the nation's highest Court sustained the use of the injunction against the *Nights of Horror* series, reference was made to the boast of an eighteen-year old killer (one who had been *amused* by horsewhipping, beating, kicking, and ultimately drowning his victim), that he had read every single one of the sado-masochistic *Nights of Horror* issues. And the parallels between his atrocities and the bizarre crudities of the books proved tragic confirmation of the boy's conceit. From time to time, teen-age sex clubs—and outrages performed by their members inspired in part by weirdly erotic reading, outrages that range from group statutory rapes through sexual attacks culminating in killings—come to newspaper readers' attention. In 1966, England's famed Moors murder case shocked the world; public horror was heightened by the apparent connection between the youthful murderers' sado-masochistic library and the sexual molestation, torture, then killing of at least two children and one teen-ager.[8]

Anecdotal evidence of this kind, standing alone, has concededly thin probative value: it proves that pornography and perverted crimes have, in a limited number of particular instances, been connected, but it does not demonstrate any overall likelihood of consanguinity between the two. Calm common sense may be far more effective for this purpose—although, granted, it is far less dramatic.

Those advocates of untrammeled free speech who minimize the ties between pornography and crime should need no persuasion to convince them that the sex drive is, as Freud has taught us, one of the child's prime drives. Inevitably, among the young will be some who, in seeking channels for the expression of their consuming sexual urges, will imitate the "sophisticated" sexuality that they read about or see pictured while immaturity still holds sway over their judgments. When their reading has gone no further than tales of intercourse, it may produce (in conjunction with the complex of confusing sexuality with which our society is crammed) teen-age "all-the-way" sex, or possibly criminal conduct along the lines of statutory rape, homosexual activity, or the impairment of a minor's morals. Former New York City mayor Jimmy Walker's flip comment, "No girl was ever ruined by a book," is an entertaining argument, and quite true in suggesting that no book could do the job unaided. But to suggest that books and movies may not ease the way would be to embrace the slogan rather than the reality. It is no answer to argue that if we permit youngsters to read books and to view films depicting murders and other non-sexual violence, we must similiarly expose them to pictured and narrated sex. Community morality has sharply etched the lesson that private killing and violence is wrong. And that lesson, generally, is one accepted by all; it is not solely the morality of a by-gone generation. The vagaries that permeate the relationship between the sexes, however, have no such universally accepted guidelines. Whether or not we approve, we accept the fact that some sexual expression among the young is likely, if not inevitable (be it necking, petting, masturbation, or intercourse). But for the young, the proper limitations of this sexuality are blurred; just how far teen-agers should go remains dubious. What is "square" morality, to be rejected by would-be youthful sophisticates, and what is realistic, far more permissive, but yet not truly "bad" (except in the eyes of the old-fashioned), is unclear. When "no" from a partner may mean "yes," or at least "maybe," is uncertain. How much force, shunned in other areas, may be appropriate in sex, how much an enjoyment of pain can be part of the sex experience, is cloudy. And so the suggestive power of books or films in this area of sexual conduct can be far more devastating to youngsters looking for non-"square" examples to follow, than the same media are likely to provide in the area of killing or non-sexual violence. Nor can this argument be fobbed off by the suggestion that books and movies are, after all, primarily "entertainment" and that they leave behind no real imprint, that they stimulate no continued thought, no imitative action. Only the bleakest pessimism, the most abject negativism, can suggest that this is so. Surely they can and they do, on at least many occasions, *both* entertain and teach. As youth is malleable, if on at least some occasions these media may be forces for good, they may also be influences for evil. And carrying all of this one step further, if the available books or movies suggest orgies, forcible rapes, and sado-masochistic details, must we not anticipate that in at least some few cases these shocking "lessons" will be aped?

Stated differently, to a large extent, people—and that includes children and teen-agers—are the products of their daily living. If that living is under bombardment from batteries steeped in all the details of sexual crime, there will be some among the young who will be susceptible, some for whom the siege, ultimately, coupled with a thousand other aspects of their lives, will overcome the resistance.

Among the claims made by those who militantly oppose any restraints upon pornography is one that rather than serving as a model for crime, or as an incitement to it, the obscene may provide a "safety valve" of sorts. Proclaiming their own Orwellian newspeak, they state that *pornography, designed to excite, really pacifies.* And to sustain that absurdity, their line of argument starts with the recognition that pornography will supply sexual fantasies and that those fantasies will sometimes lead to masturbation. From there the argument takes off, suggesting that masturbation will supplant the sexual violence in which pornography's disciples might otherwise engage. Granting that pornography may excite some non-violent youngsters to masturbate, just why rape, sadistic sex, and the whole gamut should sell masturbation as a satisfactory substitute for sexual violence among those tending toward aggression remains wholly unexplained.

That today's ready exposure of the obscene to adolescents may turn only a very few toward delinquency should not sidetrack measures designed to keep pornography from the young. Pornography's impact—dispassionately viewed—compared to slums, broken homes, and parents unfit for parenthood, is almost certainly minuscule. But from the standpoint of affected delinquent youngsters, or from that of their victims, one rape, or one sadistic sexual assault, is one too many. If without meaningful hurt to freedom, youths can be denied access to pornography in the hope that such little adolescent crime as it nourishes may be reduced, such denial may be well advised.

Although the fear of crime may supply the most dramatic reason for keeping pornographers from profiteering from their dealings with the young, it is not the only reason. Indeed, it does not seem the most persuasive reason.

19. Sales to the Young—Morality, Tensions, and Parents

My Heart Leaps Up When I Behold
The Child is father of the Man.
—William Wordsworth,

MORALITY IS LARGELY a private affair. Lawmakers cannot—indeed, should not—legislate against, nor can judges suppress, every seemingly immoral action. Sanctions can only be imposed upon obviously evil or patently dangerous activities, so shocking that virtually all right-minded citizens would agree that they are both immoral and injurious to innocent persons or those whose immaturity and susceptibility give them no protection. If pornography exposes youngsters to lasting injury, legislation to protect them is in order, *if it is feasible.*

The maturing of children along wholesome lines is in danger when their future abilities to form sound adult relationships are jeopardized by confusion in their minds of the uses of sex. Anthropologist Margaret Mead has observed that

. . . every society has the task of bringing up children who will focus their capacities for sexual feeling on particular persons, with or without overt bodily expression, and who will not only refrain from large amounts of undirected, objectless sex behavior, but will be able to produce the proper intensity of feeling expressed or unexpressed, for the proper object.[1]

Pornography, however, runs in precisely the opposite direction. It tends to depersonalize sex, to exalt it for its own sake. Rather than focusing "sexual *feeling*" upon another particular person, it tends to exalt sexual *activity* (separating it from *feelings*), and to direct it among fantasies—whether real or imagined—peopled by fully developed persons. Pornography preaches that sexual experience exists for its own sake, experience à go-go. Deeper currents are not to be pursued. Sex is not to loose its edge on mellower joys, on shared aspirations and even on those shared despondencies and frustrations that ebb and flow—not necessarily between sexual athletes—but inevitably between true lovers. Sex in pornography is an abandonment to physical experience. Period. Cerebral or true emotional sharing can only dull its excitements.

This pornographic sanctification of sex as an end in itself, of nudity for provocation's sake, of erotic adventures and of sensual experiences, is a spicy diet, gorged today, but not without its aftertaste. It takes its toll on adolescents brimming with new sexual capacities but uncertain of their appropriate use. Although pornography's impact on only rare occasions may be crime-inducing, it produces more broadly harmful, if less acute manifestations: it tends to negative true one-to-one relationships between a man and a woman, and to stunt the maturing process. Marya Mannes has commented:

. . . the strip tease, girlie magazines, and movie ads are only a few of the elements which reduce sex to a matter of measurements and calisthenics (fast, fast relief) and diminish, through contempt of all but her flesh, the image not only of woman but also of love. Between this diminution and vulgarization of the female and the rise of the male homosexual, the tie is plain.[2]

Psychiatrists have noted this perverse impact of the pornographic and have been alarmed by it. Reporting that it had reviewed "a collection of paperback books, magazines, records and illustrated advertising leaflets and folders with order forms attached," and that their contents "ranged from erotic through libidinous to outright lascivious and lecherous," the New York Academy of Medicine, in 1963, declared:

The Academy believes that although some adolescents may not be affected by the reading of salacious literature, others may be vulnerable. Such reading encourages a morbid preoccupation with sex and interferes with the development of a healthy attitude and respect for the opposite sex. It is said to contribute to perversion. In the opinion of some psychiatrists, it may have an especially detrimental effect on disturbed children.[3]

Although this statement abounds in caution, it is unequivocal in one declaration: that pornography "interferes with the development of a healthy attitude and respect for the opposite sex." Other present-day authorities on education and on mental health share these views.[4] Premised on these conclusions, the Academy recommended the prohibition of the sale of obscenity to minors. The Academy's recommendation reaffirms the early wisdom of Plato and of Aristotle, and underscores once again society's role in forfending against that continuing harm to the young that improper "literature" may inflict.

Apart from adolescent crime, from youthful immorality, and from the warping of later adult relationships, another consideration excites official action to bar smut peddlers from trafficking with the young. It is one that has been suggested earlier: the importance of giving meaningful protection to parental freedom in bringing up children.

Plato's state, in which the government was to raise the young in a community separated from their parents, has never found welcome in America. Here the parents are ostensibly in charge. True, the laws require school attendance, but even there choices may exist: public, parochial, or a range of private institutions for the children of parents who can afford them. Discipline, harsh or permissive, rests with parental choice. One set of parents may use current forms of the razor strop; another may use an incentive plan. Some parents may observe a Victorian code of sexual morality; their neighbors may be Saturday night wife-swappers. Either attitude is almost certain to be at least partly mirrored in their attitudes toward child-raising. Yet it is rare that government interferes with this individuality; parental misfeasance must be extreme before our judges will step in. The right to raise one's own children in the way one wants is sacred to our democratic way of life.

The right, however, is adulterated by materials that seep into the home and into the hands of the young, items that tug adolescent morality in a direction opposed by parents. The home is no impregnable fortress; the corner candy store and the newsstand, where a brisk, legal, *over-the-counter* trade with the young may flourish, bid defiance to even the most careful parental supervision. With the courts now protecting much that would have been declared obscene a decade ago, if a parental set of standards is to work, governmental support is necessary.

For highly permissive parents no need may exist for statutory provisions designed to interfere with sales to the young. But others, who prefer to raise their children more conservatively, need the law's aid in quarantining obscenity. The United States Supreme Court, in striking down a local statute that would have constricted adult reading to standards meant to safeguard children did *not* declare the converse: that adolescent reading, viewing, or listening were to be governed by adult standards.

Today it is clear that precisely the opposite was the Court's intention. The Court majority in its 1966 *Ginzburg* opinion, in enunciating a variable obscenity standard, examined the *audience* at whom the defendant had directed his promotional broadsides. Justice Potter Stewart, whose dissent in the same case urged that adults had a constitutional right to choose vulgarity, remarked, "Still other considerations might come into play with respect to laws limited in their effect to those deemed insufficiently adult to make an informed choice."[5] And two years earlier, two of the Justices had, even more explicitly, considered the need for special statutes shielding children. Speaking for himself and former Justice Arthur J. Goldberg, Justice William J. Brennan, in his *Jacobellis* opinion, had suggested:

State and local authorities might well consider whether their objectives . . . would be better served by laws aimed specifically at preventing distribution of objectionable material to children, rather than at totally prohibiting its dissemination.[6]

Such "bullet" statutes, aimed solely at protecting the young, and strengthening parental hands, have ample precedent. Until a few years ago, the potentially harmful effects of tobacco, although generally assumed, had not been unequivocally proven. Yet laws essentially of some aid to parents who wished to discourage their young from smoking or tippling, laws banning the sale directly to minors of tobacco and intoxicants, have been sustained for decades throughout America.

As the right to raise one's children, and to instill in them appropriate moral standards, is a parental *right*, it is one the community should be willing to take necessary legislative steps to safeguard. Without legislation and enforcement, "rights," parental or otherwise, have little real meaning. But to talk of parents' *rights* to raise their own offspring, and to instill in them strong moral codes, is an understatement. This is a parental *duty*. Platitudes about the role of the home are readily mouthed, that delinquency, addiction, and a host of unresolved social problems are traceable to inadequate family life. But only the self-blinded can claim that the family ever has *full* control. Children are not raised in test tubes. Thousands of outside factors intrude. If the family, the home, the parents, are to be the scapegoats for everything that goes wrong, the lawmakers should provide the little help they can to strain out those disruptive influences that make parental tasks more difficult.

Hopefully, even the most militant of anti-censors may find kind words for legislation that zeroes in on sales to minors, legislation protecting parental rights to give or to show their youngsters almost anything, and simultaneously penalizing smut sellers who peddle their wares directly to the young. Clearly, not all parents wish their youngsters nourished on tales of sodomy, or worse. Poet-essayist John Ciardi, for example, is one of censorship's most articulate and implacable foes. Ruminating about "book-burners" in mid-1963, when *Fanny Hill* was reissued, he ardently defended its right to be freely sold to all, *including children,* saying:

> I believe that parents who have reared their children in sympathy, and yet within a sense of this world as it goes, have nothing to fear from what the children read.[7]

Many, many months later, after his views about *Fanny Hill* had been used against its publishers in the New York trial (although Ciardi unequivocally opposed its censorship, he found inescapable the conclusion that it was pornography), he took special glee, in discussing *Last Exit to Brooklyn,* to spit his venom at censors:

> My damnation on any man who quotes me in support of any book-banner, for that man is a cheat and a liar. But now there comes upon the land the case of *Last Exit to Brooklyn,* the new best-seller by Hubert Selby, Jr., and if I may pause to wish a case of Job's boils on any prosecutor who distorts my sentiments into a legal case against the book, then let me cite Selby's effusion as the season's and the century's post-ultimate event in the literary swill-slopping contest.[8]

Yet, by the fall of 1965, when the success of *Fanny Hill* and *Last Exit* and a host of other dubious novels had led Grove to press its luck, and issue the collected works of the Marquis de Sade, parent Ciardi expressed unaccustomed doubts and backed down from his earlier bravado:

> Sade is disturbing. Let me confess that he drives me from an earlier position I once defended too smugly in this column, arguing that my children were free to read any book with my blessing so long as they would discuss it with me. I am bound to say I am not willing to have them read Sade this side of their adulthood. The details of sodomy, in-

cest, orgies, homosexuality, coprophagy, and the tortures invented in the hallucination of a demented philosopher are no diet I can endorse for those too young and too formless to have developed their own principle of selection and their own dispassion. I shall keep the book away from my children . . . .[9]

Although the shock of the Sade-Grove collaboration was to force Ciardi into this confession, his statement that he "shall keep the book away from [his] children" suggests that he had not, completely, shed the illusion of self-sufficiency. In the absence of a statutory ban on sales to the young (censorship of sorts), any local book dealer might lawfully undermine Ciardi's determination, selling de Sade directly to the poet's children (should their wholesome, parent-encouraged, curiosity lead them to seek out that one volume that, uniquely, papa had banned). The likelihood of such parental undercutting multiplies as Grove has followed its $15 hard-cover volume with a special king-sized paperback at $1.75 (as it had done earlier with *My Life and Loves* of Frank Harris).

John Ciardi's views on what is wholesome and what is bad for the young are John Ciardi's views as a parent, and as an essayist. They are highly subjective. Just as Ciardi the poet prizes his right to read as *he* pleases, and Ciardi the parent to protect his children's rights to read and to be kept from reading or viewing as *he* pleases, hopefully Ciardi the libertarian prizes the rights of other parents, whose standards may vary from his own, to place such limits upon the reading and viewing of their offspring as they may deem sound. Ciardi would let his young read *Fanny Hill* but not de Sade's *Justine*. Other critics, also fathers, and still other judges, might disallow *Fanny Hill,* but allow *Playboy.* Still others would deem *Playboy* not fit for the young. But if Ciardi is to be permitted the law's aid in keeping de Sade's works from his dependents—and such aid is probably necessary if the book is to be kept from them—less permissive parents should be entitled to similar aid to keep less putrescent items from their young. And so, in drafting a statute to protect the young against the profiteering of smut vendors, the draftsmen should strain to avoid reliance on those subjective and sharply differing personal judgments that have rendered the enforcement of existing obscenity statutes so uncertain.

But before discussing specifics concerning the content of such a statute—what such a law, designed to keep objectionable material from being *sold* to the young, should provide—one last argument for a statute protecting the young must be made.

Suppose that none of what has been said has proved convincing. Suppose that the reader remains uncertain whether parents should have the law's assistance in keeping from their children items that the parents believe are likely to prove traumatic. Suppose that the reader remains uncertain that there is any serious danger that pornography will create lacerating tensions that may harm children, or that will distort prospective adult relationships, or that it may even lead to adolescent and adult crime. Or, more to the point, suppose that not simply the reader, but *the judges* remain unconvinced. Does that mean that statutes designed to protect the young, not having been proven to be necessary, are ill-advised interferences with book-and-picture sellers' freedoms, and that if passed they must be struck down?

I suggest, no.

Children are society's most precious resource. In equipping them to grow into reasonably healthy adults, all of our errors— if any—should be on the side of caution. If, even arguably, shielding minors from pornography vendors may help the young (and is unlikely to hurt them), erring on the side of safety seems the prudent course. And if legislative bodies follow that course of prudence, and legislate in the reasonable (even though possibly mistaken) belief that their actions will protect the young, it is not for the judges to exalt their own personally held views, that such laws may not be necessary, in the place of contrary legislative judgments. As Justice Harlan, in the *Roth* case, reminded his colleagues and the nation:

In judging the constitutionality of this conviction, we should remember that our function in reviewing state judgments under the Fourteenth Amendment is a narrow one. We do not decide whether the policy of the state is wise, or whether it is based on assumptions scientifically substantiated. We can inquire only whether the state action so subverts the fundamental liberties implicit in the Due Process Clause that it cannot be sustained as a rational exercise of power.[10]

20. Sales to the Young—A Proposed Ban

... the Greek delegate (too Socratic by half) suggested that it might be a good thing to establish a preliminary definition of the word "obscene." Sir Archibald Bodkin sprang to his feet with a protest. "There is no definition of indecent or obscene in English Statute Law." The law of other countries being, apparently, no more explicit, it was unanimously decided that no definition was possible. After which, having triumphantly asserted that they did not know what they were talking about, the members of the Congress settled down to their discussion.

> —Aldous Huxley, *Vulgarity in Literature*, p. 1 (1930), describing a Geneva conference on the suppression of traffic in obscene publications

ONE CONCLUSION IS NOW INESCAPABLE in this area of obscenity and censorship; more adjective-larded legislation is not needed. In leaving such statutes on the rolls, our lawmakers have themselves created the problem that they, among others, have criticized our courts for botching so badly. A penal law that is to deter and is to be enforceable cannot be one so crammed with uncertainties that the knowledgeable policeman, lawyer, or court can only divine—more with prayer than with confidence—when it ought to be invoked.

And yet, new legislation continues to be turned out incorporating all of the unworkable ambiguities of the old. New York State's legislators, for example, while recognizing the need to concentrate on protecting the young, have lacked the invention to do so forthrightly, to scrap those evasive concepts that continue to haunt our law. In a series of statutes enacted in 1955,[1] 1963, and 1965, they have grasped at all of the tired, all-but-meaningless phrases, ranging from the original synonyms "obscene, lewd, lascivious, filthy, indecent or disgusting," through the almost equally undefined "illicit sex or sex immorality" and "appeals to lust," to those Court-given uncertainties, "appeals to the prurient interest," "patently offensive," and "utterly without redeeming social importance."

New York's 1955 venture at special legislation dealing with obscenity and the young, but using many of the tired old words and phrases, was ultimately knocked out for vagueness in 1964— the state's top court splitting four to three.[2] Then in early 1965, the New York legislature acted again in the same area of pornography and the young. It voted, and Governor Nelson A. Rockefeller endorsed into law, not one, but *two*, new laws,[3] both perpetuating some of the vagaries of the old, although this time starting to move toward desirable specificity.

Both new statutes featured careful definitions of the nudity and sexual actions that were to be kept from the contemplation of the young. But then, the lawmakers, after getting off to a fine start, threw away its advantages by embracing modifying words. The strictures of the new laws were only to apply to items of nudity, sex, and the like, that served to "exploit lust for commercial gain and which would appeal to the lust of persons under the age of eighteen years or to their curiosity as to sex." Just what the lawmakers understood about teen-age "lust" or "curiosity as to sex," or how prosecutors, booksellers, or police were to interpret these phrases or the phrase "exploit lust for commercial gain," remained a mystery. Some months later, New Jersey's legislature was to pass a similar statute; in vetoing it, Governor Richard J. Hughes noted:

The requirements that the material in question "exploit lust for commercial gain" and "appeal to the lust of persons under the age of 18 years" are so subjective as to render their application on any given occasion a matter of wide conjecture.[4]

Under the other New York State statute the ban on sales to youngsters was only to apply to an item that, in the statutory verbiage:

(i) predominantly appeals to the prurient, shameful or morbid interest of minors, and

(ii) is patently offensive to prevailing standards in the adult community as a whole with respect to what is suitable material for minors, and

(iii) is utterly without redeeming social importance for minors.

Here we *really* have it: all the words that hardly any two judges seemed to have been able to interpret alike, lifted from the welter of conflicting opinions and peppered liberally with the words "for minors."

Judges who have split bitterly in applying traditional obscenity statutes are certain to find themselves at odds under the new laws as to whether *Playboy*, with its nudes, its sex, and its sophistication and veneer, is or is not fit for the young. What about *Lady Chatterley's Lover* or *Memoirs of Hecate County?* And what about the widely advertised "how-to-do-it" guidebooks to sexual happiness, written by doctors and by psychologist-marriage counselors? Different judges will be certain to decide differently—and to rail at each other in the process.

In legislatively enacting those phrases that have nurtured so much chaos, the lawmakers have assured constitutionality.[5] What can be safer than adulating the highest Justices by molding a new statute in the very words hailed from their special Sinai? But constitutionality is hardly the prime goal of penal legislation. Utility—uniformity of understanding by police and by courts, by prosecutors, by publishers, and by booksellers, *along with hopefully persuasive arguments for constitutionality*—should be the aim.

Although perpetuating some obscurity, New York's new statutes (and others elsewhere emulating them) are not *all* bad. Applying them, courts are almost certain to find at least some items to be unsuitable for the young that some judges might deem permissible for their parents. The most tawdry of the striptease nudes, whether in glossy sets or in magazines, and sado-masochistic pamphlets—worthless smut on the borders of illegality when sold to adults—would clearly seem taboo for youngsters. To that extent the new statutes are a forward step. However, they create another of the obscenity law's paradoxes. Not telling booksellers and others precisely what it is they may or may not do discourages the cautious from selling minors questionable materials: materials that may *not* in fact be within the laws' proscriptions. "The bookseller's self-censorship," Justice Brennan had noted, commenting on this play-it-safe timidity in his *Smith* case (scienter) opinion, "would be a censorship affecting the whole public, hardly less virulent for being privately administered. Through it, the distribution of all books, both obscene and not obscene, would be impeded."[6] And so the new laws' *in terrorem* impact is likely to work a censorship on sales to the young broader than the laws intended, a censorship of a type *not reviewable* in the courts.

How much better off all would be, the prosecuted, the prosecutors, the public, and the judges, were there to be a return in the obscenity area to the customary requirement of penal statutes: that they be precise; that, in so far as is humanly possible, they put everyone on notice of exactly what is, and what is not, prohibited?

Such legislation *is* possible.

A PROPOSED STATUTE

A draft statute designed to keep professionals from pushing objectionable materials to the young—whether in writing, picture, movie, or other form, whether sold across the counter or by mail order—follows. Its strengths are twofold. *First*, its strictures are precise: it zeroes in, without ambiguity, on merchandise hawked by vendors or exhibitors for profit. *Second*, simultaneously, it guarantees the broadest freedom to parents, schools, museums, and libraries, all those charged with responsibilities in the education of the young.

As careful definition is as important to obscenity enforcement as it is throughout the criminal law, the statute on sales to minors opens with a glossary. Precise meaning is established for the terms the statute will rely upon. (The glossary also serves as the keystone to the statutes, considered in subsequent chapters, on the public display of offensive materials, and on obscenity and adults.) Then, clear definitions having been established, the restrictions are precisely set forth.

PRESENTING NUDITY OR SEXUAL ACTIVITY TO MINORS FOR PROFIT

1. *Definitions.* As used in this section:

(a) "knowingly" means having knowledge of the character of any item described in this section, or having failed to exercise reasonable care to ascertain its content;

(b) "minor" means any person under the age of eighteen years;

(c) "nudity" means uncovered, or less than opaquely covered, post-pubertal human male or female genitals, pubic areas, or buttocks, or the human female breast below a point immediately above the top of the nipple (or the breast with the nipple and immediately adjacent area only covered), or the covered human male genitals in a discernibly turgid state;

(d) "obscenities" mean those slang words currently generally rejected for regular use in mixed society, that are used to refer to genitals, buttocks, or female breasts, or excretory functions or products, or sexual conduct, either that have no other meaning, or that in context are clearly utilized for their bodily, sexual, or excretory meaning;

(e) "person" means any person, association, corporation, or business entity, or any employee thereof;

(f) "sado-masochistic abuse" means flagellation or torture by or upon a human who is nude, or clad in undergarments, or in revealing or bizarre costume, or the condition of one who is nude or so clothed and is being fettered, bound, or otherwise physically restrained;

(g) "sells or offers to sell" means giving or offering for monetary consideration or other valuable commodity or services;

(h) "sexual conduct" means human masturbation, sexual intercourse, or any touching of the genitals, pubic areas, or buttocks of the human male or female, or the breasts of the female, whether alone or between members of the same or opposite sex or between humans and animals in an act of apparent sexual stimulation or gratification; and

(i) "sexual excitement" means the condition of human male or female genitals, or the breasts of the female, when in a state of sexual stimulation, or the sensual experiences of humans engaging in or witnessing sexual conduct or nudity.

2. *Sales.* Any person shall be guity of a misdemeanor who knowingly sells or offers to sell to a minor any of the following:

(a) any picture, photograph, drawing, sculpture, motion picture, film, or other visual representation or image of a person or portion of the human body that depicts nudity, sado-masochistic abuse, sexual conduct, or sexual excitement; or

(b) any book, magazine, paperback, pamphlet, or other written or printed matter however reproduced, or any sound recording, which contains any matter enumerated in the immediately preceding paragraph, or obscenities, or explicit verbal descriptions or narrative accounts of sexual conduct, sexual excitement, or sado-masochistic abuse.

3. *Deliveries.* Any person shall be guilty of a misdemeanor who, for a monetary consideration or other valuable commodity or service, within this state, arranges for or dispatches for delivery directly to any minor, whether said delivery is to be made within or outside of this state, by post, delivery service, or any other means, any of the materials enumerated in the subdivisions of subsection two of this section; however, unless the defendant either was informed or had reason to suspect that the customer or prospective customer was a minor, he shall not be guilty of a misdemeanor when he has caused to be printed on the outer package, wrapper, or cover of the merchandise to be delivered, in words or substance, "This package (wrapper) (publication)

contains material that, by New York law, may not be sold directly to a minor"; this subdivision shall not render the carrier's conduct, or that of its agents or employees, criminal.

4. *Shows.* Any person shall be guilty of a misdemeanor who, for
a monetary consideration or other valuable commodity or service,
knowingly exhibits to a minor who is unaccompanied by his parent or guardian, or knowingly sells to a minor an admission ticket
or other means to gain entrance to, or knowingly admits a minor
who is unaccompanied by his parent or guardian to premises
whereon there is exhibited a motion picture, show, or other
presentation, whether pictured, animated, or live, which in whole
or in part depicts or reveals nudity, sexual conduct, sexual excitement, or sado-masochistic abuse, or the participants in or on-
lookers at acts in progress of sado-masochistic abuse or sexual
conduct, or which includes obscenities or explicit verbal descriptions or narrative accounts of sexual conduct.

5. *Displays.* Any person shall be guilty of a misdemeanor who,
while either operating or being employed in a sales, cashier, or
managerial capacity in any retail establishment, knowingly
suffers or permits a minor not accompanied by his parent or
guardian to enter or remain on such premises, if therein in that
portion where the minor is present:

(a) any picture, photograph, drawing, sculpture, or other visual
representation or image of a person or portion of the human
body that depicts nudity, sexual conduct, or sado-masochistic abuse is visibly displayed; or

(b) any book, magazine, pamphlet, paperback, or other written
or printed matter however reproduced is so displayed that it
visibly reveals a person or portion of the human body depicting nudity, sexual conduct, or sado-masochistic abuse.

6. *Presumptions.* The following presumptions are applicable to
this section:

(a) Any person owning, operating, or employed in the business
of selling, offering for sale, renting, or exhibiting any of the

materials proscribed by this section shall be presumed to have knowledge of the contents of all such materials offered for sale, delivered from, exhibited, shown, rented, or displayed in the premises owned or operated by him or in which he is employed.

(b) The sale, offer to sell, exhibition, show, or display to a minor of any of the items proscribed by this section, shall be presumptive evidence that the defendant knew that the person was a minor.

7. *Defenses.* The following shall be defenses to this charge, the burden of proof of which, by a preponderance of the evidence, shall be upon the defendant:

(a) That from the minor's appearance the defendant had no reason to suspect that the minor was under eighteen years of age, or that if he had reason to or did so suspect, he made reasonable efforts to determine the minor's age; reasonable effort shall not consist of merely asking the minor his age.

(b) That, in instances in which the defendant's action would not have been criminal had the minor been accompanied by his parent or guardian, the minor was accompanied by an adult, and the defendant had no reason to suspect that the adult accompanying the minor was not the minor's parent or guardian.

(c) That the defendant was in a parental or guardianship relationship with the minor.

(d) That the defendant was a bona fide school, museum, or public library, or was acting in his capacity as an employee of such organization or of a retail outlet affiliated with and serving the educational purposes of such organization.

(e) That the defendant was charged with the sale, offer to sell, showing or display of an item, those portions of which might otherwise be contraband forming merely a minor and incidental part of an otherwise non-offending whole, and serving some purpose therein other than titillation.

CONSIDERATION OF THE PROPOSAL

In defining nudity, sexual conduct, and other items taboo for sale to the immature, there is no hedging, no use of weasel words. No haze of subjectivity is imposed by suggestions that the nudes or the sex must be lust-provoking or prurience-inciting. In essence, Thurman Arnold's flip slogan, "no nudes is good nudes," has been taken seriously in this limited area of *sales* to youngsters. The draft, for example, would make it criminal for a merchant to sell sets of pictured nudes to minors. It would not matter whether they were the crassest striptease shots, or a set consisting of reproductions of a Botticelli, a Rubens, and a Goya. Were the draft to be adopted, simplicity would exist, and forecasting would become easy. Personal reactions, the bane of censorship, would finally become irrelevant. Were there a sale, were the purchaser a minor (as defined by the statute), were the merchandise to portray nudity (or one of the other carefully described categories that would be taboo for the young), neither police, nor jurors, nor judges would need to question whether the subject matter was prurient or non-prurient, patently offensive or inoffensive, socially redeemed or irredeemable. The absurdity, the annoyance, the expense, and the delay entailed in case-by-case appellate review seeking to trace undiscoverable lines ostensibly separating the artistic from the obscene would be avoided.

What about the constitutionality of such a statute? If it completely blanketed out the young from some of the artistic treasures of the centuries, the beauties of the body, and the mysteries of sex, blocking parents from giving their offspring those books the parents thought appropriate for them, it would without doubt be an unconstitutional restraint on freedom violative of the First and Fourteenth Amendments. But the draft does not do those things; it has a working safety valve. Unlike customary obscenity legislation, the proposal does *not* declare it a crime to "sell, *lend or give* away" pornography. Dealing with children as *customers* only, its verbs are solely "sells or offers to sell," and similar words connoting commercial activity. It places no blinders on the young; rather it merely channels their source materials through persons who appropriately check what should get through to them: the parents, schools, libraries, and museums; *not* police, prosecutors, and judges. The proposed statute in no way inhibits the public library or the school bookstore from lending or selling a youngster Rabelais' *Gargantua* and *Pantagruel* or even Frank Harris's *My Life and Loves* (assuming the policies of the public library or campus outlet authorize such loan or sale). Nor does it block the museum that may sell him a reproduction of a full-tone fleshy Rubens nude or of a pallid Phillipe Halsman photograph of contemporary nakedness. The John Ciardi disciple who may choose to give *Fanny Hill* to his offspring remains unpunished; raising *his* children is *his* business. But merchants, selling the same items directly to the young, violate the proposed statute. The statute's targets are those prime moral lepers, the profiteers who, pushing muck to adolescents, live off pre- and post-pubertal curiosity. With parents and appropriate institutions assured of their freedom to give their youthful charges whatever they may deem appropriate, the ban against *commercial* sales to the young of certain non-obscene items (materials not prohibited for adults) does not seem an unreasonable interference with speech and press freedoms. It should, therefore, be lawful if any interference may, constitutionally, be tolerable.

More than a score of years ago, the United States Supreme Court settled that question, holding that where protection of children was involved, the First Amendment's prohibitions could be narrowed; interferences not tolerated when adults only were in the picture would, sometimes, be appropriate when the well-being of minors was at stake. The case had originated in the town of Brockton, Massachusetts, in late 1941. There, Mrs. Sarah

Prince, who in testimony desciribed herself and her nine-year-old niece as "ordained ministers" of God, was arrested for permitting the child to distribute the Jehovah's Witness publications *Watchtower* and *Consolation* on the public streets in violation of the Commonwealth's child labor laws. "This child is exercising her God-given right and her constitutional right to preach the gospel, and no creature has a right to interfere with God's commands," Mrs. Prince had declared promptly on being accosted by the officer. And so, neatly, reflecting far greater *savoir-faire* than the slickest of professional pornographers, Mrs. Prince had preserved and specified the constitutional issue for review in the Supreme Court, where the First Amendment freedom of religion has long been equally protected with those of free speech and free press. When *Prince* v. *Massachusetts* reached the Supreme Court it ruled:

The state's authority over children's activities is broader than over like actions of adults. . . . A democratic society rests, for its continuance, upon the healthy, well-rounded growth of young people into full maturity as citizens, with all that implies . . . .

. . . The zealous though lawful exercise of the right to engage in propagandizing the community, whether in religious, political or other matters, may and at times does create situations difficult enough for adults to cope with and wholly inappropriate for children, especially of tender years, to face. Other harmful possibilities could be stated, of emotional excitement and psychological or physical injury . . . . We think that with reference to the public proclaiming of religion, upon the streets and in other similar public places, the power of the state to control the conduct of children reaches beyond the scope of its authority over adults, as is true in the case of other freedoms, and the rightful boundary of its power has not been crossed in this case.[7]

With the First Amendment's freedom of religion clause unoffended by reasonable statutory impediments to childhood religious activity, the Court, if it is to be consistent, should find the First Amendment's free speech-free press provisions unoffended by reasonable statutory impediments to childhood reading and viewing.

Apart from the free speech-free press guarantees, the draft statute may, if enacted, find its constitutionality challenged for imposing criminal sanctions on harmless conduct: the commercial sale, for example, to youngsters of pictured nudes that could not, under any contemporary standards, be deemed obscene even for those of tender years. Challengers may urge that this is an unreasonable interference with individual freedom of action, that the legislative strictures extending beyond shielding the young from pornography's harm are therefore beyond the power of any legislature to impose. However, this ignores the fact that all nudes, no matter how artistic, are likely to be sought by emotionally undeveloped youngsters for the secret sniggers they evoke. Moreover, and far more significantly, laws that ban only that which would be "obscene for minors" fail, ultimately, to draw any real lines at all. Realistically viewed, they delegate the legislature's power to decide what is to be banned and what is not to the appellate courts, there to be exercised sometime in the future. Legislation drawing precise lines—lines that will produce minimal chores for the judiciary and maximum certainty for all parties concerned—is the alternative. Attaining this precision, however, has its price. It produces those occasions, likely to be more theoretical than real, when the law may seem to interfere unreasonably with the sales of *innocent* materials. We cannot have it both ways. The highest appellate tribunals have ample grounds on which to sustain the suggested statute as reasonable legislation; it is necessarily broad in order to root out the plague of judicial subjectivity. Whether they will or not, however, involves more of crystal-gazing than of precedent-searching. Should the statute be upheld, then in the area of sales to minors no further need will exist for the labored case-by-case appellate review that has become the hallmark of obscenity enforcement.

The proposal is long—seemingly endless when compared to

more traditional "obscene, lewd, and lascivious" legislation. But if its wording imparts the certainty that is intended, it is better by far to have many paragraphs in a statute than a multitude of conflicting opinions. Several aspects of the draft call for brief comment.

The statute's term, "minor," is limited to those who are under eighteen years of age. Obviously there is no magic in this line-drawing. At what age do minors so grow to maturity that adult materials should no longer be kept from them? The eighteenth birthday seems as appropriate a cutoff point as any that might be selected. It is the age at which men may enlist in the military without obtaining parental consent. It is not uncommonly the age (and this varies from state to state) below which, for purposes of statutory rape, a girl cannot consent. It has been suggested as the desirable age at which the franchise should commence. In many states, liquor cannot be sold to younger persons. At eighteen most young people are completing high school and are starting to make their own way, or to go on to higher education. Parental supervision is rapidly attenuated once eighteen has been reached. Were the cutoff lower, hopes for the statute's constitutionality would be bolstered: the arguments would be strengthened of its purpose to safeguard *children*, not simply those who are technically minors. But, at the same time, many teen-agers would be excluded from its protections.

In enjoining sales to minors of nudity-revealing items, the draft's prohibitions are not limited to pictures showing genitalia. Partial coverings are often more erotic than complete nudity. So, for statutory purposes, "nudity" exists not only when pubic areas are revealed, but when the figure is so thinly veiled or so sparsely covered as to show the buttocks or the exposed female breasts. The statute bars sales of items containing representations by words or pictures of sado-masochistic abuse, of sexual excitement, and of sexual conduct, whether hetero- or homosexual, or that engaged in solitarily. The nature of the interdicted representations is fully specified in the definitions section of the proposed law. As drafted, the more than minor and incidental use of obscenities, defined as "slang words currently generally rejected for regular use in mixed society" and used to refer to sexual parts or excretory functions, is also barred.

The statute does not enjoin all *references* to sexual conduct. In 1964, in vitiating New York's then obscenity-to-minors statute, a scant majority of that state's highest court observed that, under that law:

> The Oedipus legend in classic Greek drama would be forbidden because it is principally devoted to incest, the Tristan and Isolde legend and Hawthorne's "Scarlet Letter" would be illicit reading for the young because it is principally made up of adultery, Bernard Shaw's "Mrs. Warren's Profession" would be outlawed for obvious reasons, as well as all writings dealing with homosexuality.[8]

This is not true of the proposal. Its ban is limited to *"explicit verbal descriptions or narrative accounts"* of sexual conduct; it does not embrace mere statements, or bare inferences, that such conduct took place.

The draft statute endeavors to get at objectionable materials no matter the means used to bring them to the attention of minors. Direct sales are, of course, the focus of its principal attack. But with motion picture classification and licensing all but a thing of the past, and with movies becoming increasingly frank and with Broadway and off-Broadway shows, nightclubs and coffeehouses running far ahead of the movies in this regard, the statutory bans extend generally to those who exhibit objectionable shows (live or pictured) to those minors who are unaccompanied by parents or guardians.

Adult anger has long centered on the candy store where teenagers cluster at racks displaying girlie magazines and erotic pulp. The draft statute makes it criminal to permit minors (unaccompanied by parents or guardians) access to those portions of retail establishments where such pictured nudity and erotica are openly displayed for all to see. This ban is limited to retail

stores; it will not bar youngsters from public buildings or bona
fide private museums in which nudes are exhibited. Nor will it
prevent retail bookstores from offering books that may contain
nudes as illustrations, and stacking those books on their open
shelves; it will merely bar the display of the photographs (*not*
the books themselves), as lures in such portions of the shops that
admit youngsters. Were it enacted, this section would keep the
young out of those tawdry bookstores and magazine shops that
choose to specialize in, and to display, titillating wares. (More
likely, were the statute to be passed in several of our larger
states, book and magazine covers would soon be so toned down
as to safely pass muster). One limitation on the proposal's impact should be noted. This portion of the draft would *not* bar
youngsters from riffling through magazines or paperback novels,
the covers of which were not taboo, but which contained matter
such that, under the statute, the publications could not lawfully
be sold to minors. A proscription broad enough to prevent that
sort of browsing would fetter studious youngsters from book-
hunting in wholesome book and paperback shops.[9] (Merchants,
however, who were to make a practice of permitting minors to
leaf through specially massed collections of erotica should find it
difficult to defend successfully against charges of "offering to
sell" objectionable items to them.)

All this takes care of face-to-face sales, exhibitions, and displays to minors. But what about the mail order vendor who,
using such mailing lists as he has purchased or compiled, is
happy to remain ignorant of the ages of his listed prospects. The
mail order retail business in borderline pornography, as the experiences of Roth and Alberts prove, has long been sizable and
lucrative. The proposed statute penalizes the shipper who either
knows or has reason to suspect that he is selling to a minor.
When sales are not face-to-face, such knowledge will be rare indeed, and proof of it will be even rarer. The statutes would,
however, eliminate the innocent-looking "brown paper wrapper";
it provides a means of putting interested parents on notice that

the material shipped to their offspring may be objectionable. Items likely to be mailed that may disturb parents will vary broadly. Some may wish to ban *Playboy* or its imitators. Others may believe it undesirable that their children receive those photo sets advertised in certain magazines: "24-year-old Exotic Dancer and pro model—has personal collections of intimate and revealing pictures for sale," or "See More of the Swedish Girls; Exclusive models offer you interesting and uncensored photos of themselves." The statute provides for alerting parents by making shippers liable once they send things to youngsters that are within the statute's interdiction and fail to mark them in substance, "This package contains material that, by law, may not be sold directly to a minor." The intercepting parent would, of course, be free to pass such packages along to his offspring, or to stop them short. He might even take the trouble to notify the vendor to discontinue future shipments.

Scienter is approached realistically in the draft statute. Judicially required since the *Smith* decision in late 1959, the prosecution has had the burden not only of showing the obscenity of the prohibited item, but also that the vendor had at least general knowledge of its content. How does one prove (beyond a reasonable doubt) what moves in the recesses of another's mind? How does one show that a bookseller knows the items in his stock, that a theater owner is familiar with the movies he exhibits, or that a newsdealer is aware of the general character of the magazines he displays? Aside from those dubious dialogues in which a dealer says how "hot" is his merchandise—conversations most unlikely to take place when the purchaser is a fifteen-year-old —scienter, realistically viewed, is rarely susceptible of sure proof. But common sense may assist. No corner hardware merchant would long prosper, lacking general familiarity with the items he had for sale. No Wall Street broker could succeed, ignorant of fluctuations in the securities he marketed. Similarly, honest book and magazine dealers have some general knowledge of the character of the wares they order, put on their shelves, sometimes display, and ultimately hope to sell. The draft statute would transmute this common sense into law; it would create a legal presumption declaring, in effect, that merchants know something about what they do for a livelihood: in the case of people in the business of selling, scienter would be presumed.

Lastly, the draft statute articulates a number of defenses. The merchant who in fact sells to a minor would be able to defend on the ground that the minor's mature appearance misled him, or that the minor was accompanied by an adult reasonably believed to be his parent, or that—as has been discussed—the defendant was an employee of the minor's school, or of a bona fide museum or library, or was himself the youngster's parent.

The proposal provides one other defense, and places the burden of proving it on the defendant. That the allegedly offending items constitute only a minor part of an otherwise inoffensive whole, and serve some purpose other than titillation, would be a valid defense against criminal charges. Assume, for example, that an issue of *Life* magazine were to portray, among its hundreds of pictures, some New Hebrides tribesmen or women so as to reveal their genitals, or the breasts of the warriors' wives. It is not too difficult to suppose a current novel, one *not* totally preoccupied with sex, nevertheless including a scene of lovemaking described in sensual detail. Consider the near subliminal, yet vital, sequences in the motion picture *The Pawnbroker*, which showed a young woman stripped to the waist. It is highly improbable that police or prosecutors would pursue vendors or exhibitors of such items, whether or not viewed by the young; much too much malodorous merchandise that makes broader, more persistent, and far less sensitive use of nudity and of sex is around. But this defense is provided lest the proposed statute's existence were to serve to spark absurdly puritanical blue-penciling by nervous publishers of general interest books and magazines, by motion picture exhibitors—or by police or prosecutors. It is an escape hatch of sorts, although one fairly narrowly defined.

ENFORCEMENT PROBLEMS

From the policeman's standpoint, enforcement of sales-to-minors statutes, even though more certain, embraces difficulties not present under the general obscenity laws. Directed at safeguarding minors, arrests under any such statute will largely be limited to situations in which there is a candy store and a youngster-customer. The retailer, the small fellow at the end of the line, will be the prime enforcement target. Today's major vendors of filth, those who plan, contract for, print, and distribute thousands upon thousands of scabrous magazines or pictures, but do so solely on a wholesale level, will remain immune from the statute's sanctions as long as their rapacity does not drive them to take on retail outlets or a mail order business.

A means does exist whereby, nominally, those wholesale operators might be brought within the law's embrace. A statute might provide that materials taboo for minors marketed for resale would have to be plainly marked "for adults only." Failure on the part of publishers, manufacturers, wholesalers, or distributors to so mark merchandise would render them criminally liable. Compliance—painlessly accomplished—would, however, negate criminality. And simultaneously the legend, serving as a lure for the young, might well make the products *more* attractive. Dean Lockhart and Professor McClure have even suggested that this labeling of forbidden fruit might stimulate adolescent shoplifting![10] It may also provoke new claims that our laws are shackling the press. On balance, such provisions seem unwise.

Police action against local merchants is apt to be fitful under any sales-to-minors statutes. Adult policemen will not be able to base arrests on their own purchases as they can and customarily do under the general obscenity laws. Nor can busy police expend endless hours of incognito lounging near rumored violators, waiting to pounce should they spot a sale being made to an underage customer. For the most part, enforcement will depend not upon police initiative, but upon sporadic complaints made by parents concerning sales to their children. Sometimes the youngsters will have been eager, well-instructed decoys, sent by citizens' groups to make purchases from merchants believed to have been peddling contraband to neighborhood teen-agers. In other cases, the youngsters may prove unwilling and inept witnesses, kids caught by their elders scanning items purchased in defiance of parental vigilance. In either event, the child's reliability will be critical. His accuracy in recollecting the offending salesman, and his ability to reconstruct the circumstances of the sale, possibly necessary to bolster proof of scienter, may be crucial. These cases will, of course, require bringing minors as witnesses into the atmosphere of the criminal courts, almost always a somewhat insensitive performance, and one never wholly desirable.

Surely no sales-to-minors statute will be foolproof. Youngsters who are so inclined are able to get tobacco and liquor, although the law stands four-square behind parental disapproval. Pruriently inclined or curious minors, even those facing the opposition of parents, are certain to have at least occasional access to forbidden items. Friends with more permissive parents may make them available; minors with non-permissive parents may find pictures or texts in their own homes that were there intended only for elder eyes, and merchants may supply books, magazines, and pictures willingly for money despite the laws, or unknowingly to precocious shoplifters. However, if precise sales-to-minors laws are sustained, such direct selling to the young that may have heretofore existed should slack off appreciably. The specter of criminal prosecution under pointed legislation should serve to deter all but the most greedy of local merchants. It is one thing to remain active in an immoral *but not illegal* occupation, rationalizing profit-making on the basis that morality is not a storekeeper's merchandise, and that "if I don't do it, someone else will." It is quite another to violate the laws knowingly, even though detection and proof of violations may be difficult.

Surely, if retail sales to the young made both by eager smut

vendors and by irresponsible merchants are curtailed through invocation of a law all can understand, the most galling aspect of
the obscenity trade will, finally, have been tackled with some
success.

21. Public Displays — Offenses Against Taste and Privacy

I don't mind at all what people do, as long as they don't do it in the streets and frighten the horses.

—remark attributed to Mrs. Patrick Campbell

PUBLIC NUDITY IS UNLAWFUL from coast to coast in America, criminal "indecent exposure" statutes being actively enforced throughout the nation. Although some nudist camps exist, and in some cities bare-bosomed waitresses stimulate the drinking trade, such exposure takes place wholly on private property. When the nudists run into town to do their shopping they wear more than their money belts, and the "topless" bar waitresses get dressed to go home. As criminal charges are pressed against both the lone publicity-seeking model who doffs her bikini top on a public beach, and the publicity-shunning, sick, old man who indecently exposes himself in a public park, why is there community *inaction* against massive, coarse, commercial, public displays of pictured near-nakedness? Concededly extensive billboard bareness is not, in these no-longer Victorian days, as startling as is momentary live exposure. Yet if the community disbelieves in public nakedness, its pictured counterpart when ungraced by any semblance of artistry and publicly displayed to attract customers, should, logically be inhibited by law.

This is not to suggest that blue-coated police go rushing
through the parks, fig-leafing Hermes' statues or draping those
of Venus. These are not the naked images that any tasteful community finds offensive. Those fittingly banned, however, are seen
on burlesque and B-girl bar billboards; they reveal the current
strippers, pastied and g-stringed. They include nudie-movie stills,
life-size, displayed under the marquees as teasers for such filmed
drivel as *Love Hunger, Nature's Playmates,* or *Sin-O-Rama.* The
tawdry "bookstore" window displays are similarly likely to offend,
as are those corner magazine stands that tender row upon row of
pictured bosoms to newspaper purchasers and passersby. That is
the stuff that makes no pretense at artistry. It is an unavoidable
peepshow assaulting the stroller's eyes, and importing the honky-
tonk of noisy, blaring, impersonal sex into our streets.

Increasingly, both the policy of government and the thinking
of progressives recognize that man lives not by bread alone. We
are experiencing a culture boom and a psychiatric boom, both
stressing the impact of environmental factors upon each of us.
Civil aesthetics are taking on new importance. The United States
Congress passes a highway beautification bill impressing controls on billboards and junkyards that deface our nation's road-
sides.[1] A citizens' committee, adamant about protecting the
beauty of the Adirondacks succeeds in blocking (at least temporarily) a powerful utility's drive to construct a hydroelectric power plant along one of America's loveliest river valleys.[2] Residents
of New York City's most artistic, liberal, non-conformist area—
Greenwich Village—petition for governmental intervention
against *non-criminal* misconduct, declaring that they find offense
in the public use of obscenities, of alchohol, and of demonstra-
tive conduct between members of the same sex, all in the area's
favorite park; in their petition they note that the actions complained of "shock and disgust visitors . . . and make the park
an unsuitable place for children."[3] Lady Bird Johnson plants
azaleas and cherry trees in parks and squares scattered about
the nation's capital, and philanthropist Mary Lasker places mag-

nolias and dogwoods along New York City's Park Avenue and in the United Nations garden.[4]

With all this stress on civic beauty, on eliminating (or at least keeping out of view) the seamier side, why—in the name of free speech—our communities should remain impotent to eliminate repellent public displays is not clear. The right to read freely, to speak freely, and to publish freely does *not* mean the right to do so anyplace at anytime. Justice William J. Brennan, Jr., the Justice to write the prevailing opinions for the high Court in *Roth, Jacobellis, Fanny Hill, Mishkin,* and *Ginzburg,* noted recently:

> I may say that whatever theory of the first amendment's scope is championed, all schools of thought . . . are in substantial agreement . . . that government has some power to regulate the "how" and "where" of the exercise of the freedom; government is not powerless to say that you cannot blare by loudspeaker the words of the first amendment in a residential neighborhood in the dead of night, or litter the streets with copies of the text. In other words, though the speech itself be under the first amendment, the manner of its exercise or its collateral aspects may fall beyond the scope of the amendment.[5]

And Justice Potter Stewart, whose spring 1966 opinions were to see him moving close to making a triumvirate of the Black-Douglas duo, remarked in his *Ginzburg* dissent, after avowing the sacredness of freedom of expression:

> Different constitutional questions would arise in a case involving an assault upon individual privacy by publication in a manner so blatant or obtrusive as to make it difficult or impossible for an unwilling individual to avoid exposure to it.[6]

Should the clear majority of a community deem pruriently appealing billboards and window displays repulsive (and existing legislation against certain displays would seem to reflect that popular feeling[7]), anti-display statutes, if sufficiently clear and precise, should be sustained as constitutional. They would curtail, not essential freedom of expression, but only the foisting of erotica on the public at large. The statutes would, in short, regulate only "the 'how' and 'where' of the exercise of the freedom," not the freedom itself. Such restrictions would not interfere with the rights of adults to gobble up such magazines as they may wish to devour, to squirm to their hearts' contents in nudie-movie theaters, or to gaze at strategically sequined strippers performing in the flesh; only the street-corner displays would be banned.

Concepts of "nuisance" and zoning afford precedent for anti-display legislation. The drunk roistering in the streets, the tannery fanning noxious odors into the neighboring air, and the late dance hall blaring its unmuted discord at nearby householders represent some annoyance, some public nuisance. Under varying circumstances, such nuisances have been enjoined, have given rise to civil or even criminal liability, or have been zoned out of certain neighborhoods.

Whether or not something exceeds the bounds of mere inconvenience and becomes actionable has been determined by weighing its social usefulness and its suitability to its locale against that degree of annoyance that would have to be tolerated were it to continue; or, if an annoyance's usefulness can be preserved, its injurious aspects eliminated, that is the ideal solution.[8] Using these legal standards to test the sex-and-nudity displays suggests that the vexation worked by the displays is clearly not as intolerable as is that of nerve-shattering or nightmarishly incessant sound, or acrid odors. On the other hand, by hypothesis the artless signs and billboards against which an anti-display statute might be directed have themselves no real social value, nor are they likely to be aesthetically desirable on *any* public street.

A novel appellate case provides a strange but strong precedent, suggesting that punitive legislation directed against eyesores, although they inflict no real injury, would be constitutional. Starting in 1956, a strong-minded couple named Webster and

Marion Stover in suburban Rye, New York, adopted their own brand of demonstration, protesting against what they regarded as unconscionably high local taxes. They deliberately cluttered the *front* yard of their otherwise pleasant private home with multiple clotheslines, and on those clotheslines they hung a steadily thickening jungle of tattered clothing, old underwear, and assorted rags. In 1961 Rye finally responded. It enacted an ordinance prohibiting front yard clotheslines, except with permits to be issued where necessary for drying clothes when other facilities were not available. The Stovers duly applied for a permit, but as was anticipated their application was denied. No true need for it existed. The irate couple failed to appeal the denial, but instead persisted in their protest. Both man and wife were therefore promptly charged with violating the new ordinance, and in due course both were convicted. The Stovers ignored the wisdom in the age-old vaudevillian's skit, "Pay the two dollars." They appealed the case all the way to New York's highest court, urging that their conviction deprived them of the free enjoyment of property without due process of law, and that it interfered unconstitutionally with their right to free speech, their right to protest.

Judge Stanley Fuld, liberal partisan of the broadest view of the Bill of Rights, writing for the court, *upheld* the ordinance as one that, "based on what may be termed aesthetic considerations, proscribes conduct which offends sensibilities and tends to debase the community. . . ."[9] So doing, Judge Fuld quoted and relied upon language used some nine years earlier by Justice William O. Douglas in an opinion that spoke for the United States Supreme Court:

. . . The concept of the public welfare is broad and inclusive . . . . The values it represents are spiritual as well as physical, aesthetic as well as monetary. It is within the power of the legislature to determine that the community should be beautiful as well as healthy, spacious as well as clean, well-balanced as well as carefully patrolled. . . .[10]

Judge Fuld said:

Once it is concluded that aesthetics is a valid subject of legislative concern, the conclusion seems inescapable that reasonable legislation designed to promote that end is a valid and permissible exercise of the police power. . . .

. . . Moreover, the ordinance imposes no arbitrary or capricious standard of beauty or conformity upon the community. *It simply proscribes conduct which is unnecessarily offensive to the visual sensibilities of the average person.* It is settled that conduct which is similarly offensive to the senses of hearing and smell may be a valid subject of regulation under the police power . . . and we perceive no basis for a different result merely because the sense of sight is involved.

This language, along with experience with nuisance ordinances and with zoning, suggests that a statutory ban directed against exposing pictured nudity and sex to public view for commercial purposes would be sustained, even though the items against which it would be directed would not constitute actionable obscenity were they privately sold or shown to adults. Anti-display legislation would be premised on the reasonable belief that, using Judge Fuld's phrase, such nudity-and-sex displays were "unnecessarily offensive to the visual sensibilities of the average person." If the visitor from Keokuk shepherding his wife and camera laden youngsters past nudie-movie marquees feels the need to engage in some diversionary tactics, if the native adult takes less pride in his city because of the coarseness of the displays at its busiest intersections, why must we put up with it? Why tolerate such streetside peepshows? What value have they? As the late Professor Zachariah Chafee, of the Harvard Law School, noted two decades ago:

. . . the law wants to prevent the sense of citizens from being offended by sights and sounds which would be seriously objectionable to a considerable majority and greatly interfere with their happiness. From this standpoint, a nasty word in a streetcar is treated like a lighted cigar—the law is interested in the immediate effect on the sensibilities of others.[11]

Realistically, free speech and free press can be fully protected and these crude displays can still be eliminated. Any city's moral tone, intangible but nonetheless very real, would be raised without them, and nothing would truly be forfeit in obtaining the improvement.

Anti-display statutes might even perform yeoman duty in removing irritants from public view and thus calming advocates of more and more censorship. By driving merchandise, not underground, but into *discreet* channels, the temper-taunting red flags will disappear and pro-censorship pressures should be lessened. Were legislative enactment to succeed in driving objectionable items from public *view*, while permitting adults *privately* to buy, to read, to see, or to hear far more objectionable materials, the *meaningful* rights of all would be reconciled. The majority would be spared the discomfort of being forcibly confronted by the depersonalizing, the embarrassing, the crude; the minority would, as part of the same legislative framework, be freed to enjoy more of what it wished, quietly and without fanfare.

A PROPOSED STATUTE

A proposed anti-display penal statute follows. Its approach, and much of its terminology, parallels the sales-to-minors draft. Precision, once again, is attained through careful definitions of terms and through the elimination of those hedging phrases and adjectives, so dear to legislators and judges, that experience has shown to have little clear meaning:

PUBLIC DISPLAYS OF NUDITY OR SEXUAL ACTIVITY FOR ADVERTISING PURPOSES.

1. *Definitions.* As used in this section:
(a) "advertising purposes" means purposes of propagandizing in connection with the sale commercially of a product or type of product or products, or the offering commercially of a service, or the exhibiting commercially of an entertainment;

(b) "displays publicly" means the exposing, placing, posting, exhibiting, or in any fashion displaying in any location, whether public or private, an item in such a manner that it may be readily seen and its content or character distinguished by normal unaided vision viewing it from a public thoroughfare, depot, or vehicle; it shall also include the giving out of handbills in a public thoroughfare, depot, or vehicle; and

(c) "public thoroughfare, depot, or vehicle" means any street, highway, park, arcade, depot, or transportation platform, or other place, whether indoors or out, or any vehicle for public transportation, owned or operated by government, either directly or through a public corporation or authority, or owned or operated by any agency of public transportation, that is designed for the use, enjoyment, or transportation of the citizenry.

(The other definitions, appearing in the proposed sale-to-minors statute, will also apply.)

2. *Public Displays.* Any person who for advertising purposes knowingly displays publicly or causes to be displayed publicly any picture, photograph, drawing, sculpture, or other visual representation or image of a person or portion of the human body that depicts nudity, sado-masochistic abuse, sexual conduct, or sexual excitement, or any page, poster, or other written or printed matter bearing such representation or a verbal description or narrative account of such items or activities, or any obscenities, is guilty of a misdemeanor; any person who shall knowingly permit such display on premises owned, rented, or operated by him shall be guilty of a misdemeanor.

3. *Presumptions.* The following presumptions are applicable to this section:

(a) Any employee of any person operating premises wherein a public display in violation of this section takes place who is on the premises at the time of the violation shall be presumed to have been the operator of the premises.

(b) The owner, lessee, or operator of premises wherein a public display in violation of this section takes place shall be presumed to have knowingly caused that public display to have been made, to have had knowledge of the nature of the items publicly displayed, and to have known that they could have been seen and distinguished from an adjoining public thoroughfare or depot.

4. *Defenses.* The following shall be defenses to this charge, the burden of proof of which, by a preponderance of the evidence, shall be upon the defendant:

(a) That the public display, even though in connection with a commercial venture, was primarily for artistic purposes or as a public service.

(b) That the public display was of nudity, exhibited by a bona fide art, antique, or similar gallery or exhibition, and visible in a normal display setting.

CONSIDERATION OF THE PROPOSAL

One special problem pervades the display area. In terms of banning sales to children, the artistic was *not* excepted from the proposed statutory interdiction. In dealing with public displays, however, a distinction *must* be made between the image of the partly draped heroic female seen in a railroad station (the "Spirit of Transportation"), and the color billboards flanking a burlesque entrance showing sparsely spangled ecdysiasts. Talking in terms of "artistic value" or alleged "redeeming importance" not only might not make the needed distinction (civic artistry is often hotly disputed), but would, once again, bring the issue down to one of individual taste. The draft public display statute chooses a simpler means of drawing lines that give the broadest latitude to civic projects while striking at the real evil: the entrepreneur publicly flaunting nudity-and-sex images to make a dollar on his sensationalism.

The proposed ban is applied to that nudity and sex that is so displayed *commercially* for advertising purposes as to be visible to the passing public. By focusing this way on the apparent *purpose* of the presentation, questions of taste are avoided. The civic monument is given immunity, while items condemned will include pictures found on burlesque billboards, in nudie-movie teaser montages, and in the Times Square bookstores' window displays. The draft provides a safety valve so that bona fide art displays, privately sponsored but in public view, will not be endangered. Suppose, for example, that a Fifth Avenue specialty shop's spring windows were to feature manikins grouped about a reproduction of Botticelli's *Birth of Venus,* from which the spring finery was to draw its colors; or suppose that an art gallery's paintings, including nudes, were to be visible to passing window shoppers. It is unlikely that busy police would concern themselves, the artistic purposes and appropriate tone being obvious. But should they, the draft affords protection. It supplies a defense, the burden of proving which would be upon the defendant, that the display was primarily for artistic purposes, was a public service, or was that of a bona fide art gallery.

So much for the irritant that is public display. The proposed statute, as drafted, is designed to remove the most blatant aspects without invading the right of private in-the-store displays and of private sales. It would accomplish this by the threat of punishment. But along with criminal sanctions, a procedural statute might separately provide for injunctive relief, within the discretion of appropriate governmental agencies, to be invoked in lieu of criminal penalties under circumstances in which the penal provisions, although in order, might seem needlessly harsh.

Obviously, in this advertising and public relations conscious age, with sensational displays toned down, certain impulse buying would slack off. Such slacking off would take profits with it. And with profits would go much of the motivation to publish, to film, or to sell. This progression might lead the affected entrepreneurs to claim that anti-display statutes would tend to force them out of business. And this may be so. Further, they might claim that in so doing the statutes would interfere improperly with their freedom of speech and of the press. But "Government has some power to regulate the 'how' and the 'where' of the exercise of the freedom," Justice Brennan has noted, referring to the freedom of speech and press. The freedom to publish does not necessarily involve the freedom to use any and all means to *force* gaudy reflections of one's products down the craws of a disinterested public.

22. Indecency and Adults — the Argument for Intervention

We . . . who profess to deal neither in poison nor in pap, may not unwillingly stand aside. Let those read who will, and let those who will abstain from reading. *Caveat emptor.* No one wishes to force men's food down the throats of babes and sucklings.

—Algernon Charles Swinburne, *Notes on Poems and Reviews*

WERE LAWS TO BE ENACTED that carefully trained their sights upon materials sold to children and on items publicly displayed, would any need—or even any worthy arguments—remain favoring censorship of adult entertainments? Author-editor John Chandos summed it up:

It is not an offence in England or America to entertain thoughts of a heterosexual nature, it will be an ominous day when it is. It is not an offence to engage in heterosexual intimacy. If there is a valid argument why it is unlawful to publish matter which may influence people to commit an act which is not in itself unlawful, I have yet to hear it.[1]

Many, with Chandos, insist that adults be given *carte blanche*, unless some sure cause and effect can be adduced showing that obscenity is harmful to them. Such evidence does not exist; such harms as there may be are largely to morality, an intangible. But much of our law is triggered by the safeguarding of intangibles, including morality. Supreme Court Justice Abe

Fortas voiced this, prior to ascending the high Bench, when in discussing the privilege against self-incrimination he observed, "The fundamental value that the privilege reflects is intangible, it is true; but so is liberty, and so is man's immortal soul."[2]

Current legal debate yields a number of instances in which our most ardent libertarians press this ascendancy of moral action in fixing our law's outlines. The scrapping of the so-called "separate but equal" doctrine in favor of integrating the public education of Negroes and whites is primarily the substitution of morality for tradition. And, in the area of the criminal law, libertarian voices consistently urge "morality," as they see it, deeming it so important as an ideal that they acknowledge that the community must be willing to sacrifice some degree of safety at its altar. Wiretapping, as an example, used against major criminal suspects, produces proof of crime; but its use is branded "dirty business" ignobly exercised by a moral society. The death penalty, with grim finality, precludes any murderer from killing again; but it is deplored as the ultimate in immorality, coarsening and brutalizing the community that makes use of it. *Non-coercive* prisoner interrogation often produces reliable confessions, evidence upon which the admittedly guilty may be convicted and incarcerated when the protection of all seems to require it; yet many urge that it is immoral for police and prosecutors to question suspected wrongdoers. And a police officer, armed with a search warrant, may seize a quantity of heroin such that mere proof of its possession would convict its custodian of a felony; but if, on some technicality, the warrant proves defective, the officer's act becomes unlawful, and as the law today deems it immoral that the state should rely upon lawlessness in proving its case, the evidence is excluded. I do not here quarrel with any of these assertions of "morality." Clearly, however, they underscore the sophistry of many who would write off the significance of morality when dealing with obscenity, and who, *in that context only*, insist both that morality cannot be legislated, and that the community refrain from censorship unless it can produce *tangible* evidence that obscenity harms grown-ups.

Sexual morality, and obscenity's impact upon it, is a traditional and appropriate concern of society. The recognition of this by anthropologist Margaret Mead and former federal Judge Thurman Arnold, who clearly are neither bluenoses nor friends of broad state censorship, has been noted earlier.[3] Recently, Britain's Sir Patrick Devlin, commenting on England's Wolfenden Report (which advocated removing the criminal onus from private homosexual conduct between consenting adults), observed:

. . . an established morality is as necessary as good government to the welfare of society. Societies disintegrate from within more frequently than they are broken up by external pressures. There is disintegration when no common morality is observed and history shows that the loosening of moral bonds is often the first stage of disintegration, so that society is justified in taking the same steps to preserve its moral code as it does to preserve its government and other essential institutions.

• • •

Not everything is to be tolerated. No society can do without intolerance, indignation, and disgust; they are the forces behind the moral law. . . .[4]

Anti-pornography measures, then, although not to be too readily indulged, should be available to protect "established morality," and when that morality has been attacked, to respond to, or to anticipate and to head off community indignation. Supreme Court Justice John M. Harlan has commented on the propriety of anti-obscenity legislation, although no crime-obscenity nexus may be demonstrable:

. . . even assuming that pornography cannot be deemed ever to cause, in an immediate sense, criminal sexual conduct, other interests within the proper cognizance of the States may be protected by the prohibition placed on such materials. The State can reasonably draw the inference that over a long period of time the indiscriminate dissemination of materials, the essential character of which is to degrade sex, will have an eroding effect on moral standards.[5]

In brief, our states appropriately grapple with moral, as well as with air and water, pollution.

To what extent is pornography polluting? In its acceptance and promotion of indiscriminate sex, it tends to dehumanize the sex relationship. "We may define pornography, cross-culturally," according to Margaret Mead, "as words or acts or representations that are calculated to stimulate sex feelings independent of the presence of another *loved and chosen* human being."[6] Pornography promenades and trumpets sex, rather than holding it close. And something of this is bound to rub off on those who wallow in it. The eroticist's approach to sex feeds on pornography and, in turn, grows fat by what it feeds on. "Eroticism, unlike sex and love, apparently offers something for nothing," commented novelist-critic J. B. Priestley, adding:

It is sexual pleasure without sexual responsibility . . . . Unlike sex, it is not completely natural and it is at the furthest possible remove from love, which is supremely personal . . . . More and more men are crowding into this blind alley, not demanding more life, richer relationships, but only a barren titillation. The encouragement and exploitation of eroticism, sometimes out of hatred of Woman and fear of real sex and love, but mostly for commercial gain, now constitutes one of the worst features of our Western civilization.[7]

Pornography's barrenness, its self-centeredness, was more recently inspected by Priestley's countryman, Pamela Hansford Johnson. Reflecting on the Moors murder trial, in which children were the victims of pornographically inspired carnage, Miss Johnson commented:

We are in danger of creating an Affectless Society, in which nobody cares for anyone but himself, or for anything but instant self-gratification. We demand sex without love, violence for "kicks." We are encouraging the blunting of sensibility: and this, let us remember, was not the way to an Earthly Paradise, but the way to Auschwitz.

When the Nazis took on the government of Poland, they flooded the Polish bookstalls with pornography . . . . They did so on the theory that to make the individual conscious only of the need for personal sensation would make the social combination of forces more difficult. The more we withdraw into the shell of self, breeding like tapeworms upon self alone, the less likely we are to face the problems that do not directly relate to ourselves. The Nazi scheme was the deliberate use of pornography to the ends of social castration. The theory was, and it is worth considering, that—permit all things for self-gratification, and you are likely to encourage withdrawal from any sort of corporate responsibility.[8]

Pornography not only coarsens, but it invades that precious privacy that, in our Western culture, coexists with sexual intimacy. Katherine Anne Porter, in her reflective essay about *Lady Chatterley's Lover* and the litigation that cleared it, expressed this:

. . . the unbelievably grotesque episode of this besotted couple weaving flowers in each other's pubic hair, hanging bouquets and wreaths in other strategic bodily spots, making feeble little dirty jokes, inventing double-meaning nicknames for their sexual organs, and altogether, though God knows it is an imbecilic harmlessness, and is meant in all solemn God's-earnestness to illustrate true passion at lyric play, I for one feel that I have overheard talk and witnessed acts never meant for me to hear or witness. . . . Love-making surely must be, for human beings at our present state of development, one of the more private enterprises. Who would want a witness to that entire self-abandonment and helplessness? So it is best in such a case for the intruder to tip-toe away quietly, and say nothing. I hold that this is not prudery nor hypocrisy; I still believe in the validity of simple respect and regard for the dark secret things of life—that they should be inviolable, and guarded by the two who take part, and that no other presence should be invited.[9]

Miss Porter's plea that we be spared these invasions of sexual privacy is no lone expression tendered by a prominent literary lady. In June 1965, in voiding Connecticut's law that banned the use of contraceptives, the United States Supreme Court lent its aid in protecting what it termed the "zone of privacy" that surrounds the sex act. In an opinion written by Justice William O. Douglas, the high Tribunal declared that the sex relationship involved "a right of privacy older than the Bill of Rights."[10] Granted, there is a vast difference between the right to sexual privacy of married persons to use such contraceptives as they may choose, and asserting the right of sexual privacy to bar novelists, autobiographers, or photographers and their models. from portraying sex acts. Nevertheless, the Supreme Court's blessing supports a premise that tends to justify restrictions upon adult pornography: public policy favors protecting inviolate the privacy of sex.

Further arguments, not crucial but contributory, favor imposing some limitations on pornography's exposure to adults. Age does not magically transform all young people, in all ways, to maturity. There are many adults who are no better able than children to handle the internal conflicts, pornographically intensified, that disturb their sexual daydreams. Pornography, for certain adults, will inflame drives that they may prove unable to handle, or that they may seem to control only at the cost of inner tensions.

That pornography breeds adult crime has been contended, but it seems dubious at best. The latest Kinsey report, *Sex Offenders,* uniquely combining underplayed wit with interminable statistical analysis, concludes that it does not:

There is nothing pathological or antisocial in enjoying and owning pornography. . . .

When one reads in a newspaper that obscene or pornographic materials were found in an individual's possession, one should interpret this information to mean that (1) the individual was probably a male of an age between puberty and senility, and (2) that he probably derived pleasure from thinking about sex. No further inferences are warranted.[11]

Yet the researchers' underlying data cast some doubt on this conclusion; the data suggest that pornography, as a factor in adult sex crime, cannot be written off completely. Institutionalized white males over sixteen years of age, classified by the Kinsey Institute as "heterosexual *aggressors*" against children, minors, and adults (those serving time for forcible sex acts against little girls, adolescent females, and grown women) reported a high arousal rate from sado-masochistic pictures and stories.[12] For instance:

In keeping with their offense, they [heterosexual aggressors vs. minors] had the largest proportion (21 per cent) of men who were sexually aroused by sadomasochistic pictures and stories, and by far the largest proportion (13 per cent) who were strongly aroused . . . . The aggressors vs. minors also rank first in the number (74 per cent) who were sexually aroused by pornography, and first again in the number (44 per cent) who were strongly aroused.

Moreover, our law is paternalistic. It does *not* permit us to go to hell in a handbasket simply because, as individuals, we may choose to do so. It protects us from our own follies, or at least from those that our legislators deem follies, although we may not believe that we are in need of that protection. The government compels salaried persons to salt away an income for their old age through Social Security, although many might prefer living wholly for today, or may have plenty in reserve for tomorrow without forced saving. The penal laws bar us from gambling, although we may have ample means and may crave its excitement. Contemporary Mormons may have only one wife. We may not use marijuana, although we are permitted to use the more habit-forming and, for many, less pleasurable tobacco. The law bars us from partying with ready, willing, and agile prostitutes. It has even made suicide criminal. As British editor C. H. Rolph has said:

It does not . . . follow that because a man wants something it is good for him, even in this post-Puritan age, and society is within its rights in acting on its belief that it is not—again in the absence of proof to the contrary. If there really is anyone who "needs" striptease shows, one suspects that, like a drug addict, his more genuine need is for treatment.[13]

One further consideration exists, one that cannot stand alone, favoring banning the most unredeemed pornography from adults. Some of whatever is readily at hand for elders is likely to trickle down to their and their neighbors' offspring. This runoff takes two forms. One is tangible: some youngsters, inevitably, will get copies of whatever pornographic books or paraphernalia have been freely sold to their parents; the quarantining of children is certain to have some leaks. The other is intangible: the young emulate the smart, the sophisticated, the "advanced" tastes of their forbears. Should, for example, raw and obscene talk prove the path to reputation among the cognoscenti (as, for a while, it did for Lenny Bruce), it may be difficult to convince the younger generation that filthy conversation is socially unacceptable, that chronic reliance on it may mirror an inability to use effectively ordinary powers of speech. If the search for erotica leads adults to stag movies and to topless bars, it may seem disingenuous to try to convince children that sex is really an expression of love and that female modesty may prove more desirably feminine than exhibitionism. Ophelia observes (while still quite sane) that no one can effectively show "the steep and thorny way to heaven, whilst . . . himself . . . the primrose path of dalliance treads." This is not to take issue with the Supreme Court's obviously sound and necessary observation, in the *Butler* case, that no law should "reduce the adult population . . . to reading only what is fit for children."[14] But if, *for other reasons,* limited restrictions upon adult reading or viewing seem appropriate, such fitness may be reinforced by adding this factor to the scales.

These arguments for censoring adult reading or other entertainments do *not* prove that such censorship is *essential* if society, as we know it, is to survive. Ever present, and pulling in the opposite direction, is the need to safeguard the freedom of speech and press, although we know from a long line of high Court decisions that obscenity is not constitutionally shielded. And so the problem of the impact of pornography on adults is one of reaching a balance between two interests, neither of which is truly compelling; on the one hand the desire of majorities (existing legislation in almost every state reveals their numbers) in our communities to root out pornography; on the other the minority's espousal of uninhibited freedom to enjoy even the most depraved pornography, conceding that such freedom cannot *today* be bottomed upon sound constitutional claims.

A balance, of course, must be struck, but the fear haunting any censorship of adult entertainment is this, that once it starts it may spin out of hand. Objectively examined, what cubit of culture or what iota of literary tradition would our Western civilization have lost if *Lady Chatterley's Lover* had remained under banishment? To libertarians, the importance of the *Lady Chatterley* litigation was not that the book itself was spun gold, but if the novel could have been lawfully cast out, what might next have followed? Yet as long as censorship's boundaries are sketched only by such vague words as "obscene," "lewd," and "lascivious," and by the equally uncertain opinions that interpret them, the fear of any censorship and the fear that once started its confines are dangerously uncertain make sense. Under this vague vocabulary the ultimate decision hinges on the unforeseeable membership of the Supreme Court. Although during the last decade the Justices have generally shown themselves to be far more the friends of the libertarians than of the Philistines, they have not established metes and bounds so clearly mapped as to answer the anti-censors' question, "Where will censorship, once started, stop?" The imposition of some limitations on freedom of speech and press does not mean, of course, that the barriers are up and that the next order of business is general state control over all expression. This fear that any control may ultimately mean broad restraints is unworthy of those trained in the law. Much of the business of lawyers, particularly that of legislators, is the drawing of lines. Heneage Finch, the first Earl of Nottingham and later Lord Chancellor of England, faced with a similar contention almost three centuries ago (in a quite different sort of a case), gave answer, "I will tell you where I will stop: I will stop where-ever any visible Inconvenience doth appear."[15] Truly liberal legislators might better make this their watchword than the absolutist slogans and the accompanying fears they so commonly mouth. Rather than making no law because of paralyzing fears as to a stopping place, legislators should so carefully draw lines that the judiciary, with all of the uncertainty of judge-made law, will not be obliged to putter and patch. If *some* restrictions upon adult access to pornography are desirable, but *severe* restriction would be dangerous, legislators should decide the point at which "any visible Inconvenience doth appear."

23. Indecency and Adults —
Precise Limitations

I should say that there is a very wide distinction between what is
read and what is seen. In a novel one may read, "Eliza stripped off
her dressing-gown and stepped into her bath," without any harm;
but I think that if that were presented on the stage it would be
very shocking.

—Sir William S. Gilbert, in testimony before the *British
Joint Select Committee on the Stage Plays (Censorship),*
p. 192 (1909)

WHETHER ADULT VIEWING, reading, and listening should be
state-inhibited, in any fashion, is a question on which different
legislative bodies can, quite understandably, reach varying results. To pose a simple contrast: the views of representatives
from the Granite State, New Hampshire, and those of their
counterparts from the Silver State, Nevada, might diverge.
The inheritors of New England's puritanical tradition would
almost certainly be far harder on bare-breasted bar waitresses
than would Nevadans, for whom female nudity may conjure
visions of cash registers clinking with tourist dollars.

If priorities are to be assigned in the battle against indecency,
laws protecting the young and statutes safeguarding community
sensibilities against offensive displays, are more urgently needed
than are those imposing restrictions on adult off-the-street behavior. But if there are to be laws in this area of adult indecency, they should strive to avoid the absurdities that generally
mock present-day anti-obscenity provisions.

First, insofar as is possible, a proper law should shun today's imprecise vocabulary. The words and phrases "obscene," "patently offensive," "hard-core," "redeeming social importance," and "appeals to prurient interests," emphasize personal *tastes,* not legislative *standards.* Testifying in Britain in 1909, in opposition to the Lord Chamberlain's authority to censor plays (authority that is still there existant), but favoring some controls, George Bernard Shaw said:

I strongly protest against anything that is not quite definite. You may make any law you like defining what is an incentive to sexual vice, but to lay down a general law . . . with regard to unspecified incentives to sexual vice is going too far, when the mere fact of a woman washing her face and putting on decent clothes, or anything of the kind, may possibly cause somebody in the street who passes to admire her, and to say, "I have been incited to sexual vice." These definitions are too dangerous. I do not think that any lawyer should tolerate them.[1]

Second, the law should recognize that there is a vast gulf between what one does or sees in private and what is done or seen in public. *Private* entertainment, ranging from reading through *dolce vita* private parties, should be largely immune to regulation. Such activities are, essentially, one's own business. Quite different are those entertainments that take place at the "publick house." Inns and theaters have always been subject to regulation, and publicly advertised entertainments held in them are not private in any meaningful sense of the word. All adults for whom there is space and who can pay the price of admission are admitted, and the shows play to audiences of strangers —strangers both to each other and to the performers. The impact of the public show is likely to radiate far beyond these immediate audiences. Such shows, for continued life, depend on their financial success; that, in turn, depends upon the critical and popular splash the show makes. It is not sufficient that the first audience approves. The community outside must be informed, in the hopes that more of it will attend in the future.

If such shows are sufficiently at odds with morality, and their ballyhoo has been successful, they may become an "in" topic of cocktail chatter, often by people who have never seen them. And their success is likely to proliferate imitations. Obviously, the mere fact that an admission may have been charged does not make it private, if that word is to have other than economic significance. The gulf, then, between the truly private and what realistically considered is public should be acknowledged in any proper adult anti-obscenity statute.

Third, any new statute should build on the differences among those media through which seeming pornography is presented. Statutes too commonly lump together books, motion pictures, live shows, and other means of presenting the possibly offensive, applying the same language in testing each for obscenity. Yet sex, sexual intercourse or oral-genital contact for example, staged as *live* entertainment for third persons, strains at depravity; it is a far greater affront to community mores than would be *pictured* sex. And *pictured* sex, in turn, is appreciably more shocking than *literary* sex.

Fourth, a wise adult obscenity law must take stock of the particular audience at whom the disputed items are directed. Not only is there a difference between adolescents and adults, but there may be differences between varying adults. In his *Hicklin* opinion, Lord Chief Justice Sir Alexander Cockburn had anticipated such distinctions:

A medical treatise, with illustrations necessary for the information of those for whose education or information the work is intended, may, in a certain sense, be obscene, and yet not the subject of indictment; but it can never be that these prints may be exhibited for anyone, boys and girls, to see as they pass. The immunity must depend on the circumstances of the publication.[2]

In March 1966, Justice Brennan's *Ginzburg* opinion, speaking for a majority of the American high Bench, brought this thinking up to date in noting, as to one of the publications:

The solicitation was indiscriminate, not limited to those, such as physicians or psychiatrists, who might independently discern the book's therapeutic worth.

• • •

Petitioners, however, did not sell the book to such a limited audience, or focus their claims for it on its supposed therapeutic or educational value; rather, they deliberately emphasized the sexually provocative aspects of the work, in order to catch the salaciously disposed.[3]

As has been seen, judicial majorities in the *Mishkin* and the *Ginzburg* cases (and three of the Justices in the *Fanny Hill* case) ruled that when borderline obscenity was involved, the nature of the marketing efforts and of the prospective audiences were relevant factors in reaching a decision. Dean William B. Lockhart and Professor Robert C. McClure, the most careful American scholars in the obscenity field, have extensively discussed the idea of *variable obscenity*, of which the pandering test is a preliminary wrinkle. They favor the concept, and have urged that it "provides solutions to most of the problems that constant obscenity leaves unresolved."[4] Two years before the 1966 decisions, the United States Supreme Court, by implication, indicated its recognition that differences in *media* markedly affected judgments concerning obscenity. Seven of the high Judges (all except Hugo L. Black and William O. Douglas) had, by earlier rulings sustaining some obscenity enforcement, tacitly expressed their views that at least the very roughest of traditional hard-core, genital-revealing photographs of people sexually rampant were subject to banning as pornographic.[5] Yet, in June 1964, a majority of the Justices ruled, in the *Tropic of Cancer* case, that *written descriptions of precisely the same conduct* were *not* actionably obscene. And so high Court sanction exists for attaching major significance to the choice of means used in depicting any items of alleged obscenity. This needs no laboring: *a Fanny Hill* movie, with shots zoomed in to faithfully reflect the book's genital details, would far outdo the most vulgar stag motion picture ever made, and would, beyond all question, be ruled to be hard-core; this although the book has been cleared by the nation's highest court.

If the obscenity standard is to be a variable one, with numerous decisions being made that classify media, audiences, advertising, and the items that may or may not be portrayed, it is more fitting that it be legislatively designed than relegated by legislative inaction to the courts. Legislators, elected for limited terms, are necessarily in close touch with community standards. Besides, line drawing should be, in the first instance, a legislative and not a judicial function. "I recognize without hesitation," said Justice Oliver Wendell Holmes, "that judges do and must legislate, but they can do so only interstitially; they are confined from molar to molecular motions."[6] Creative legislation can do far more. It can effectively construct new standards, and can do so explicitly and in advance of the sheer exhaustion that litigation entails. Justice John M. Harlan, who of all the high Court's Justices has most consistently pursued a course that would retain anti-obscenity enforcement while minimizing the claims upon the high Court's time entailed by case-by-case review, stressed this legislative role when, in dissenting in the *Ginzburg* case, he noted

Were a State to enact a "panderer" statute under its police power, I have little doubt that—subject to clear drafting to avoid attacks on vagueness and equal protection grounds—such a statute would be constitutional . . . . What I fear the Court has done today is in effect to write a new statute, but without the sharply focused definitions and standards necessary in such a sensitive area.[7]

"Sharply focused definitions and standards" are the essence of the proposed variable obscenity statute that follows. As formulated, it is not tendered as an immutable solution, one that *must* be adopted in every particular. Even if it is agreed that *some* censorship is to be imposed upon adults, legislators from varying areas may deem the suggested standards far more, or far less, sophisticated than those palatable to the adults in their home communities. They may vary its particulars accordingly. Moreover, it is obvious that our mores will continue to change— the sexual turbulence of the last twenty years seems headed for no repose—and the specifics of any closely worded statute will, in the future, have to be modified. But in the obscenity field we are enjoined by the courts to embrace a *contemporary* community standard, and the proposal is an effort to do just that. It does not crystal-gaze, predicting tomorrow's morality or tolerance. Statutes are for today; unlike constitutions they need not serve omnisciently for posterity. Posterity will have time enough to do its own legislating.

Over-all, the constitutionality of the proposal should not be seriously in question. Although the anti-obscenity vocabulary spun by the high Court and by both state and federal legislative bodies has been abandoned in the draft, that vocabulary's underpinnings are not ignored. Rather the proposal substitutes specifics for the accustomed generalities. In creating this precision, constitutionality should be bolstered. Trial judges should welcome it; it would rid them of much of the absurdity of trying to guess what appellate courts may say is or is not obscene. And appellate tribunals would find their role in reviewing obscenity shrinking to what it was in pre-*Roth* days. Passing on whether an indecency crime has been committed would become only slightly more difficult than determining whether or not such crimes as robbery or assault have been established.

So much for generalities. Specifically, how does the proposal plan to do all this?

A PROPOSED STATUTE

1. *Definitions.* As used in this section:
   (a) "public show" means any entertainment or exhibition advertised or in other fashion held out to be accessible to the public, whether or not an admission or other

charge is levied or collected; an entertainment or exhibition shall be deemed a public show although access to it is only granted to members of a club or other association, when membership in such organization is obtained upon payment of an admission price or contribution or token dues or other small fee, and the organization in fact exists primarily for sponsoring or arranging admissions to such performances; and

(b) "live public show" means a public show in which human actors, dancers, or other performers, employees, or other persons appear in person before spectators or customers. A bona fide drawing, painting, photography, sculpture, or other art class utilizing human models and admitting only participating instructors, students, and models shall not be deemed a live public show.

(The other definitions, appearing in the proposed sale-to-minors statute, will also apply.)

2. *Facilitating live public shows.* Any person shall be guilty of a misdemeanor who, in any capacity, knowingly directs, gives, manages, participates in, prepares, or presents, or who employs others so to do, any live public show explicitly showing sado-masochistic abuse, sexual conduct, or nudity, or containing explicit verbal descriptions or narrative accounts of sado-masochistic abuse, sexual conduct, or sexual excitement or utilizing obscenities.

3. *Presenting pictured material and other images.* Any person shall be guilty of a misdemeanor who, in any capacity, knowingly:

(a) directs, distributes, exhibits, manages, photographs, produces, sells, or shows, or possesses with intent to sell or to show, or participates in the creation, presentation, sale, or transfer, of any motion picture, or of any photograph, or any book, magazine, or other item, containing one or more photographs, of humans:

i. that, showing sado-masochistic abuse, sexual conduct,

or defecation or urination, explicitly reveals genital areas; or

ii. that, intended to be presented at a public show, explicity reveals acts of sado-masochistic abuse, sexual conduct, defecation, or urination, or persons so positioned as to appear to be engaged in such conduct, and that shows the nude or nearly nude body, although genital areas are not pictured; or

(b) with intent to present same at a public show, directs, distributes, exhibits, manages, photographs, produces, sells, shows, or possesses, or participates in the creation, presentation, sale, or transfer, of any motion picture of humans:

i. that explicitly reveals genital areas; or

ii. that either reveals sexual acts of homosexual or bestial contact, or that shows the participants in or witnesses to such suggested acts moments prior to, or during, or moments after such suggested acts; or

(c) draws, exhibits, paints, presents, sculpts, sells, shows, or participates in the creation or presentation of any drawing, picture, sculpture, or other essentially non-photographic visual representation or other image, or any book, magazine, or other item containing one or more such images that, presented at a public show, shows sado-masochistic abuse, sexual conduct, defecation, or urination, so as to reveal genital areas.

4. *Publishing and selling written or recorded materials.* Any person shall be guilty of a misdemeanor who, in any capacity, knowingly distributes, leases, sells, or otherwise commercially markets or rents any book, magazine, pamphlet, paperback, or other written or printed matter however reproduced, or any sound recording, or who possesses such item for purposes of so disposing of it, under circumstances demonstrating his intention to exploit commercially a morbid interest in sado-masochistic abuse, sexual conduct, sexual excitement, defecation, or urination.

Among those circumstances that may, taken together, serve to demonstrate the actor's intention are:

(a) the content of the item with regard to materials it contains in the enumerated proscribed areas;

(b) the content of the item, if any, apart from those materials it contains in the enumerated proscribed areas, and the relative significance of that content in the advertising or marketing of the item;

(c) the artistic, scientific, historical, or other social values of the item, and the relative significance of such values in the advertising or marketing of the item;

(d) the general character of the advertising or marketing of the item, and that of other items jointly advertised or marketed with the item;

(e) the format, price, and distribution of the item.

This subsection shall not, however, render criminal the distribution, selling, or otherwise commercially marketing or renting a book, magazine, pamphlet, paperback, or other written or printed matter that is a serious and bona fide treatise or handbook on sexual functioning, guidance, hygiene, or problems, and is advertised and marketed as such.

5. *Presumptions.* The following presumption is applicable to this section:

Any person owning, operating, or employed in the business of selling, offering for sale, renting, or exhibiting any of the materials proscribed by this section shall be presumed to have knowledge of the contents of all such materials offered for sale, delivered from, exhibited, shown, rented, or displayed in the premises owned or operated by him or in which he is employed.

6. *Defenses.* The following shall be defenses to this charge, the burden of proof of which, by a preponderance of the evidence, shall be upon the defendant:

(a) That those aspects of any item that would otherwise appear to be actionable under this section form merely a minor and incidental part of an otherwise non-offending whole, and serve some purpose therein other than titillation, except that no sexual conduct beyond an apparent touching of the unexposed buttocks or female breast shall be permitted in any live public show, nor shall any sexual conduct that explicitly reveals genital areas be permitted in any public show, nor shall any book, magazine, or other item contain any photograph of humans that, showing sado-masochistic abuse, sexual conduct, defecation or urination, explicitly reveals genital areas.

(b) That a bona fide governmental, scientific, or other similar justification for the defendant's conduct exists, demonstrated by the content, format, and price of the work itself, the circumstances of the item's marketing and intended use, and the defendant's conduct concerning it.

CONSIDERATION OF THE PROPOSAL

In separate provisions the draft deals with live public shows, with photographs and moving pictures, with non-photographic images, and with written or recorded materials. It does not deal with radio and television; they are effectively regulated by the Federal Communications Commission, and—playing to mixed audiences, to adults and to children, in their own homes as well as in public places—hew to standards far more inhibiting than any here contemplated. As to each media considered, the proposal states what sexual, excretory, or nude presentations are banned. It focuses upon *public* matters, permitting adults almost complete freedom, unimpeded by anti-obscenity laws, in their private actions. (Separate statutes may, of course, perpetuate inhibitions on prostitution and other privately indulged conduct that legislators may believe necessitates enforcement interference; however, it is generally impracticable as to non-commercial wholly private action.) The proposal recognizes, however, that regardless of the most careful draftsmanship, in some circumstances materials seemingly proscribed should not be. Photographs or movies of intercourse and sodomy when collected by the Kinsey Institute for Sex Research would provide one example of a necessary exception; the obviously non-prurient momentary male nudity, rear viewed, in the recent Broadway theatrical experience *Marat/Sade* (*The Persecution and Assassination of Marat as Performed by the Inmates of the Assylum of Charenton under the Direction of the Marquis De Sade*) is another. Defenses, carefully circumscribed, are therefore provided. One of them comes into play when the nature of the item's intended use *proves* its bona fide educational, governmental, scientific, or other similar justification; the other when the proscribed facets of a seemingly improper item are minor only, and are incidental to otherwise inoffensive materials.

LIVE SHOWS

When sex is performed in the flesh for an audience, even be the action partially shielded by a burlap bag as in the Parisian happening early in this decade, two things that seem to remain uninvolved are free speech and free press. The founding fathers, neither by design nor inadvertance, created any constitutional right to such public displays. (The First Amendment's protection of "the right of the people peaceably to assemble" is a limited one; it is ". . . to assemble *and* to Petition the Government for a redress of grievances"; it does not assure the right to assemble in any place for any possible purpose.) And so, unprotected by the First or any other amendment, such performances may be outlawed completely and are banned under the draft statute without any need being specified of proving that they have obscene or prurient appeal.

As proffered, the draft similarly bans female nudity and semi-nudity, live, in public, whether or not an admission price is charged, or the façade of a "private" club or association is created to mask the operation. No proof is required of the show's obscene character. Both the burlesque stripteaser and the bare-breasted topless bar waitress would be outlawed. Here, too, no First Amendment issue seems to exist. Other than that we have learned that the courts may do nearly anything (the late Supreme Court Justice Robert H. Jackson observed "We are not final because we are infallible, but we are infallible only because we are final"[8]), how can an appellate court rule it *unreasonable,* and therefore unconstitutional, when a community—one that has been wearing clothes, indoors and out, summer and winter, ever since it drove out the Indians—legislates that live adult nudity in the presence of strangers of the opposite sex, regardless of the form it takes, is an affront to decency and is therefore a penal offense? There is no need to require, and to get hung up on, findings of prurience. Dispensing with that requirement avoids not only subjective personal judgments, but those absurd, awkward, and embarrassing spectacles in which hefty police officers attempt to mime the bumps and gyrations of "exotic dancers," to prove that their disrobing was obscenely accompanied. This is not to suggest that nudity *per se* is offensive. It is not. Once again, surroundings are all. Nudity can be highly appropriate in the artist's studio or in his classroom, in the privacy of the bedroom, or in nudist camp woodlands shared by participants and not paraded before clothed spectators. Society may, however, without acting unreasonably, reject it completely as a live spectator sport.[9]

What about other live and entertaining presentations of nudity and semi-nudity: the bare-bosomed show girls of the Folies-Bergère, the nude modern dance team of the Buffalo *Festival of the Arts Today,* the bare beer bathers of Milwaukee, the bra-less dancers of *Les Ballets Africains* cavorting to savage rhythms on American platforms as part of an international cultural exchange? In each, semi-nudity being more than merely minor and incidental to the performance, the bans of the proposed statute would apply. Yet, concededly, for only a small segment of the audience would these shows share the burlesque

stripper's shabby appeal. The statute's impact on such performances may be unfortunate, but a statute that is to be effective
in banning the tawdry in public nudity would, were it to avoid
the hazards of personal tastes (euphemistically labeled "artistic
judgments") also have to bar semi-nudity in "nicer" events.
Theory aside, how much *serious* cultural deprivation would be
involved by insistence that all public performers, even those
for whose performances toplessness was indigenous, be draped
with a tiny swatch or two? Were the African tribal dancers
to be permitted to disport in topless non-attire, what about such
other tribesmen and women whom American audiences might
enjoy watching and whose primitive dances, authentically presented, would require complete undress? "When you realize that
you are dealing with a matter of degree," Justice Holmes has
noted in another context, "you must realize that reasonable men
may differ widely as to the place where the line should fall."[10]
And it is not the bench's function to void statutes merely because the judges prefer their own judgments to those of the
legislators. Moreover, the fact that in minor respects a carefully drawn statute declares conduct criminal that may seem
harmless is not a basis for voiding it. Such penal provisions are
not uncommon. Speed limits and traffic lights, necessary to
control masses of cars during busy hours, still pertain on lonely
streets and highways at four in the morning when no other
cars or pedestrians are to be seen. Our laws against statutory
rape make it criminal to share sex with a long initiated full-
bodied teen-age hustler who happens to be just the tender side
of the age of consent.

As proposed, the draft would also ban the Lenny Bruce kind
of public show in which a live entertainer regales his audience
with the shock humor of massed obscenities and the prurient
details of sexual and excretory experiences. Here, as the ruckus
during the Bruce prosecutions witnessed, is an area in which
a number of articulate and thoughtful persons believe the
law has no business; that if adults wish to pay to hear this, it

is wholly a matter of their personal choice and should be their business. Different legislatures may differently view the wisdom of a provision aimed at such a show. Those who may wish it included within their anti-obscenity statute, those who may deem it expressive of their community standards, may enact it with some confidence that at least reasonable arguments exist to sustain it constitutionally. The charging of an admission price alone should not immunize such a performance. The aura generated by any show open to the ticket-buying public is likely to extend, as has been seen, far beyond the show's immediate audiences. Moreover, the *personal* impact of a *live* entertainment on those actually present is not cavalierly to be undersold. Why do road show and little theater performances draw audiences, when the same spectators often might catch better-acted versions at their local movie houses? In part because live acting has the potential for telegraphing a personal response across the footlights; it can generate a person-to-person magic through the theater. Spectators become, after a fashion, participants. These personal reactions are compounded when fired by something as personal, as intimate, as sex. Self-conscious excitement may be stirred by an audience's awareness of each others' and of the performers' presence, of the scorning of societal taboos, and of the daring to do so publicly in the presence of numbers of listeners. One of the ills of pornography is its invasion of the privacy of sex. How much greater that invasion becomes when the materials are simultaneously shared at public performances than when they are absorbed by the solitary reader, poring alone in his home over the pages of a book! (There is, of course, a contrary argument: audience response may suggest a hearty ribaldry; private pursuit of the pornographic hints at a secret eroticism and masturbation fantasies.) Old words, words that all have heard before, stories of primal sex play and of changeless bodily functioning are likely to assume special shock impact hurled live at the paying public. Pornography has been defined as "the blow to sense, not merely to sensibility."[11] Administered through a live, three-dimensional show, that blow is far more resounding than when transferred from the pages of even the most pungent of volumes. The performers and the audience become joint actors in a verbal orgy of sorts, one stripping the privacy and much of the decency from normally covert concepts. If being a "volunteer" has any relevancy whatsoever in terms of actionable obscenity, it is markedly easier to beg off when a book is involved, it need only be shut, than when attending a public performance. Walking out on a sharp tongued entertainer may call for a courage likely to keep all but the heartiest captives in their seats.

A ban on live performances steeped in obscenities or sexual or excretory detail would not bowdlerize every play or performance that made use of them. The defenses already noted would apply. Edward Albee's play, *Who's Afraid of Virginia Woolf?* or LeRoi Jones's *The Toilet*, both invoking dialogue strewn with obscenities *incidental* to character, plot, and situation, would *not* run afoul of the suggested statute.

MOVING PICTURES, PHOTOGRAPHS, AND OTHER IMAGES

"One picture," runs the Old Chinese proverb, "is worth more than ten thousand words." So saying, the Chinese combined words and pictures in a pictographic written tongue. In the West our words are not self-illustrating, and our invention of photography was to further compound the Oriental odds. Particularly in the area of sex, snapshots and the movies have the capacity for being far more vivid, far more personal, and far more pruriently appealing, than paragraphs of written words. To entertain those for whom pornography is manna, photographs require no literacy, only momentary attention, and little imagination. Genital-revealing shots (whether stills or motion pictures) of people engaging in sex are hard-core at its most ruttish. No need, no justification, for them has ever been tendered. They intrude not only upon the persons photographed (who, paid for their prostitution, are pleased to waive their privacy), but they profane the intimacy of sex itself. Legislators, therefore, might reasonably find the camera's lens does that which is inherently indecent and irredeemable. And so the proposal outlaws such pictures completely, even when prepared for adult private viewing, allowing only their collection for scientific purposes, as when assembled for the Kinsey Institute's library in Bloomington, Indiana, or when taken and privately used to further the work of the Reproductive Biology Research Foundation headed by Dr. William H. Masters in St. Louis, Missouri.[12] The law's ban would range from the crude stag movies and "playing cards" through any claimed avant-garde "artistry" that might spotlight the same subject matter. One example of the latter would be those scenes of masturbation and oral-genital stimulation seen in Jack Smith's *Flaming Creatures*, that led to the arrest and conviction of film critic Jonas Mekas.

The work of contemporary motion picture directors, magazine publishers, and artists has, however, spotlighted some of the fine gradations that may exist in this area of photographed sex. Ralph Ginzburg's last and most controversial issue of *Eros* (the one on which a portion of his conviction was to rest), in pictures that Ginzburg termed a "photographic tone poem," showed a nude couple with torsos belly-to-belly, so positioned that genital contact, although uncertain and unrevealed, was not unlikely. In the spring of 1964 Grove Press's avant-garde monthly, *Evergreen Review*, featured a photographic portfolio of mixed nudes, processed as if taken under water or through a bubbly haze. The pictures showed bodies so juxtaposed that sexual contacts of various sorts were not improbable, but the distortion left wholly to the imagination precisely who was doing what (if anything), how, and to whom. (Criminal litigation charging that issue of *Evergreen Review* with obscenity was disposed of on procedural grounds.[13]) The widely distributed Ingmar Bergman motion picture, *The Silence*, closed in on the facial ecstacy of a woman while masturbating, and the film, *A Stranger Knocks*, cleared by the Supreme Court in March 1965,[14] showed the head and shoulders of its heroine while, off camera, the rest of her was engaging in sexual intercourse. These peepshow suggestions, all barely avoiding the explicit, veered from traditional concepts of photographic pornography sufficiently to create uncertainty as to obscenity. They suggest how specific a meaningful statutory definition of variable obscenity must be if it is to avoid personal judgments.

The proposed statute attempts to produce order out of this chaos. It provides that items that are explicit are more offensive than those that are only implicit; that photographs of people sexually engaged are more vivid, and to be more tightly controlled, than are drawings or other non-photographic images; that moving pictures are far more real than are stills; that nude figures, sexually positioned, are of greater potential prurience than clothed ones in similar poses; and that pictured bestiality and homosexuality are more repugnant than pictured heterosexual activity.

Specifically, the proposal bars any use, public or private, of genital-revealing photographs of people engaged in sexual activity. True artistry hardly requires the freedom, or rather the licentiousness, to be that explicit. Father John Courtney Murray, the Jesuit scholar-priest whose outcry *against* both private pressure group and governmental censorship was to see him in conflict with the prelates of his Church, has observed that "the genuine artist knows instinctively that, although art may 'say all,' there are certain things it is never allowed to say explicitly."[15] The draft statute would permit photographs in books and magazines (where ordinarily they might be privately, not publicly, perused), of grouped nudes sexually positioned although no genitals were revealed—the *Eros* and *Evergreen Review* photographs, for example. But moving pictures of nudes showing genitals, even if no sexual activity were to be suggested, would be barred from public exhibition. Photographs showing neither genitalia nor nudity, but nevertheless suggesting sexual activity,

as in *The Silence* and *A Stranger Knocks,* might be publicly
shown; they require imagination to complete the picture, and
themselves do little to satisfy lewd tastes; the controversy sur-
rounding their banning gives them their only measure of prurient
appeal. Photographs, however, unmistakably suggesting bestiality
or homosexuality, sexual deviations disgusting and repugnant
to the overwhelming majority of our communities, would be
barred from public shows. (In late 1965 a federal judge, in
excluding a Swedish film, *491*, from America, until his ruling
was reversed by a split higher federal court, noted that it
included the following:

The Inspector is shown with his head between the thighs of the boy.
The movie stops just short of showing the culmination of the homosexual act . . . . A naked prostitute is the subject of the sex orgy.
She is shown leaning over the rail in a naked condition while a
member of the crew commits sodomy with her . . . . The boys
got angry with her [the prostitute] and vented their anger by holding
her and forcing a large dog they had picked up into position to have
sexual relations with her. The movie stops just short of showing
the culmination of sexual relations, but all of the witnesses who testified as to that happening testified that the culmination of the sexual
relations was not left as a matter of mere speculation.[16])

The proposal is more permissive when wholly creative imagery
is involved, rather than photographs of flesh-and-blood men
and women. Such imagery is less real, less personal. The draft
authorizes *private* enjoyment by adults of paintings, drawings, or
sculpture, showing people engaging in sexual conduct, and
permits pictures of such creative works as may appear in books
or magazines. This would legitimatize, for adult private viewing,
things such as ornately embellished versions of the *Kama Sutra,*
pictorially detailing its multiple approaches to physical love,
with genital activity basic to the illustrations. But the proposal
would bar showings of the same sorts of figures as part of *public*
entertainments, be they art exhibits or art movies. Making
something dealing with sex available in a privately read book,

and displaying it to be gaped at, clucked over, and *publicly* shared by galleries of strangers, are two quite different things. The proposal (were this aspect of it to be adopted) would not ban any American counterparts that time might coin of the massive and powerfully executed granite nude figures that dominate Oslo's Frogner Park, the lifework of the late Gustav Vigeland. In these statues genitals are shown, and nudes are sculpted in close embrace; but genital activity is not revealed. Quite different, however, were the works publicly exhibited in San Francisco in 1964 by auto-fender-and-hood artist, Ron Boise. These the proposal would ban from public showing (although under then existing legislation a California jury did not sustain the obscenity charge that had been leveled). Boise's medium was junked auto parts; his end products were carefully and actively equipped males and females, quite explicitly engaged in intercourse, fellatio, and cunnilingus.[17]

As the proposal stands, it would enjoin the public display of works such as Boise's of at least arguably artistic merit. This raises the question of whether the law may validly ban the *public* showing of any creative work without regard to its aesthetic appeal. Once again, dealing with original paintings or sculpture, neither freedom of speech or press seems necessarily to be involved. We are left, therefore, not with the question of obscenity, but whether an appellate court might hold it to be unreasonable, and therefore void, for a state to ban public showings of art that graphically depict acts either condemned completely by community taboos or reserved for wholly private enjoyment. Whether or not reviewing judges would themselves deem such legislation either wise or necessary, as *it would only enjoin showings to which the public was invited,* and not private possession, sale, or display to friends, the proposed statute would not seem beyond the realm of reasonable legislative action. Sir Patrick Devlin, charging a British trial jury in a 1954 obscenity case, pointed out:

. . . a creative writer or a creative artist, one can well understand, naturally desires a complete freedom within which to express his talents or his genius. But he is a member of the community, and like any other member of the community he is under the same obligation not to do harm, either mentally or physically or spiritually. If there is a conflict in an artist or a writer between his desire for self-expression and the sense that morality is fundamental to the well-being of the community (if there is such a conflict) then it is morality that must prevail.[18]

The plan here suggested draws lines that in creating precision will, to some, seem completely arbitrary. But this is true of much of the law's delineation of criminal conduct. The classifications here are no more absurd than are those that make the theft of one hundred and one dollars, cash, a felony, while stealing an irreplaceable keepsake of lesser appraised value may, in the same jurisdiction, be only a misdemeanor; burglary— a serious crime—exists if the miscreant pushes open a door in entering, but should he find it ajar his crime in most jurisdictions is considerably less serious. And any legislature might vary this draft, adjusting it to local concepts of what it deemed offensive in the home community.

A detailed statute along these lines, enacted jointly with a law protecting the young against the commercial exploitation of nudity and sex, would go far toward filling the needs that have kept motion picture licensing, the *pre-release censorship* of films, alive. The proposals would put the movie moguls, as well as police and prosecutors, on fairly precise notice of the items that, appearing in films, would bar children from paying their own way, and would with equal clarity declare just what was banned as adult fare. Boards of censors dictating the film footage that was to be snipped under the influence of their personal tastes would become anachronistic Mrs. Grundys. Criminal actions, which could be objectively instituted under the proposed statutes, would suffice. (Although the drafts do not expressly provide for the use of injunctions, separate legislation might create this remedy as an alternative to criminal enforcement.)

In any case film licensing in America seems outdated. With movies made from volumes as varied as the Bible and *Sex and the Single Girl,* little logic—other than having gotten used to it—remains in rejecting prior restraint on all media except the movies. In 1965, possibly recognizing this absurdity, the United States Supreme Court whittled down the role of film censor.[19] The high Tribunal requires that the censors move so rapidly that no movie's release will be significantly delayed, and that any censoring board see to it that its own actions are reviewed by the courts before they are given any impact. Charging prosecutors or other officials with bringing allegedly offending films into the courts, even though they are already being shown, will be far less complicated and less costly, and almost as effective in keeping the obscene from view, as would be perpetuating boards of moving picture censors.

BOOKS, MAGAZINES, AND RECORDINGS

For the past half dozen years, busy presses have been grinding out vast numbers of books that a scant decade ago most American publishers would not have dreamed of issuing. Whether this has been for good or bad, to suggest that the law should now retreat to something appreciably less than "anything goes," would be to propose that an army of police should mobilize enforcement brooms in a quixotic effort to sweep back the oceans.

Were legislators and book banners to face up to this squarely, and to concentrate their fire on the more damaging areas of pornography, then much of the trouble that simmers constantly between the censors and the literati might be cooled. What *most* annoys the liberal is the interference by others with his right *to read privately* anything he may wish. And that includes much that were it not for the censors he would find boring. To see his selections in literary fare undermined by what often seem the lack of taste and the personal biases of others is demeaning. Besides, he is stridently aware that the written word has been foundational to freedom, and that its censorship, far more than censorship in any other area, suggests thought control.

Books provide the medium of contact between a writer and his readers, and these contacts should remain as free of censorship as are all personal conversations. The most avid censorship advocate is quick to concede that his own perusal of pornography has done him no personal harm; questioned as to why the same materials must be kept from other adults, his response is likely to be sputtering confusion.

But simply declaring that "anything goes" as to the written (or recorded) word sold to adults for private use, is not quite acceptable. Hordes of contemporary Mishkins, Roths, Albertses, Ginzburgs, Rossets, and Girodiases would come teeming out of the woodwork, with ever greater promotional campaigns touting more openly than ever the joys of titillation. A way, then, of having our cake and of eating it too, is needed; a method of permitting adults to devour any and all published materials, while simultaneously keeping the community from being saturated with all the van-loads of prurience that the boldest huckstering might produce. That way has been found; at least its embryo was produced by the United States Supreme Court in its March 1966 decisions. The pandering test, by focusing on the advertising and merchandising of borderline pornography, provided the means for giving adults maximum freedom to read everything, including the obscene, while inhibiting the pornography huckstering campaigns that would otherwise attend such freedom.

In its *Fanny Hill* decision, the Supreme Court took special cares to stress that the book was not being given clear sailing everywhere under any circumstances:

On the premise, which we have no occasion to assess, that *Memoirs* has the requisite prurient appeal and is patently offensive, but has only a minimum of social value, *the circumstances of production, sale and publicity* are relevant in determining whether or not the publication and distribution . . . is constitutionally protected.[20]

But how can publicity, particularly advertising stressing sex appeal, be *reasonably* policed in this age when frank erotic provocation sells almost everything, it sometimes seems, except Levy's Jewish Rye Bread? Dissenting in both the *Mishkin* and the *Ginzburg* cases, Justice William O. Douglas observed:

This new exception condemns an advertising technique as old as history. The advertisements of our best magazines are chock-full of thighs, ankles, calves, bosoms, eyes, and hair, to draw the potential buyer's attention to lotions, tires, food, liquor, clothing, autos, and even insurance policies.[21]

This argument by Justice Douglas points up the desirability, the *necessity* as viewed by his colleague Justice John M. Harlan, for clarifying legislation if the pandering test is to be part of our obscenity law. The action by the high Court's majority has only paved the way for such new statutes, having itself provided no formula for judging "pandering," for distinguishing an appeal to the sex drive from an appeal to prurience. Careful drafting is needed. The draft statute so serves. If the prosecutor can prove an intention *"to exploit commercially a morbid interest"* in sexual or other lurid detail, then, and only then, can he succeed in establishing guilt. Proof of such intention, the proposal provides, is to be based upon the interaction of several listed factors.

One is surroundings. Times Square bookstores offer an extreme example of how surroundings may pander to prurient tastes. Their display windows shout an appeal compounded inside the store by rack-loads of cellophane-sealed, highly priced, paper-covered booklets, and nude and near-nude photo sets. The total vividly demonstrates the "intention to exploit commercially a morbid interest in sado-masochistic abuse [and] sexual conduct."

Under the draft statute, interacting factors that may prove an intent to exploit morbid sex interests are format, price, and mode of distribution. Quite apart from content, a suggestion of illegality is proffered when cheaply photo-offset paper-covered booklets are priced to sell at five, ten, and fifteen dollars each. Undated magazines tender a similar suggestion. At the other extreme, displays of ninety-five cent paperbacks, not only at book and paperback stores, but on drug counters and supermarket shelves, may argue convincingly against claims that they are supplied to meet the demands of recondite literary tastes.

Using *Fanny Hill* as an example, the draft statute (were it enacted) would *not* be violated by a campaign—book jackets, window displays, newspaper and trade journal ads—that stressed those historical and artistic factors so heavily relied upon by the publishers when they have found themselves in court. However, were these factors to be ignored, yielding to promises of that erotica that have led to the novel's repeated outlawry, then it would be clear that the advertiser's intent was to pander: to exploit prurience, not redeeming importance. The Illinois high court, in its opinion holding *Tropic of Cancer* to be obscene (withdrawn when, within the week of its issuance, five Justices of the United States Supreme Court held the book *not* to be obscene) commented:

Intervenor-plaintiffs seek to portray this book as one intended primarily for the intellectually sophisticated, who would presumably be able to recognize the claimed philosophic theme despite the vivid descriptions of sexual activity. This attempt seems to be fatally inconsistent with the fact that this book was being offered in a paperback edition selling at 95¢, was being distributed in train stations, drug stores, and newsstands throughout Chicago by the hundreds, and was being advertised with such slogans as "Damned and Banned for 27 years, Now Available."[22]

Had the pandering test been announced earlier, and had the draft statute been the law in Illinois, a reaffirmance of the *Tropic* conviction would have been appropriate. As recited by the Midwestern tribunal, here was a book available on a scale, in a format, and at a price encouraging to thrill-seekers and tending to controvert any claim that it was offered for the "intellectually sophisticated"; it was attractive by its "vivid descriptions of sexual activity" and was marketed to underscore these aspects.

Borderline books such as the *Tropics* and *Fanny Hills* would, under the pandering test and the draft, have to be advertised with circumspection. But, Justice Douglas notwithstanding, the high Court's standard should strike no terror in the hearts of advertisers of non-prurient books (or other wares) who seek simply to interject a certain spice into their promotional appeals. Art Buchwald has suggested how paperback publishers might subtitle some of our nursery classics:

Snow White and the Seven Dwarfs—The story of a ravishing blond virgin who was held captive by seven deformed men, all with different lusts.

Cinderella—A beautiful passionate woman bares her naked foot to the man she loves while her stepmother and stepsisters plot to cheat her out of the one memorable night in her life.

Alice in Wonderland—A young girl's search for happiness in a weird depraved world of animal desires. Can she ever return to a normal happy life after falling so far?

Little Red Riding Hood—A girl goes to visit her grandmother only to discover a wolf in her bed. Read what happens when the girl refuses to get into bed with the wolf.[23]

Buchwald's parody is one of degree only. If Buchwald's blurbs were to be used to test the proposed statute's impact, the proposed law would *not* be violated. The tales themselves are lacking in that content—sado-masochistic, sexual, or the like, as carefully defined in the draft—necessary to the finding of a violation.

Concededly, the standard the proposed statute poses for judging promotional efforts is not as precise as the rest of the draft legislation suggested here. Nevertheless it should, in practice, help provide the precision to render workable the high Court's talk of "pandering," "commercial exploitation of erotica solely for the sake of prurient appeal," "exploitation of interests in titillation," and "emphasis on the sexually provocative."

Moreover, it is not the exploitation of a *healthy and normal* interest in sex that the draft statute bans; that broad a ban would almost obliterate that world Justice Douglas so graphically described. The proposal would enjoin only the exploitation of *"morbid"* sexual interests. And "morbid," although a word not mathematically measurable, means, "unhealthy," "diseased," or "abnormal." Put differently, the draft statute condemns only that advertising and merchandising (of dubious books and recordings) that is *abnormally* crammed with sexual or excretory promise.

Even so, there is no getting around the fact that some fuzziness would remain. It would inevitably attend any test that does not size up the product solely, but examines it against the context in which it is offered to the public. Yet this uncertainty would not be such a major blight on the proposed series of statutes as to endanger our press freedoms. Such fuzziness as would exist would be of *secondary* impact only; the *prime* item, the book, pamphlet, or recording, could be *freely* produced. And the publisher or dealer who wished to avoid conflict with the law would only need to base his ballyhoo on such non-sexual (or, at least, such non-*morbidly* sexual) values as he might be able to find.

Granted, for some publishers it would not be that simple. What values could be found, other than those of morbid, unrelieved sex, in Mishkin's books, for example, or in much of the worst of the paperback erotica, or in the most offensive of the girlie magazines? The merchandising of all of these items has consisted largely of their lurid covers, their suggestive titles, their willfully massed displays, and the sordid ads for them that appear in other books and magazines issued by the same publishers. Thus unless their content were to be adulterated, and their titles and covers to be changed, they would—under the pandering test and the proposed statute—be courting trouble. To this extent the draft, while seeming to grant adults complete freedom in their choice of reading, and publishers in their decisions as to what to issue, would be a means of giving with the right hand what in part, was taken back with the left. But if the most crassly useless of publications were to be forced either to adulterate their offensiveness in order to find some decent values to be stressed, or were to be driven out of business, what would be the loss?

As some inhibitions upon adults and pornography exist today throughout the nation, and whether or not sensible, seem destined to stay with us at least a while longer, this chapter has formulated an orderly scheme for them. It is one tendered, hopefully, as a replacement for the chaos that today is ours. It may be that government regulation of adult conduct is simply not worth the effort. Yet repeal of all adult restraints is highly improbable. And if legislators believe that the desires of some adults to enjoy the crassest obscenity are not to be tolerated, then this chapter's suggestions provide an approach for legislative thinking and action.

PART V

The Future

24. Legislative—and Other—Realities

I never admired politicians, though they are generally kindly and genial, and often very intelligent; but seldom is there one with real courage.
—Clarence Darrow, *The Story of My Life,* p. 52 (1932)

THE TRIUMVIRATE OF LAWS here proposed would, were they enacted, effect a great forward stride toward reasonable precision in dealing with the pornographic. But were precision the sole accomplishment, it would not be worth the candle; *absolute* precision would be easily achieved if all bans on obscenity were eliminated, or, at the opposite extreme, if the Constitution's free speech-free press provisions were modified by a new amendment authorizing Draconian-anti-filth statutes and enforcement.

The merit of these three proposals is that a high degree of precision is achieved without rocketing to either extreme; obscenity enforcement is neither abandoned nor is the First Amendment (as it is now understood) short-circuited. Clear *legislative* declarations of what is deemed so obscene that it is not to be tolerated strike a balance far more firmly than do the personal judgments of the judges—judgments that change from bench to bench, varying with shifts in judicial manpower.

Unhappily the advantages of such legislation do not necessarily presage its passage. Using neither the accustomed statutory language nor the phrases handed down by our nation's highest Court, the proposed statutes are novel. Twentieth century Cassandras are sure to wail at the "obvious" lawlessness of these untested drafts: the most ardent of the bluenoses will do so, deeming them too permissive; civil libertarians, sniffing ultimate victory (despite their 1966 high Court setbacks), will want them rejected as needless compromises. Even should statutes along the lines of these proposals, or facets of them, ultimately be held to be unconstitutional—and that is *not* impossible—pontification of *certain* unconstitutionality from biased sources is quicksand upon which to base any rejection of them. "We are under a Constitution," Charles Evans Hughes observed more than fifty years ago, "but the Constitution is what the judges say it is."[1] Their decisions in no area of law better prove this than in that of obscenity. Novel proposals advanced to solve hitherto unsolved legal conundrums and supported by arguments showing their reasonableness ultimately *are* constitutional only on one condition: *if five of nine Justices of the high Court, believing that they should be, say that they are.*

SCIENTER AND BURDEN OF PROOF

Two aspects of the proposals are sure to furnish fuel to any who might wish to urge unconstitutionality. One is their provision that persons in the business of selling or exhibiting items that may turn out to be pornographic will be presumed to have knowledge of the nature of their stock; that as to such defendants proof of scienter may *not* have to be tendered unless the defense first tenders some proof of non-knowledge. The other specifies that an item's scientific, artistic, or other justification is something for the defense to prove; the prosecution need not show the utter lack of such justification. Quarrels with these provisions of the drafts cannot be dismissed cavalierly. After all, in the case in which the Supreme Court first advanced the scienter requirement, *Smith* v. *California*, the defendant was a book dealer. And in March 1965, in curtailing the pre-censorship of the movies, the Justices declared that "the burden of proving that the film is unprotected expression *must rest on the censor.*"[2]

Experience shows that merchants are in fact almost certain to know at least the general nature of each of the items that they sell. And of all items, pornographic books are least likely to be sleepers. As our courts of law uphold legal presumptions soundly grounded on experience, any statute that presumes dealers' knowledge of their stocks should be sustained. California, however, lacked such a statutory presumption in 1959 at the time of the *Smith* case, and in deciding that case the high Court took care to state that it was leaving unresolved:

. . . whether there might be circumstances under which the State constitutionally might require that a bookseller investigate further, or might put on him the burden of explaining why he did not, and what such circumstances might be.[3]

Again resorting to common sense, the state can only prove a defendant's knowledge *inferentially,* but any defendant can, should he so choose, testify *directly* concerning it. Why, then, should he not be called upon to speak out, or to risk the penalties of silence, when the *act* that damns him has been proven, but he hopes that the courts will, in reliance upon his supposed pure heart, relieve him of its consequences?

That the *Smith* decision did not doom such legislation is supported by the views of many of America's foremost legal scholars and appellate judges, banded together as the American Law Institute. Sometimes looked upon as more distinguished for its theory and scholarship than for its sense of reality, the Institute responded to practical needs in 1962—three years after the *Smith* decision—in proposing that "A person who disseminates or possesses obscene material in the course of his business *is presumed to do so knowingly* or recklessly."[4] This proposal would hardly have been advanced by such a distinguished group were its members not of the view that the presumption could be sustained as constitutional.

Despite the Supreme Court's recent general statement in a censorship case that "due process certainly requires . . . that the State bear the burden of persuasion," giving the defense the chore of showing social importance should not brand the proposals as unconstitutional. The high Tribunal's statement was made in the absence of any separate *statutory* earmarking of proof of obscenity and proof of either the existence or absence of redeeming social importance. Although the concept of obscenity assumes the lack of any redeeming social importance, more closely viewed two findings emerge that must largely be independently made. One is whether, under all the circumstances, the item is repulsive, filthy, or disgusting. The other is, if so, are there special factors of artistry, historical content, or others, that redeem it. The proposed statute underscores the separateness of these two findings. In the 1960 British trial of Penguin Books, arising from that publishing house's reissue of *Lady Chatterley's Lover,* the trial judge put it this way in his charge to the jury on the question of artistry:

Whether the book is obscene or not—there the onus of proof is put upon the Prosecution. The Prosecution, as you know, have to prove "beyond reasonable doubt." If there is a reasonable doubt, the Jury acquit. In this Section the *defendants* had to prove these matters, and that means they had *not* got to prove beyond reasonable doubt; all they have to do is to satisfy you as to the probability of the matter which they are called upon to establish. Thus, if you come to the conclusion that this book is obscene, you must ask yourselves this further question. . . . Have the defendants established the probability that the merits of the book as a novel are so high that they outbalance the obscenity, so that its publication is for the public good?[5]

That jury charge followed a 1959 British statute that *placed on the defendant* the burden of establishing that seeming pornography was in fact "for the public good . . . in the interests of science, literature, art or learning."[6] Another portion of that "model" legislation that was proposed by the American Law Institute does substantially the same thing.[7]

The defense, in practice, generally comes first with its experts, because the trial courts assume that seeming obscenities are unredeemed until their values have been *affirmatively* shown. Thus the proposed statutes would conform American legislation with existing practice, with the recommendations of leading legal theorists, and with what is at present the law of England.

LEGISLATIVE RESPONSIBILITIES

Years ago, when ideas concerning accepted moral behavior were more broadly shared than they are today, words like "obscene," "lewd," and "lascivious" had rather clear and certain meaning. But the last several decades have seen such major ferment in sexual morality that the only thing that now seems clear is that the statutory words harbor many diverse meanings to many different people. Laws resting on them, then, *should be void for vagueness.* The judiciary could well toss the whole problem back at the lawmakers with a single explosive decision, one voiding all statutes that rest on those amorphous concepts. But the judges, particularly the Justices of the United States Supreme Court, have been courageously trying to salvage something of the anti-pornography laws. In the process they have burdened themselves with interminable censorship chores, have been beset with abuse for their opinions, and have ended up giving little true guidance to anybody.

Pornography legislation along the lines of the proposals would return the lawmaking functions to our legislative halls, where they belong. But saddling our statutes with specifics would require legislators to make innumerable small decisions; a multitude of detailed inclusions and exclusions would have to be weighed and debated. With each would come myriad pressures from churchmen and from civil libertarians, from police and from publishers, from artists, editors, and educators, from psychologists, psychiatrists, and sociologists, and from other variously assorted experts, organizations, and "men-in-the-street." Reaching substantial legislative agreement upon such proposals, were it to be ventured at all, would be extremely difficult. Far easier it is for our elected lawmakers to stand fearless and four square behind simple statutes that express unalterable opposition to the "obscene," letting the judges, who cannot legislate along broad schematic lines but can only rule on what is before them on a case-by-case basis, struggle with the rest. It is almost as simple as opposing sin, and favoring motherhood, the flag, and hot apple pie.

Excuses for such legislative lassitude come readily to hand. There are the myriad questions of constitutionality which may be avoided by not budging from the status quo. Moreover, concededly, the draft statutes do not wrap obscenity with a neat blue ribbon. Although providing far more clarity than now exists, there is still some distance to be traveled before mathematical accuracy could be achieved. The least precise aspect of the proposals, for example, their suggestion that an "intention to exploit commercially a morbid interest" in sexuality be declared criminal, although as enunciated, a marked improvement over a mere pandering standard, does not achieve ideal specificity.

Should legislators continue along the comfortable road, failing to seize the initiative, failing to come up with specific anti-indecency laws, the state appellate courts and the United States Supreme Court have the means in their power of sparking constructive legislative action. If the courts are irritated with their own roles as censors, their own service as local and national High Courts of Obscenity, yet are not prepared to rule with Justices Black and Douglas that pornography *is* protected free speech, they may take steps to force the issue. Obscenity is not the only area of the law in which social changes have rendered local action unconstitutional today, although to earlier generations the very same action had seemed lawful and appropriate.

In two far more significant legal areas, the education of white and Negro children and the apportionment of our state legislatures, state conduct formerly deemed constitutional was, upon reinspection, held to be inadequate under present conditions, and was struck down.[8] In each instance, the underlying problem required corrective action of such detail and precision that it could only be accomplished legislatively and administratively, and not by simple judicial decree. And so, although holding existing laws and methods repugnant to the United States Constitution, the high Court—aware that instantly voiding them would create chaos—gave local legislative bodies time in which to act, obliging them to do so "with all deliberate speed." The highest appellate courts, state and federal, might similarly determine that with the passage of time terms such as "obscene, lewd, and lascivious" had become so amorphous as to have developed increasing repugnance to constitutional standards of definiteness in penal legislation, and that should the state or federal governments wish to salvage any restraints on pornography they would have to draft more pointed statutes.

OTHER "SOLUTIONS" TO THE OBSCENITY MUDDLE

Other modes of resolving the obscenity dilemma have been proposed. Among the foremost is one suggesting that criminal charges not be authorized until after the courts had, in noncriminal proceedings, determined that an item was obscene and prospective dealers had, in some fashion, been given notice of that ruling.[9] Another suggests that boards of specially skilled persons—artists, writers, professors, psychologists, clergymen—determine what is to be censored, and in so doing provide guidance for judicial action.[10] These suggestions may render censorship slightly more palatable than it has been for some in the artistic and literary community; that community may prefer the censor-aesthete to the censor-cop. But regardless of who wields the blue pencil, and regardless of the nature of the procedure that invokes it, at the heart of both of these proposals is their continued reliance on *personal tastes,* rather than a limited control based upon well-articulated standards that play down individual preferences and that consider each item in its setting. Moreover, these "solutions" derive from viewing censorship and obscenity largely in terms of occasional works like *Lady Chatterley's Lover* or *Tropic of Cancer,* or even of deliberately polished products such as *Eros.* But vast hordes of dubious materials would be the grist that would cause these proposals to bog down were they enacted. The profusion and variety of items that exist necessitate—if we are to have real improvement—clear but broad principles, and preclude item-by-item non-punitive litigation that would see each, in each of fifty states, going up through the appellate courts before anything was really decided. That same profusion would so preoccupy handpicked censors that they would be interminably detained from whatever creative, instructive, or social service that had led to their selection to the censorship board.

THE ROLE OF VOLUNTEERS

This book has concentrated on obscenity, today, and the law. But the law, the criminal law, does not exist to regulate every heartbeat in our moment-to-moment existence. This is not "1984." Penal statutes are designed to play a role when things have gotten badly out of joint. When the deterioration has so advanced that the intervention of some *deus ex machina,* the state, is needed, then the criminal law provides the means for that intercession. Essentially, however, the law leaves people to their own devices; the police and the courts cannot, and clearly should not, be monoliths casting shadows over our every waking action.

In rural areas and the small cities of America neither anti-obscenity statutes nor volunteer citizens action committees are required to exclude things that may offend the community. The community's standards become the community's practice. The daily, friendly, informal, personal relationships of merchant-townspeople are such that, like members of a family, without prompting, each is ordinarily sensitive to his neighbor's feelings. Each realizes that all are mutually dependent. Anyone who would, for profit, offend those about him, dares not; it would soon prove unprofitable as well as uncomfortable.

But in the impersonal metropolis there is no such spontaneous ebb and flow. The citizenry, more often than not, live in one part of town but work elsewhere. Merchants and customers are likely to remain mere faces, unnamed and often unrecognized by one another. Volunteer committees have sprung into action to simulate the small town's sense of merchants' responsibilities in those larger cities, to awaken parents to those items that might (in the view of some) endanger youth, and to jog sometimes seemingly sluggish police and prosecutors. The role of the citizenry in the fight on pornography goes back almost two hundred years (indeed, its roots seem to reach to those ancient scribes and Pharisees who on setting before Jesus the woman taken in adultery, evoked the response "He that is without sin among you, let him first cast a stone at her"[11]) to London's Proclamation Society, founded in 1787, and numbering Dr. Thomas Bowdler among its promoters. Later, replaced by the Society for the Suppression of Vice, its aims included the suppression of blasphemous publications, the prosecution of blasphemy, and the halting of the trade in obscene books.[12] A namesake group founded by Anthony Comstock in 1873, the New York Committee for the Suppression of Vice, continued the Bowdler battle in America. Comstock claimed to have been responsible, both through his own crusades and his pressures on legislatures, police, and prosecutors, for having destroyed one hundred and sixty tons of obscene literature and pictures.[13]

In 1938, under Catholic hierarchal sponsorship, the National Organization (later, "Office") for Decent Literature was formed, functioning across America on a local diocesan level. It had followed by five years the creation of the National Legion of Decency (recently baptized the National Catholic Office for Motion Pictures), that concentrated upon film classification. In Cincinnati a score of years later Charles H. Keating, Jr., an Ohio attorney, organized a non-sectarian citizens' group, Citizens for Decent Literature; within a few years, it too was to go national. Wholly unaffiliated local groups have also proliferated. Among the most active of them has been Operation Yorkville, on New York City's upper East Side, concentrating on protecting the neighborhood's youngsters from newsstand filth, and, on the West Coast, CLEAN—the California League to Enlist Action Now.

These groups, complementing the quite dissimilarly oriented civil liberties committees, may serve valid ends. Through their own publications, press releases, and public meetings, they have sought to alert parents and their communities generally to some of the apparently unredeemed trash that has been so freely available. Simultaneously, the libertarians have used like means to alert the same audiences to censorship dangers. The decent literature committees have met with big city retail merchants to convince them that they are not without responsibility in shaping community morality. Many, in particular several of the nation's largest retail drug chains, have voluntarily determined upon prophylaxis, and have removed the most offensive paperbacks and girlie magazines from their display racks. Through national bulletins these volunteer committees have kept local police and prosecutors informed of how other communities have been battling pornography. They have also played a direct role in the courts—as have the opposing libertarian organization—by filing "friend of the court" briefs in litigated obscenity cases. In some instances they have been instrumental in provoking test cases. (New York's case that ultimately led to the invalidation of the state's 1963 statute making criminal the sale of pornography to the young, the case arising from the sale of *Fanny Hill* to a sixteen-year-old, was sparked by Operation Yorkville; OY personnel had schooled the teen-age purchaser in her role, and had sent her in to make the buy.) And just as do the civil liberties groups, the censorship committees send their leaders to testify and to lobby in the legislative halls whenever proposed anti-pornography laws start moving through the legislative hopper.

In the continuing war between the literati and the Philistines, these volunteer committees have been subjected to withering attacks for using the boycott to force their own ideas concerning book, magazine, and film decency upon their neighbors. Although no longer as common as they were a decade ago, boycotts have been a weapon of the National Office for Decent Literature, used in order to force merchants to discontinue selling reading matter that NODL deemed objectionable.[14] Some of the most articulate leaders in the fight on pornography continue to urge the boycott. New York's Francis Cardinal Spellman, addressing a national fraternal meeting in Denver, Colorado, in mid-1964, exhorted:

In terms of direct action, I urge all to refuse to support dealers who traffic in pornography. This is not a welcome method these days, but this approach may be the only weapon the interpreters of the law have left to us and perhaps the only language some people understand. Once it becomes clear to the neighborhood shopkeeper, the corner news-dealer and the local drug store owner, that we will use it, then the purveyors of filth will be dealt a stunning and maybe even a fatal blow.[15]

The outraged outcries of the literati against such boycotts seem a little hollow in this age when far more militant action by private pressure groups has often been the order of the day. To achieve urgent goals in race relationships, for example, it has not been little square placards posted in the windows of cooperating stores that have given notice as to who is and who is not to be shunned, but numbers of vocal pickets, parading—sometimes singing or shouting—before the non-cooperating establishments. Quite appropriately picketing has been used to

build economic pressures; and, sometimes, when peaceful picketing has failed to obtain integration, sit-ins have followed, in
order to force retail operations to a standstill until demands
have been met. Today, most progressives would agree that the
goal of racial integration is far more serious and urgent than is
that of weeding some supposed trash out of candy-store literature. But one of the greatest beauties of our democracy is the
freedom it guarantees men in choosing their own hobby horses
and in protecting equally their rights to ride them, sometimes in
the damnedest directions. If extreme tactics seem appropriate
in achieving the aims of integrationists, how can far milder
tactics be chastised as *grossly improper* when invoked by those
worried about our community's sexual morality?[16] Whether such
tactics are *wise* or not, however, is something else.

Committees of private citizens, exerting economic pressures
to force merchants to stop selling trash, "trash" being defined
neither by statute nor by decision but solely by values personal
to the committee members, represent an insidious sort of private
enforcement. The "law" this makes is privately made. Yet its
public impact may be considerable. Enacted by no legislature,
reviewed by no court, such "law" may keep the words of hacks,
or those of gifted writers, from adults as well as from children.
Book boycotters' targets have included volumes penned by
Mishkin-recruited scribblers, by the tramp publishers of the
Nightstand and Kozy stamp, and by such banned and litigated
authors as Frank Harris, John Cleland, and Henry Miller. But
along with these have been varied and important works by
observers of the sexual scene: Alfred Kinsey, Mary McCarthy,
James T. Farrell, Lawrence Durrell, Richard von Krafft-Ebing,
J. D. Salinger, and William Faulkner are a handful. This private,
unofficial censorship is so readily abused that committees toying
with thoughts of its use would do well to pause and to question
whether boycotts may not discredit, rather than serve, any anti-
indecency campaign in which they are invoked.

A decade ago, when the boycotts sparked by the National

Office for Decent Literature were most widespread, Jesuit Father John Courtney Murray suggested four rules for the reasoned guidance of religious groups in their public actions concerning questions of morality and of censorship. Father Murray's four guides (and any citizens' action committee concerned with obscenity would do well to keep them in mind) were:

First . . . each minority group has the right to censor for its own members, if it so chooses, the content of the various media of communication, and to protect them, by means of its own choosing, from materials considered harmful according to its own standards.

Second . . . no minority group has the right to demand that government should impose a general censorship, affecting all the citizenry, upon any medium of communication, with a view to punishing the communication of materials that are judged to be harmful according to the special standards held within one group.

Third, any minority group has the right to work toward the elevation of standards of public morality . . . through the use of the methods of persuasion and pacific argument.

Fourth . . . no minority group has the right to impose its own religious or moral views on other groups, through the use of the methods of force, coercion, or violence.[17]

THE ROLE OF LAW—THE RULE OF LAW

Even with Father Murray's wise lesson before them, mortals cannot always be counted upon to act this calmly, this rationally. If the law supplies a safety valve, it will help, however. Statutes dealing effectively with indecency may provide such a fuse. As long as our legislators outlaw excesses against public morality, and our police and prosecutors enforce those statutes, formal legal channels will siphon off community rage at items that so greatly exceed contemporary standards as to rub raw the remnants of puritanism that are still part of our culture. "The first requirement of a sound body of law," the then Professor Oliver Wendell Holmes, Jr., of the Harvard Law

School wrote in 1881, in *The Common Law*, "is that it should correspond with the actual feelings and demands of the community, *whether right or wrong*. If people would gratify the passion of revenge outside of the law, if the law did not help them, the law has no choice but to satisfy the craving itself, and thus avoid the greater evil of private retribution."[18] When the law provides no adequate redress, the citizenry may not always be rational in its resort to self-help.

Acknowledgments

A GENEROUS GRANT from the Walter E. Meyer Research Institute of Law made this book possible. As initially envisioned, it was to wrestle with a range of enforcement problems that are today in flux: from Arrest, Bail, and Confessions, through Vice and Wiretapping. But as the work got under way it became apparent that the obscenity confusion was so monumental that a meaningful contribution might best be made by focusing upon that area. I am deeply indebted to the institute's exceedingly trustful trustees and directors for their confidence—and for the complete independence afforded me.

I could not have written this book had it not been for Frank S. Hogan, District Attorney of New York County, and one of America's great prosecutors. From 1953 through 1964 I served as an assistant district attorney on his staff; during portions of that service as his administrative assistant and chief of his Criminal Court Bureau, I profited not only from my warm association with him but from that unique vantage point from which I observed—and participated in—some of the churning that has been taking place in the administration of criminal justice. I am, of course, deeply grateful to the police, prosecutors, judges, defense lawyers, and court personnel who, over the years, have been my fellows and my teachers in the courts and whose lessons this book reflects.

Particularly helpful to me in tracking down elusive materials, whipping my thoughts into shape and from them evolving this book, have been Professors Robert McKay and Edward Bander, and Joseph P. Foley and Lewis R. Friedman, Esqs., and Mrs. Anna Marie Carrilo. And most encouraging, most helpful, and most important of all, was—and is—my wife, Joyce.

Notes

CHAPTER 1　The Antagonists in the Obscenity-Censorship Battle

1. Distinctions have been made between "pornographic" and "obscene." St. John-Stevas, *Obscenity and the Law* 2 (1956), notes:

> A pornographic book can be easily distinguished from an obscene book. A pornographic book, although obscene, is one deliberately designed to stimulate sex feelings and to act as an aphrodisiac. An obscene book has no such immediate and dominant purpose, although incidentally this may be its effect.

(Unfortunately the St. John-Stevas book, the finest contemporary history of this corner of the law, is out of print. It is so good that the libraries of the New York University Law School, the Bar Association of the City of New York, and the New York County Lawyers' Association all report their copies to be "missing.")

Walter Allen, British editor and critic, has commented on the distinct origins of "pornography" and "obscenity":

> The law makes no distinction between pornography and obcenity; yet, while it is true, so much are we in the realms of the subjective here, that one man's obscenity may be another's pornography, the words are anything but synonomous. It seems to me that the distinction between them is valid and necessary. By derivation, pornography means, literally, brothel writing, the description of the lives, manners and habits of prostitutes and their clients. Obscenity seems originally to have meant that which could not be represented upon the stage. It is related to ancient Greek theories of drama, according to which the pluck-

ing out of Gloucester's eyes in *King Lear* is obscene. By extension, the word covers a whole range of human functions which are neither good nor bad in themselves but natural, but which must be performed in privacy. They are obscene if they are not. The act of defecation is the obvious instance. The connotations of obscenity are far from being exclusively sexual. In origin, pornography is a concept in morals, obscenity is a concept in aesthetics.

To Deprave and Corrupt . . . 147 (Chandos, ed., 1962). But as the law makes no distinction between the two terms, they are used interchangeably in this book.

2. See, e.g., the opinions of Justices Black and Douglas in Roth v. United States, 354 U.S. 476, 508 (1957); Smith v. California, 361 U.S. 147, 155, 167 (1959); Jacobellis v. Ohio, 378 U.S. 184, 196 (1964); A Book Named "John Cleland's Memoirs of a Woman of Pleasure" v. Massachusetts, 383 U.S. 413, 424 (1966); Ginzburg v. United States, 383 U.S. 463, 477, 482 (1966); Mishkin v. New York, 383 U.S. 502, 515 (1966).

3. This was the position taken by Ephraim London, an attorney active in defending criminal obscenity cases, during a televised discussion, "The World at Ten," on January 7, 1965 (New York City channel 13).

4. "A Letter from Allen Ginsberg," 1 *Eros* 24 (Winter, 1962).

5. E. & P. Kronhausen, *Pornography and the Law* 66–67 (Rev. ed., Ballantine, 1964).

6. Id. at 346–47.

7. Appellant's New York State Court of Appeals brief 9–10, in People v. The Bookcase, Inc., 14 N.Y.2d 409, 201 N.E.2d 14 (1964).

8. People v. The Bookcase, Inc., 14 N.Y.2d 409, 201 N.E.2d 14 (1964).

9. N.Y. *Times*, May 28, 1962, 23, cols. 4–5.

10. Haight, *Banned Books* 12–13 (1955).

11. Hyde, *A History of Pornography* 9 (1965).

12. *Senate Report no. 2381, Interim Report of the Committee on the Judiciary by Subcommittee to Investigate Juvenile Delinquency (Obscene and Pornographic Materials)*, 84th Cong., 2d Sess., 3, 61 (June 28, 1956).

13. January 1960 Federal Bureau of Investigation *Law Enforcement Bulletin*.

14. Hall, "Poison in Print—and How to Get Rid of It," May 1964 *Reader's Digest* 94.

15. Larkin v. G. P. Putnam's Sons, 14 N.Y.2d 399, 408, 200 N.E.2d 760, 765–66 (1964).
16. The decision in Kingsley International Pictures Corp. v. Regents, 360 U.S. 684 (1959).
17. *Hearings on Control of Obscene Material, Before Subcommittee on Constitutional Amendments and Subcommittee to Investigate Juvenile Delinquency of the Senate Committee on the Judiciary,* 86th Cong., 1st & 2d Sess. 57–58 (1960).
18. The cases were Jacobellis v. Ohio and Grove Press, Inc. v. Gerstein, both of June 22, 1964, discussed in Chapter 7.
19. Address, August 6, 1964, before the Order of Eagles Convention, Denver, Colorado.
20. Lockhart & McClure, "Literature, the Law of Obscenity, and the Constitution," 38 *Minn. L. Rev.* 295, 320, 371–72 (1954).
21. Hyde, *A History of Pornography* 18 (1965).
22. Dunne, *Mr. Dooley on Ivrything and Ivrybody* 153 (Dover ed., 1963).
23. *Man and Superman,* Act III, 101 (Brentano's, 1915).
24. See *Survey of New Jersey Psychiatrists and Psychologists Pertaining to the Proscription by Legislation of Sexually Oriented Publications for Persons Under 18 Years.* (New Jersey Committee for the Right to Read, 1967).
25. *Hearings on Obscene Matter Sent Through the Mails, Before Subcommittee on Postal Operations of the House of Representatives Committee on Post Office and Civil Service,* 86th Cong., 1st Sess. 175 (1959).
26. *Hearings on Juvenile Delinquency (Obscene and Pornographic Materials) Before Subcommittee to Investigate Juvenile Delinquency of the Senate Committee on the Judiciary,* 84th Cong., 1st Sess. 217–21 (1955).
27. Larkin v. G. P. Putnam's Sons, 14 N.Y.2d 399, 407, 200 N.E.2d 760, 765 (1964).
28. *To Deprave and Corrupt . . .* 142–43 (Chandos ed., 1962).
29. Crosby, "Movies are Too Dirty," November 10, 1962 *Saturday Evening Post* 8.

CHAPTER 2   Underpinnings of the Obscenity Law

1. Butler v. Michigan, 352 U.S. 380 (1957).
2. Near v. Minnesota, 283 U.S. 697 (1931).
3. Winters v. New York, 333 U.S. 507 (1948).
4. Hannegan v. Esquire, Inc., 327 U.S. 146 (1946).

5. Regina v. Hicklin [1868] L.R.3 Q.B. 360.
6. See Broun & Leech, *Anthony Comstock* (1927).
7. United States v. Kennerley, 209 Fed. 119 (S.D.N.Y. 1913).
8. United States v. One Book Entitled Ulysses, 5 F. Supp. 182 (S.D.N.Y. 1933), *affirmed, 72 F.2d 705 (2d Cir. 1934).

CHAPTER 3   The *Roth* and *Alberts* Cases

1. Roth v. United States and Alberts v. California, 354 U.S. 476 (1957).
2. Alberts v. California, 354 U.S. 476 (1957) record on appeal 91.
3. Brief for the United States 35–39, in Roth v. United States, 354 U.S. 476 (1957).
4. Letter from the Solicitor General of the United States to the Clerk of the United States Supreme Court, April 19, 1957, cited in Lockhart & McClure, "Censorship of Obscenity: The Developing Constitutional Standards," 45 *Minn. L. Rev.* 5, 26 n. 119 (1960).
5. 18 U.S.C. § 1461.
6. *West's Calif. Penal Code Ann.* § 311 (1955).
7. 17 U.S. Law Week 3117, 3119 (October 26, 1948), reporting oral argument of People v. Doubleday & Co., 335 U.S. 848 (1948), involving Edmund Wilson's *Memoirs of Hecate County.*
8. In United States v. 31 Photographs, 156 F. Supp. 350 (S.D. N.Y. 1957), Judge Edmund L. Palmieri strained the statute's wording to reach a desirable result, and held that otherwise "hard-core" items, imported by the Kinsey Institute, were not obscene under the circumstances.
9. "Sex and Censorship in Contemporary Society," *New World Writing* 7, 19 (New Amer. Library, 1953).
10. Commonwealth v. Gordon, 66 D. & C. 101, 137–38 (Penn. 1949).
11. Roth v. United States, 354 U.S. 476, 487 n. 20.
12. But see the later opinions of Justice Brennan in Jacobellis v. Ohio, 378 U.S. 184 (1964), and A Book Named "John Cleland's Memoirs of a Woman of Pleasure" v. Massachusetts, 383 U.S. 413 (1966).
13. Sontag, "A Feast for Open Eyes," April 13, 1964 *The Nation* 374.

CHAPTER 4   The *Nights of Horror* Case

1. Kingsley Books, Inc. v. Brown, 354 U.S. 436 (1957).

2. Burke v. Kingsley Books, Inc., 208 Misc. 150, 158–59, 142 N.Y.S.2d 735, 742 (Sup.Ct. N.Y.Co. 1955).
3. See statement of Dr. Frederic Wertham, quoted in Report of the New York State Joint Legislative Committee to Study the Publication of Comics, 1955, at 15–17.

CHAPTER 5   The Unknowing Pornographer

1. Smith v. California, 361 U.S. 147 (1959).
2. Redrup v. New York and Austin v. Kentucky, 386 U.S. 767 (1967).

CHAPTER 6   Pictured Male Nudes

1. Marcus v. Search Warrant, 367 U.S. 717 (1961).
2. Manual Enterprises v. Day, 370 U.S. 478 (1962).
3. Mishkin v. New York, 383 U.S. 502, 509 (1966).
4. People v. Richmond County News, Inc., 9 N.Y.2d 578, 175 N.E.2d 681 (1961).
5. Greater specificity was provided in the dissenters' description of the magazine's contents:

An article . . . describes an experience between a married man and a young woman. It tells how, while walking to her apartment, he "absorbed the view of her breasts standing out in bold relief. In his haziness, he pictured her naked from her fleshy shoulders to her liquid underbelly." . . . then, later, she "expertly worked [her hand] down his body. Her palm pushed in his belly slightly. . . . Her breathing was louder now, and she wriggled to get into a more erotic position." . . . He "let his finger toy with her nipples until they stood up like pencil erasers. He grabbed her, and drove his tongue to the roof of her mouth. She did it back, and soon they were rubbing and kissing and feeling, and undressing each other. They thrashed on the bed until their rhythmic animal convulsions propelled them to the floor."

CHAPTER 7   The *Jacobellis* and *Tropic of Cancer* Decisions

1. Jacobellis v. Ohio, 378 U.S. 184 (1964).
2. Kingsley International Pictures Corp. v. Regents, 360 U.S. 684 (1959) in which the Court, writing six separate opinions, reversed the action of the New York State Board of Regents, which had withheld a license from the motion picture of *Lady*

Chatterley's Lover. See also Joseph Burstyn, Inc. v. Wilson, 343 U.S. 495 (1952).
3. Besig v. United States, 208 F. 2d 142 (9th Cir. 1953) (unanimous); State v. Huntington, no. 24657, Super. Ct., Hartford County, Conn. (1962); Grove Press, Inc. v. Florida, 156 So. 2d 537 (Fla. Dist. Ct. App. 1963); Haiman v. Morris, Ill. Sup. Ct., June 18, 1964 (opinion not printed; later withdrawn); Commonwealth v. Robin, no. 3177, C. P. Phila. Co. Penn. (1962); People v. Fritch, 13 N.Y.2d 119, 192 N.E.2d 713 (1963) (four to three decision).
4. Zeitlin v. Arnebergh, 31 Cal. 800, 383 P.2d 152 (1963) (unanimous); Attorney General v. Book Named "Tropic of Cancer," 345 Mass. 11, 184 N.E.2d 328 (1962) (four to three decision); McCauley v. Tropic of Cancer, 20 Wisc. 2d 134, 121 N.W.2d 545 (1963) (four to three decision).
5. Grove Press, Inc. v. Gerstein, 378 U.S. 577 (1964).
6. October–December 1963 and January–March 1964 *Playboy;* published in book form in 1965.
7. This opinion, later having been withdrawn, has not been officially published.
8. People v. Bruce, 31 Ill.2d 459, 461, 202 N.E.2d 497, 498 (1964).

CHAPTER 8   Pandering to Prurience

1. Lochner v. New York, 198 U.S. 45, 78 (1905).
2. A Book Named "John Cleland's Memoirs of a Woman of Pleasure" v. Massachusetts, 383 U.S. 413 (1966).
3. Mishkin v. New York, 383 U.S. 502 (1966).
4. Ginzburg v. United States, 383 U.S. 463 (1966).
5. Lewis, *Gideon's Trumpet* 166 (1964).
6. People v. Richmond County News, Inc., 9 N.Y.2d 578, 175 N.E.2d 681 (1961).
7. People v. Mishkin, 15 N.Y.2d 671, 204 N.Y.2d 209 (1964).
8. Jacobellis v. Ohio, 378 U.S. 184, 199–200 (1964).
9. "The Big Fine," reprinted in *Mr. Dooley on the Choice of Law* 41, 42 (Bander ed., 1963).
10. 17 U.S. Law Week 3117, 3119 (October 26, 1948), reporting oral argument of People v. Doubleday & Co., 335 U.S. 848 (1948).

CHAPTER 9   An Enforcement Philosophy

1. See Smith v. California, 361 U.S. 147 (1959), opinions of Justices

Frankfurter (at 164–67), and Harlan (at 172). See also People
v. Finkelstein, 11 N.Y.2d 300, 305, 183 N.E.2d 661, 663–64
(1962), and concurrence of Judge VanVoorhis (at 308, 183
N.E.2d at 665–66), and dissent of Judge Dye (at 309–10, 183
N.E.2d at 666).

CHAPTER 10 Sex-in-Action Photographs

1. Rolph, *The Trial of Lady Chatterley* 27 (1961), quoting from
   charge of Mr. Justice Stable in Reg. v. Martin Secker & War-
   burg [1954] W.L.R. 1138.
2. The Post Office order, banning the book from the United States
   mails, was reversed by the federal courts. Grove Press, Inc. v.
   Christenberry, 175 F. Supp. 488 (S.D.N.Y. 1959), *affirmed*, 276
   F. 2d 433 (2d Cir. 1960). The right to exhibit a motion picture
   dealing frankly, if not quite explicitly, with the book's theme
   of adultery was sustained by the United States Supreme Court.
   Kingsley International Pictures Corp. v. Regents, 360 U.S. 684
   (1959). See discussion of *Lady Chatterley's Lover* in Chapter 13.
3. "Pornography and Obscenity," republished in Lawrence, *Sex,
   Literature, and Censorship* 69 (1959).
4. People v. Jacobs and Mekas, 154 N.Y.L.J. no. 111, 16, col. 1
   (Dec. 10, 1965). The Supreme Court dismissed the appeal 387
   U.S. —— (June 12, 1967). An intermediate Cailfornia appellate
   court, in the Fall of 1966, affirmed the finding that another art
   movie, Jean Genet's *Un Chant d'Amour,* was obscene; see Landau
   v. Fording, 54 Cal. Rptr. 177. The court commented that the picture depicted "male masturbation, fellatio, oral copulation, voyeurism, nudity, sadism and sodomy."

CHAPTER 11 The Offbeat Smut Merchants

1. *Hearings on Juvenile Delinquency (Obscene and Pornographic
   Materials) Before Subcommittee to Investigate Juvenile Delinquency of the Senate Committee on the Judiciary,* 84th Cong.,
   1st Sess. 158–60, 239–42 (1955).
2. *Senate Report no. 2381, Interim Report of the Committee on
   the Judiciary by Subcommittee to Investigate Juvenile Delinquency (Obscene and Pornographic Materials),* 84th Cong., 2d
   Sess., 39–40 (June 28, 1956).
3. Kingsley Books, Inc. v. Brown, 354 U.S. 436 (1957).
4. People v. Mishkin, 15 N.Y.2d 671, 204 N.E.2d 209 (1964)
   record on appeal, fol. 1187.

5. Id. at fols. 1231–42.
6. People v. Mishkin, 26 Misc. 2d 152, 156, 207 N.Y.S.2d 390, 395 (1960)
7. *In Cold Blood* 330 (1965).
8. People v. Mishkin, 15 N.Y.2d 671, 204 N.E.2d 209 (1964). The trial court had not only convicted Mishkin for violating the obscenity law, but also on a number of charges of violating New York State's General Business Law requiring all publications to bear "conspicuously printed" the true name and address of the publisher or printer. But the United States Supreme Court had held a similar California statute unconstitutional in Talley v. California, 362 U.S. 60 (1960). Relying on that case, the intermediate appellate court had vacated the conviction on those charges, but that modification did not bear on Mishkin's sentence other than to reduce his fine from $12,500 to $12,000. People v. Mishkin, 17 A.D.2d 243, 234 N.Y.S.2d 342 (1st Dep't 1962).
9. United States v. Mishkin, 317 F. 2d 634 (2d Cir.), *certiorari denied,* 375 U.S. 827 (1963).
10. A Quantity of Copies of Books v. Kansas, 378 U.S. 205 (1964).
11. Marcus v. Search Warrants, 367 U.S. 717 (1961).
12. Mapp v. Ohio, 367 U.S. 643 (1961).
13. Linkletter v. Walker, 381 U.S. 618, 622 (1965).
14. Snyder v. Massachusetts, 291 U.S. 97, 122 (1934).
15. People v. Richmond County News, Inc., 9 N.Y.2d 578, 175 N.E.2d 681 (1961). See text pp. 58–59. Judge Fuld's opinion, speaking for himself and Judge VanVoorhis, said, in defining "hardcore":

It smacks, at times, of fantasy and unreality, of sexual perversion and sickness, and represents, according to one thoughtful scholar, "a debauchery of the sexual faculty."

Chief Judge Desmond, concurring, for himself and Judge Dye, said:

The inquiry for the court, therefore, is whether the publication is so entirely obscene as to amount to "hard-core pornography" (not necessarily dealing with deviate sex relations since while there is a pornography of perversion, "pornography" is not limited to the depiction of unnatural acts).

Three judges dissented.
16. People v. Genova, 15 A.D.2d 44, 222 N.Y.S.2d 437 (1961).

17. People v. Fried, 18 A.D.2d 996, 238 N.Y.S.2d 742 (1st Dep't 1963).
18. New York v. Fried, 378 U.S. 578 (1964).
19. An exception to the rule against proving other criminal acts, that is sometimes recognized, permits proof of prior crimes to show a particular state of mind, and for other limited purposes. See People v. Molyneaux, 168 N.Y. 264, 61 N.E. 286 (1901). But the courts are understandably chary in recognizing this exception because of the strong prejudice involved. The writer knows of no obscenity prosecution in which proof of other criminal convictions to show scienter was even tendered. Of course, should a defendant testify, he may then be cross-examined concerning his prior criminal acts and convictions.
20. Reeve v. Dennett, 145 Mass. 23, 28, 11 N.E. 938, 943–44 (1887).
21. See Lockhart & McClure, "Censorship of Obscenity: The Developing Constitutional Standards," 45 *Minn. L. Rev.* 5, 44 (1960).
22. People v. Finkelstein, 11 N.Y.2d 300, 183 N.E.2d 661, *certiorari denied,* 371 U.S. 863 (1962).
23. See, e.g., People v. Waldman, 152 N.Y.L.J. no. 82, 1, cols. 1–2 (October 26, 1964)

CHAPTER 12 Paperback Erotica

1. See Kuh, "The Grand Jury 'Presentment': Foul Blow or Fair Play?" 55 *Colum. L. Rev.* 1103, 1106–10 (1955).
2. Talley v. California, 362 U.S. 60 (1960).
3. People v. Mishkin, 17 A.D.2d 243, 234 N.Y.S.2d 342 (1st Dep't 1962), *affirmed,* 15 N.Y.2d 671, 204 N.E.2d 209 (1964).
4. People v. Birch, 40 Misc. 2d 626, 629, 631, 243 N.Y.S.2d 525, 530, 532 (Sup. Ct. Queens Co. 1963).
5. People v. Birch, 25 A.D.2d 854, 269 N.Y.S.2d 752 (1966).
6. Redrup v. New York, 386 U.S. 767 (1967).

CHAPTER 13 "Pornographic Classics," Old and New

1. Ed Zern in November 1959 *Field and Stream* 152.
2. Grove Press, Inc. v. Christenberry, 175 F. Supp. 488 (S.D.N.Y. 1959).
3. Grove Press, Inc. v. Christenberry, 276 F.2d 433 (2d Cir. 1960).
4. Rolph, *The Trial of Lady Chatterley* 17 (1961).
5. King & Hawkins, "Lady Chatterley," 48 *A.B.A.J.* 43, 47 (1962).
6. People v. Fritch, 13 N.Y.2d 119, 125, 192 N.E.2d 713, 717 (1963)

7. N.Y. *Times,* April 12, 1963, 25, col. 1.

8, N.Y. *Herald Tribune,* June 28, 1963, 19, cols. 1–6.

9. Chandos, *To Deprave and Corrupt . . .* 182 (1962).

10. Commonwealth v. Holmes, 17 Mass. 336 (1821). See also Hyde, *A History of Pornography* 99 (1965). A case reported six years earlier involved the exhibition of a painting "representing a man in an obscene, impudent, and indecent posture with a woman." Commonwealth v. Sharpless, 2 S. & R. 91 (Penn. 1815).

11. N.Y. *Times,* Sunday Book Section, June 9, 1963, 8, cols. 1–2.

12. Larkin v. G. P. Putnam's Sons, 40 Misc. 2d 25, 243 N.Y.S.2d 145 (Sup. Ct. N.Y. Co. 1963).

13. Larkin v. G. P. Putnam's Sons, 14 N.Y.2d 399, 200 N.E.2d 760 (1964) record on appeal, 84–85.

14. Id. at 65–66.

15. "The Present and Future of Pornography," 4 *Show* 54 (June 1964).

16. Ciardi, "Manner of Speaking," July 13, 1963 *Saturday Review* 20.

17. Larkin v. G. P. Putnam's Sons, 40 Misc. 2d 28, 242 N.Y.S.2d 746 (Sup. Ct. N.Y. Co. 1963).

18. See Irving, Hall & Wallington, *Anatomy of a Scandal: A Study of the Profumo Affair* (1963).

19. Larkin v. G. P. Putnam's Sons, 20 A.D.2d 702, case no. 2, 247 N.Y.S.2d 275 (1st Dep't 1964).

20. N.Y. *Times,* March 2, 1964, 29, col. 8, and March 3, 1964, 26, col. 8.

21. Larkin v. G. P. Putnam's Sons, 14 N.Y.2d 399, 200 N.E.2d 760 (1964).

22. Larkin v. G. P. Putnam's Sons, 14 N.Y.2d 399, 200 N.E.2d 760 (1964) record on appeal, 27.

23. People v. Doubleday & Co., Inc., 272 App. Div. 799, 71 N.Y.S.2d 736 (1st Dep't), *affirmed,* 297 N.Y. 687, 77 N.E.2d 6 (1947).

24. New York v. Doubleday & Co., Inc., 335 U.S. 848 (1948).

25. See text p. 83.

26. See text p. 34.

27. Attorney General v. A Book Named "John Cleland's Memoirs of a Woman of Pleasure," 349 Mass. 69, 206 N.E.2d 403 (1965).

28. See Cowper, *London Letter,* 151 N.Y.L.J. no. 47, 4, cols. 4–6 (March 9, 1964); N.Y. *Times,* February 11, 1964, 36, cols. 4–5; N.Y. *Times,* Sunday Book Section, March 15, 1964, 4.

29. "A Country and Some People I Love," September 1965 *Harper's* Magazine 58, 68.

30. March 19, 1965 *Time* 47, col. 2; October 2, 1965 *Saturday Review* 46, 61; N.Y. *Times,* May 5, 1966, 56, cols. 1–3.
31. "Literature, the Law of Obscenity, and the Constitution," 38 *Minn. L. Rev.* 295, 373 (1954).
32. N.Y. *Times,* March 11, 1965, 30, col. 1.

CHAPTER 14   The Girlie Magazines

1. N.Y. *Times,* December 6, 1960, 1, cols. 3–4.
2. People v. Richmond County News, Inc., 9 N.Y.2d 578, 175 N.E. 2d 681 (1961). See text pp. 58–59.
3. Commonwealth v. Forever Amber, Mass. Super. Ct., 1947, opinion in 32 Mass. L. Q. no. 2, 79, at 83 (May 1947).
4. Tenney v. Liberty News Distributors, Inc., 27 Misc. 2d 692, 694, 211 N.Y.S.2d 733, 736 (1960).
5. Near v. Minnesota, 283 U.S. 697 (1931). See text pp. 18–19.
6. Tenney v. Liberty News Distributors, Inc., 13 A.D.2d 769, case no. 9, 215 N.Y.S.2d 661 (1st Dep't 1961).
7. *N.Y. Code of Criminal Procedure* § 22-a.
8. *Pornography and the Law* 18–24 (Rev. ed., Ballantine, 1964).
9. Dr. Beigel's testimony appears in Larkin v. G. I. Distributors, Inc., 14 N.Y.2d 869, 200 N.E.2d 768 (1964) record on appeal, fols. 133–286, 394–436; see particularly fols. 160, 180–85, 223, 255–56, 400–04, 422–24.
10. Larkin v. G. I. Distributors, Inc., 41 Misc. 2d 165, 167, 245 N.Y.S.2d 553, 555 (1961).
11. Monfred v. Maryland, 226 Md. 312, 173 A.2d 173 (1961), *certiorari denied,* 368 U.S. 953 (1962).
12. New Jersey v. Hudson County News Co., 78 N.J.Super. 327, 332, 188 A.2d 444, 447 (1963).
13. New Jersey v. Hudson County News Co., 41 N.J. 247, 196 A.2d 225 (1963). The search was held to be unlawful because of the non-compliance with the requirements of Marcus v. Search Warrants, 367 U.S. 717 (1961).
14. Connecticut v. Andrews, 150 Conn. 92, 186 A.2d 546 (1962).
15. Wisconsin v. Chobot, 12 Wisc.2d 110, 106 N.W.2d 286 (1960), *appeal dismissed,* 368 U.S. 15 (1961).
16. Larkin v. G. I. Distributors, Inc. 14 N.Y.2d 869, 200 N.E.2d 768 (1964).
17. Austin v. Kentucky and Gent v. Arkansas, 386 U.S. 767 (1967).
18. "Some Reflections on the Reading of Statutes," 47 *Colum. L. Rev.* 527, 529 (1947).

19. That the judges' votes tend to be a reflection of personal philosophies toward censorship is underscored by a consideration of their actions in two other cases each of which *ostensibly* was not decided on obscenity grounds. In People v. The Bookcase, Inc., 14 N.Y.2d 409, 201 N.E.2d 14 (1964), decided the same day as was the *Fanny Hill* case involving Putnam's Sons, the court reversed a conviction for the violation of a New York statute barring the sale of indecent items to minors. The particular item in question happened to be *Fanny Hill*, and the purchaser was a sixteen-year-old girl. The bench did not rule on the fitness of the particular book for minors, but the opinions dealt with the constitutionality of New York's sale-to-minors statute. The same four judges who held *Fanny Hill not* obscene in the Putnam's case held the statute to be *void*, thus vacating this conviction also. The same three who had urged that *Fanny Hill* was *obscene*, and who would have sustained that conviction, in this case urged that the statute was valid, and would have affirmed this conviction as well. See text p. 250. And in People v. Finkelstein, 11 N.Y.2d 300, 183 N.E.2d 661 (1962), in reviewing an obscenity conviction, the court split, not on the question of the obscenity of the materials, but on the admissibility of other controversial items to prove community standards. Judges Burke, Foster, and Desmond all supported Judge Froessel's opinion for affirmance. Judges Dye and Fuld voted to reverse the conviction. And Judge VanVoorhis broke ranks, in part, in concurring in the affirmance of the conviction, but in a separate opinion in which he held the court below to have erred, but deemed the error not prejudicial to the defendant.

20. West Virginia State Board of Education v. Barnette, 319 U.S. 624, 647 (1943).

CHAPTER 15 Sophisticated Sexuality: *Eros*

1. Much of this statistical data is of uncertain accuracy, its source being Ginzburg's own polemic against his treatment in the federal courts. "Eros on Trial," May–June 1965 *Fact*. *Fact* is a magazine Ginzburg has published since January 1964. See also Collier, "Ralph Ginzburg: Eros Revisited," November 1964 *Cavalier* 10; Wakefield, "An Unhurried View of Ralph Ginzburg," October 1965 *Playboy* 95.

2. March 23, 1962 *Time* 77.

3. *An Unhurried View of Erotica* 16 (Ace Star ed., 1958).

4. "Eros on Trial," May–June 1965 *Fact* 19.

5. United States v. Ginzburg, 224 F. Supp. 129, 135–36 (E.D. Penn. 1963).
6. N.Y. *Times*, December 20, 1963, 27, col. 6.
7. *The Prophet* 77 (Knopf ed., 1961).
8. United States v. Ginzburg, 338 F.2d 12 (3d Cir., 1964).
9. *Amicus curiae* brief of the American Civil Liberties Union, in support of petition for certiorari, 1–2, in Ginzburg v. United States, 383 U.S. 463 (1966).
10. Manual Enterprises, Inc. v. Day, 370 U.S. 478 (1962). See Chapter 6. See also One, Inc. v. Olesen, 355 U.S. 371 (1958), *reversing*, *241* F.2d 772 (9th Cir. 1957); People v. Urban, 15 A.D.2d 480, 222 N.Y.S.2d 461 (1961).
11. Sunshine Book Co. v. Summerfield, 355 U.S. 372 (1958), *reversing*, *249* F.2d 114 (D.C.Cir. 1957); Excelsior Pictures Corp. v. Regents, 3 N.Y.2d 237, 144 N.E.2d 31 (1957).
12. People v. Cohen, 22 Misc. 2d 722, 205 N.Y.S.2d 481 (Queens Co. Ct. 1960).
13. People v. Cohen, 22 A.D.2d 932, case no. 7, 255 N.Y.S.2d 813 (2d Dep't 1964).

CHAPTER 16 Live Entertainment

1. "The Trial of Lenny Bruce," September 12, 1964 *New Republic* 13. Contrast with the same critic's comments of a year earlier: "The Comedy of Lenny Bruce," October 1963 *Commentary* 312. See also, re Bruce's decline as a comedian, J. Miller, "On Lenny Bruce (1926–1966)," October 6, 1966 *New York Review of Books* 10.
2. See, e.g., N.Y. *Times*, June 14, 1964, 75, cols. 1–2.
3. Hentoff, "Burt Lancaster, Abraham Lincoln and Lenny Bruce," December 20, 1964 *This Week* (N.Y. *Herald-Tribune*) 9:

"By June, moreover, Allen Ginsberg, the city's primary lay evangelist for free speech in the arts, had assembled a huge list of prestigious supporters of Lenny's right to deliver his message without disabling static from fuzz in the audience. Such luminaries as Reinhold Niebuhr . . . had agreed. . . ."

See also James Wechsler, "On Lenny Bruce," N.Y. *Post*, December 23, 1964, 24, col. 1; N.Y. *Times*, August 4, 1966, 33, cols. 2–3.
4. N.Y. *Times*, November 5, 1964, 47, col. 8.
5. 152 N.Y.L.J. no. 108, 1, cols. 4–5, December 4, 1964.

6. The decisions below, of the federal district court on December 14, 1964, affirmed by the Court of Appeals for the Second Circuit on December 16, 1964, are unreported. In the Supreme Court, certiorari was denied in 1965; see Bruce v. Hogan, 381 U.S. 946.

7. N.Y. *World-Telegram*, December 28, 1964, 26, cols 1–2.

8. N.Y. *Herald Tribune*, July 4, 1964, 8, cols. 1–3.

9. June 4, 1965 *Time* 26.

10. Adams Newark Theater Co. v. City of Newark, 22 N.J. 472, 126 A.2d 340 (1956).

11. Adams Newark Theater Co. v. City of Newark, 354 U.S. 931 (1957).

12. The statute, N.Y. Penal Law §1140-a, was before New York's highest court in People v. Weinberger, 239 N.Y. 307, 146 N.E. 434 (1925) and People v. Wendling, 258 N.Y. 451, 180 N.E. 169 (1932). Although in both cases that court reversed convictions, in Wendling the court specifically noted:

We do not purport to sanction indecency on the stage by this decision or to let down the bars against immoral shows. . . .

The relevant statutory language makes it criminal to present or participate in "any obscene, indecent, immoral or impure . . . show or entertainment," or in any show "which would tend to the corruption of the morals of youth or others." Clearly, this last provision, that would reduce adults to viewing standards fit for the young, is invalid. See Butler v. Michigan, 352 U.S. 380 (1957). But the invalidation of that portion does not invalidate the entire statute.

13. The Bruce trial testimony not having been collated and paginated for the intermediate reviewing tribunal, is referred to herein by witnesses, dates, and page numbers, as initially provided by the transcribing reporters. Kilgallen July 1, 1964, direct examination, at 23.

14. Kilgallen July 1, 1964, cross-examination, at 76–82. (Colloquy between court and counsel are omitted from this and from other trial excerpts.) Portions of the Kilgallen cross-examination are reprinted in 10 *Am. Jur. Trials* 232–49 (1965).

15. United States v. One Book Entitled Ulysses, 72 F.2d 705, 706–07 (2d Cir. 1934).

16. "Out of Step," N.Y. *World-Telegram*, January 11, 1965, 17, col. 1.

17. "The Trial of Lenny Bruce," September 12, 1964 *New Republic* 13, 14.

18. Kilgallen July 1, 1964, cross-examination, at 52–56, 61. See to the same effect, Richard Gilman, July 1, 1964, cross-examination, at 56–57.
19. N.Y. *World-Telegram*, July 29, 1964, 16, cols. 1–4.
20. October 1956 *Harper's* Magazine 14.
21. Fischer July 28, 1964, cross-examination, at 27.
22. See Chapter 7, note 7.
23. People v. Bruce, 31 Ill. 2d 459, 461, 202 N.E.2d 497, 498 (1964).
24. *An Unhurried View of Erotica* 62 (Ace Books ed., 1958).
25. Sociological Research Film Corp. v. City of New York, 83 Misc. 605, 606–08, 145 N.Y.S. 492, 493–94 (1914).
26. "A Wreath for the Gamekeeper," February 1960 *Encounter* 69, 70–71.
27. People v. Richmond County News Co., 9 N.Y.2d 578, 587, 175 N.E.2d 681, 686 (1961).
28. Kilgallen July 1, 1964, cross-examination, at 69–72.
29. "Burt Lancaster, Abraham Lincoln and Lenny Bruce," December 20, 1964 *This Week* (N.Y. *Herald Tribune*) 9, 18.
30. N.Y. *Times*, June 21, 1964 (entertainment section), 1, col. 8.
31. Quoted in Hentoff, "Where Liberals Fear to Tread," June 23, 1960 *Reporter* 50, 51.
32. *Village Voice*, April 9, 1964, 6.
33. See Wilson v. United States, 221 U.S. 361 (1911); Bleakley v. Schlesinger, 294 N.Y. 312, 62 N.E.2d 85 (1945).
34. See Loth, *The Erotic in Literature* 174 (MacFadden, 1962).
35. People v. Bruce transcript, April 15, 1964, 3–5.
36. *Village Voice*, July 16, 1964, 3.
37. July 3, 1964, cross-examination of Professor Daniel B. Dodson, of Columbia University, at 132.

CHAPTER 17   The Easy Course—Anything Goes!

1. N.Y. *Times*, August 7, 1964, 16, cols. 1–5.
2. See Freedman v. Maryland, 380 U.S. 51, and Trans-Lux Distributing Corp. v. Regents, 380 U.S. 259.
3. N.Y. *Times*, March 30, 1965, 51, cols. 2–8.
4. N.Y. *Times*, July 22, 1964, 32, col. 3.
5. Schenck v. United States, 249 U.S. 47, 52 (1919).
6. Dissenting, in Hyde v. United States, 225 U.S. 347, 391 (1912).
7. Roth v. United States, 354 U.S. 476, 482–83 (1957).
8. See Heartman, *John Peter Zenger and His Fight for the Freedom of the American Press* (1934).

9. Kingsley International Pictures Corp. v. Regents, 360 U.S. 684, 688–89 (1959).
10. Jacobellis v. Ohio, 378 U.S. 184, 191 (1964).
11. "Down With Sex!" February 1965 *Esquire* 72.
12. Iverson, *The Pious Pornographers,* (1963); "The Pious Pornographers Revisited," September–October 1964 *Playboy* 92 September), 116 (October).
13. N.Y. *Times,* March 26, 1965, 27, cols. 3–4; see also N.Y. *Times,* March 8, 1965, 34, cols. 1–3, and April 23, 1965 *Life* 64.
14. N.Y. *Times,* May 4, 1966, 49, col. 4.
15. See In re Davis, 242 A.C.A. 760 (Cal. 1966); see also May 28, 1965 *Time* 70.
16. *Variety,* December 21, 1966, 2, cols. 1–2.
17. Rolph, *The Trial of Lady Chatterley* 229 (1961).
18. Esquire, Inc. v. Walker, 151 F. 2d 49 (D.C.Cir. 1945), *affirmed sub nom.* Hannegan v. Esquire, Inc., 327 U.S. 146 (1946).
19. Brief in Verham News Co. v. Vermont, quoted in Arnold, *Fair Fights and Foul* 173–74 (1965).
20. "Sex and Censorship in Contemporary Society," *New World Writing* 7 (New Amer. Library 1953).
21. *N.Y. Penal Law* § 2120.
22. May 2, 1965 radio discussion (New York City, WBAI) "Pornography and the Law."
23. Redrup v. New York, Austin v. Kentucky, and Gent v. Arkansas, 386 U.S. 767, 769 (1967).

CHAPTER 18 Sales to the Young—the Crime Danger

1. Plato, *The Republic* 72 (Jowett translation, Modern Library Paperback).
2. Aristotle, *The Politics,* Book 7, 297 (T. A. Sinclair translation, Penguin Books).
3. See, e.g., *Senate Report no. 2381, Interim Report of The Committee on the Judiciary by Subcommittee to Investigate Juvenile Delinquency (Obscene and Pornographic Materials),* 84th Cong., 2d Sess. (June 28, 1956), particularly at 62; testimony taken at *Hearings on Obscene Matter Sent Through the Mails, Before Subcommittee on Postal Operations of the House of Representatives Committee on Post Office and Civil Service,* 86th Cong., 1st Sess. (1959); *New York Legislative Document no. 83* (1964), *Report of the New York State Joint Legislative Committee to Study the Publication and Dissemination of Offensive and Obscene Ma-*

terial, and earlier reports of same committee; Kilpatrick, *The Smut Peddlers* 7–9 (1960); Hoffman, "A Psychiatric View of Obscene Literature," 10 *Bulletin of Guild of Catholic Psychiatrists* 223 (1963); Armstrong, "The Damning Case Against Pornography," December 1965 *Reader's Digest* 131; Mussmanno, Address, October 23, 1965, before the Citizens for Decent Literature Convention, New York City.

4. *Cock-a-Doodle Dandy,* scene 2, 64 (Macmillan 1949).
5. See N.Y. *Post,* November 15, 1965, 6, col. 1.
6. Gebhard, Gagnon, Pomeroy & Christenson, *Sex Offenders* (Kinsey Institute 1965) considers *adult* male sexual offenders, and among other items discusses their own statements as to the impact pornography has had upon them. How reliable such personal evaluations may be is questionable. See Lockhart & McClure, "Literature, the Law of Obscenity, and the Constitution," 38 *Minn. L. Rev.* 295, 383–85 (1954).
7. See references to the studies of Sheldon and Eleanor Glueck in E. & P. Kronhausen, *Pornography and the Law* 343 (Rev. ed. Ballantine, 1964), and St. John-Stevas, *Obscenity and the Law* 200 (1956).
8. See Hansford Johnson, *On Iniquity* 38–40, 115 (1967).

CHAPTER 19   Sales to the Young—Morality, Tensions, and Parents

1. "Sex and Censorship in Contemporary Society," *New World Writing* 11 (New Amer. Library 1953).
2. *But Will It Sell?* 190 (1964).
3. "On Salacious Literature, A Statement by the New York Academy of Medicine, Prepared by the Committee on Public Health," 39 *Bulletin of the N.Y. Academy of Medicine, 2d Series* 545 (1963).
4. See, e.g., testimony of Dr. Benjamin Karpman, Chief Psychotherapist of St. Elizabeth's Hospital, Washington, D.C.:

Unfortunately [pornography] is often given to people of adolescent ages, which from our point of view is a very unstable period of life. Anything may happen during adolescence. You can take a perfectly healthy boy or girl and by exposing them to abnormalities you can virtually crystallize and settle their lives for the rest of their lives.

Hearings on Juvenile Delinquency (Obscene and Pornographic Materials) Before Subcommittee to Investigate Juvenile Delin-

quency of the Senate Committee on the Judiciary, 84th Cong., 1st Sess. 81 (1955).

Dr. William C. Kvaraceus, Tufts University Professor of Education, addressing the American Library Association's Conference on Intellectual Freedom (and, generally, strongly criticizing censors and censorship), noted:

It is true that unstable, confused, and emotionally disturbed children (and adults), who have difficulty in distinguishing clearly between the world of fantasy and the world of reality, can be further disturbed and confused by an exciting book. . . . Just as we keep sweets out of the reach of a young diabetic, we may also need to take similar precautions with certain vulnerable children.

"Can Reading Affect Delinquency?" 16 *Juvenile Court Judges Journal* 67, 69–70 (Summer, 1965). But see *Survey of New Jersey Psychiatrists and Psychologists Pertaining to the Proscription by Legislation of Sexually Oriented Publications for Persons Under 18 Years* (New Jersey Committee for the Right to Read 1967).

5. Ginzburg v. United States, 383 U.S. 463, 498 n.1. (1966).
6. Jacobellis v. Ohio, 378 U.S. 184, 195 (1964).
7. "What is Pornography?" July 13, 1963 *Saturday Review* 20.
8. "Last Exit to Nowhere," April 3, 1965 *Saturday Review* 12.
9. "The Marquis de Sade," II, October 2, 1965 *Saturday Review* 36.
10. Roth v. United States, 354 U.S. 476, 501 (1957).

CHAPTER 20   Sales to the Young—A Proposed Ban

1. Chapter 836, New York Session Laws of 1955, initially *Penal Law* § 542. Reenacted by chapter 548, New York Session Laws of 1963 as *Penal Law* § 484-h.
2. People v. The Bookcase, Inc., 14 N.Y.2d 409, 417, 201 N.E.2d 14, 18–19 (1964). Later, also with the same four to three line-up, the same court was to knock out what it had earlier left of the statute for "defects in draftsmanship" in a case involving girlie magazines. People v. Kahan, 15 N.Y.2d 311, 206 N.E.2d 333 (1965).
3. Chapters 327 and 372, New York Sessions Laws of 1965, enacting new *Penal Law* §§ 484-h, 484-i.
4. January 11, 1966 veto message of Assembly Bill no. 768.
5. Both statutes have been sustained by New York's highest court. See The Bookcase, Inc. v. Broderick, 18 N.Y.2d 71, 218 N.E.2d 668 (1966), appeal dismissed, 385 U.S. 12 (1966), and People

v. Tannenbaum, 18 N.Y.2d 268, 220 N.E.2d 783 (1966), appeal dismissed, 387 U.S. —— (June 12, 1967).

6. Smith v. California, 361 U.S. 147, 154 (1959).

7. Prince v. Massachusetts, 321 U.S. 158, 167–70 (1944).

8. People v. The Bookcase, Inc., 14 N.Y.2d 409, 417–18, 201 N.E.2d 14, 19 (1964).

9. In Police Commissioner of Baltimore v. Siegel Enterprises, Inc., 223 Md. 110, 126–28, 162 A.2d 727, 735–36 (1960), *certiorari denied,* 364 U.S. 909, a Maryland statute was held unconstitutional that, among other things, barred dealers from offering for sale within adolescent view items that could be sold only to adults. And New York State's governor has twice vetoed bills that would have penalized persons operating premises that sold books dealing with illicit sex and admitted children to those premises. See memorandum no. 196 of July 28, 1966, vetoing A. Int. 1239, and memorandum no. 112 of June 14, 1965, vetoing A. Int. 3727.

10. "Censorship of Obscenity: The Developing Constitutional Standards," 45 *Minn. L. Rev.* 5, 86 (1960).

CHAPTER 21 Public Displays—Offenses Against Taste and Privacy

1. Highway Beautification Act of 1965, P.L. 89–285, 79 Stat. 1028.

2. N.Y. *Times,* December 30, 1965, 1, col. 4.

3. N.Y. *Times,* July 14, 1965, 39, col. 8.

4. N.Y. *Times,* November 25, 1965, 46, cols. 2–4; June 4, 1965 *Time* 43.

5. "The Supreme Court and the Meiklejohn Interpretation of the First Amendment," 79 *Harv. L. Rev.* 1, 5 (1965).

6. Ginzburg v. United States, 383 U.S. 463, 498 n.1 (1966).

7. Some statutes directed against public display presently exist. But, typically, they focus on displays that "tend to demoralize the morals of youth or others or which shall be lewd, indecent, or immoral. . . ." N.Y. *Penal Law* § 1141-a. And so the more familiar general obscenity statutes, using similar language, are more likely to be invoked than the special display provisions; the general statutes also make it a crime to "show" to another an obscene item.

8. Concerning the law as to nuisances, see 4 *Restatement, Torts,* Explanatory notes to chapter 40, and §§ 826–31 (1939).

9. People v. Stover, 12 N.Y.2d 462, 191 N.E.2d 272 (1963); see also Cromwell v. Ferrier, 19 N.Y.2d 263 (1967).

10. Berman v. Parker, 348 U.S. 26, 33 (1954).
11. 1 Chafee, *Government and Mass Communications* 196–97 (1947).

CHAPTER 22   Indecency and Adults—the Argument for Intervention

1. Chandos, *To Deprave and Corrupt* . . . 45–46 (1962).
2. "The Fifth Amendment, *Nemo Tenetur Prodere Seipsum*," 25 *Jnl. Cleveland Bar Assoc.* 91, 99–100 (1954).
3. See text pp. 227–28.
4. Devlin, *The Enforcement of Morals* 13, 16–17 (1965).
5. Concurring, in Alberts v. California, 354 U.S. 476, 502 (1957).
6. "Sex and Censorship in Contemporary Society," *New World Writing*, 7, 18 (New Amer. Library 1953).
7. "Eroticism, Sex and Love," April 27, 1963 *Saturday Evening Post* 10.
8. Hansford Johnson, *On Iniquity* 26 (1967).
9. "A Wreath for the Gamekeeper," February 1960 *Encounter* 69, 74.
10. Griswold v. Connecticut, 381 U.S. 479, 485–86 (1965).
11. Gebhard, Gagnon, Pomeroy & Christenson, *Sex Offenders* 404 (1965). See also Cairns, Paul & Wishner, "Sex Censorship: The Assumptions of Anti-Obscenity Laws and the Empirical Evidence," *46 Minn. L. Rev.* 1009 (1962).
12. Gebhard et al. at 138, 170, 193.
13. *Does Pornography Matter?* 105 (1961).
14. Butler v. Michigan, 352 U.S. 380, 383 (1957); see text pp. 17–18.
15. Duke of Norfolk's Case [1682] 3 Ch. Cas. 1, 49.

CHAPTER 23   Indecency and Adults—Precise Limitations

1. Testimony before the *Joint Select Committee on the Stage Plays (Censorship)* 49, Great Britain, Parliamentary Paper no. 303, vol. 8 (1909).
2. Regina v. Hicklin [1868] 3 Q.B. 360, 367.
3. Ginzburg v. United States, 383 U.S. 463, 469–70, 472 (1966).
4. "Censorship of Obscenity: The Developing Constitutional Standards," *45 Minn. L. Rev.* 5, 77–88 (1960); see also Lockhart & McClure, "Obscenity Censorship: The Core Constitutional Issue— What is Obscene?" *7 Utah L. Rev.* 289, 298–302 (1961).
5. Such pictures, when intended *solely* for scientific use, have been held not to be obscene. United States v. 31 Photographs, 156 F. Supp. 350 (S.D.N.Y. 1957). This strains the wording of existing statutes, but comes up with a sound result.

6. Southern Pacific Co. v. Jensen, 244 U.S. 205, 221 (1917).

7. Ginzburg v. United States, 383 U.S. 463, 494 (1966).

8. Brown v. Allen, 344 U.S. 443, 540 (1953).

9. In declaring unconstitutional for vagueness a statute that was directed at conduct "which openly outrages public decency," and was invoked to convict a California topless "fashion model" and her bar-restaurant proprietor husband, the court expressly noted that it was not ruling whether a carefully drawn statute could constitutionally prohibit such exhibitions. In re Davis, 242 A.C.A. 760, 782 (Cal. 1966). See also account of somewhat similar New York action. N.Y. *Times,* January 13, 1967, 43, col. 5.

10. Schlesinger v. Wisconsin, 270 U.S. 230, 241 (1926).

11. People v. Richmond County News, Inc., 9 N.Y.2d 578, 587, 175 N.E.2d 681, 686 (1961); People v. Fritch, 13 N.Y.2d 119, 124, 192 N.E.2d 713, 717 (1963).

12. See Masters & Johnson, *Human Sexual Response* (1966).

13. Evergreen Review, Inc. v. Cahn, 230 F. Supp. 498 (E.D.N.Y. 1964).

14 Trans-Lux Distributing Corp. v. Regents, 380 U.S. 259 (1965).

15. "Literature and Censorship," 14 *Books on Trial* 393, 446 (1956).

16. United States v. One Carton Positive Motion Picture Film Entitled *491,* 247 F. Supp. 450 (S.D.N.Y. 1965), *reversed,* 367 F.2d 889 (2d Cir. 1966), two of the three judges of the appellate court ruling that the film was not "utterly without redeeming social value."

17. Photographs of this sculpture appeared in June 1965 *Evergreen Review* 64–65, and Gerber, *Sex, Pornography & Justice* 320–21 (1965).

18. The case was Regina v. Baxter, in the Old Bailey, October 1954, quoted in Rolph, *The Trial of Lady Chatterley* 15 (1961).

19. See Freedman v. Maryland, 380 U.S. 51, and Trans-Lux Distributing Corp. v. Regents, 380 U.S. 259. Previously, in 1961, the high Court had held that films were subject to pre-release licensing restraints. See Times Film Corp. v. Chicago, 365 U.S. 43.

20. A Book Named "John Cleland's Memoirs of a Woman of Pleasure" v. Massachusetts, 383 U.S. 413, 420 (1966).

21. Ginzburg v. United States, 383 U.S. 463, 482 (1966).

22. Haiman v. Morris, Ill. Sup. Ct., June 18, 1964. Opinion withdrawn and unreported.

23. *. . . and Then I Told the President* 121–22 (1965).

CHAPTER 24 Legislative—and Other—Realities

1. Address, May 3, 1907, at Elmira, New York, by New York State's then Governor, Charles Evans Hughes.
2. See Freedman v. Maryland, 380 U.S. 51, 58 (1965).
3. Smith v. California, 361 U.S. 147, 154 (1959).
4. *Model Penal Code* § 251.4(2) (Proposed Official Draft 1962). The English Obscene Publications Act, 1959, 7 & 8 Eliz. 2, c. 66, section 2(5) provides:

    A person shall not be convicted of an offence against this section *if he proves* that he had not examined the article in respect of which he is charged and had no reasonable cause to suspect that it was such that his publication of it would make him liable to be convicted of an offence against this section.

5. Rolph, *The Trial of Lady Chatterley* 233 (1961).
6. Obscene Publications Act, 1959, 7 & 8 Eliz. 2, c. 66, section 4(1).
7. *Model Penal Code* § 251.4(3)(a) (Proposed Official Draft 1962).
8. Brown v. Board of Education, 347 U.S. 483 (1954) and 349 U.S. 294 (1955); Baker v. Carr, 369 U.S. 186 (1962).
9. See, e.g., Lockhart & McClure, "Censorship of Obscenity: The Developing Constitutional Standards," 45 *Minn. L. Rev.* 5, 103–08 (1960); see also Ernst & Schwartz, *Censorship, the Search for the Obscene* 136 (1964).
10. Elliott, "Against Pornography," March 1965 *Harper's* Magazine 51, 57–58; Hook, "Pornography and the Censor," N.Y. *Times* Sunday Book Section, April 12, 1964, 1.
11. St. John 8: 7.
12. St. John-Stevas, *Obscenity and the Law* 34–35 (1956).
13. Gerber, *Sex, Pornography & Justice* 90–92 (1965); Hyde, *A History of Pornography* 15–16 (1965).
14. See Fischer, "The Harm Good People Do," October 1956 *Harper's* Magazine 14.
15. Address, August 6, 1964, before the Order of Eagles Convention, Denver, Colorado.
16. There are no definitive opinions establishing that such *private* action can be enjoined. For a discussion of the problem, see Gerber, *Sex, Pornography & Justice* 243–50 (1965). Wholly private boycotts by citizens' committees should not be confused with threats to distributors and dealers by district attorneys, police, or licensing officials, that if listed items continue to be sold prosecutions will follow. The use of such *ex cathedra* notices to remove dubious items from the marketplaces is unlawful. Officials may

act only through official channels; these informal methods that scare merchants into removing merchandise from circulation to avoid the expense, nuisance, and dangers of prosecution are defective in that they at the same time avoid judicial review of the public official's judgments as to what may be obscene. Bantam Books, Inc. v. Sullivan 372 U.S. 58 (1963).

17. "Literature and Censorship," 14 *Books on Trial* 393, 444–45 (1956).

18. *The Common Law* 41–42 (1881).

Index

Index*

---

*(Notes are not indexed.)